John Davidson

AF282521

Belief - what is it?

Salzwasser

John Davidson

Belief - what is it?

1. Auflage | ISBN: 978-3-84605-548-9

Erscheinungsort: Frankfurt, Deutschland

Erscheinungsjahr: 2020

Salzwasser Verlag GmbH

Reprint of the original, first published in 1869.

BELIEF—WHAT IS IT?

BELIEF—WHAT IS IT?

OR

THE NATURE OF FAITH

AS DETERMINED BY THE FACTS

OF

HUMAN NATURE AND SACRED HISTORY

———————

PREFACE.

THE task attempted in the following chapters is to make a natural history of religious faith, describing the matters with which religious faith occupies itself, and the mental experience of its dealing with them. The writer has endeavoured to treat the subject purely in this light, avoiding all help or entanglement which might arise in considering faith in its connection with any religious or philosophical system; and with the same view has avoided the use of conventional language on the subject, which might be suggestive of theoretical thought. The means of investigation are the authentic history of religious experience contained in the Bible, and the explanatory analogies by which revelation instructs mankind in the nature of the religious relationship.

The order of treatment is analytical. The Introductory Chapter notices how man's peculiar connection with God determines the subject of his religious thinking, and makes it necessary that his thoughts shall be instructed by God. Chapter II. is taken up with the

subject of religious faith's thoughts — namely, God's
peculiar affection towards man, in the historical form
in which it is presented to us. Chapter III. is an
attempt to trace generally the communication of true
thoughts of God, and His love of man as it was made
to the portion of mankind selected to receive that direct
instruction; and to trace also the progress of those
true thoughts in being appreciated by the selected line.
Chapter IV. notices the concomitant dissemination
of the elements of that religious truth through the
world of the time, both directly and indirectly, by
means of those to whom it was revealed at first, and
with the occasional help of separate revelation made to
other peoples. Chapters V. and VI. discuss successively
what the rational process is by which religious truth
becomes in any individual mind what is called faith,
and what is the mental experience of acquired faith in
contemplating that truth. To these is added a Chapter
(VII.) of verifications of obtained results by the general
descriptions and analogies and particular expressions of
faith used in the sacred writings. Chapter VIII. attempts to show that in all periods of believing in the
true God believers have contemplated the same personal
object of faith, humanly known as Jesus of Nazareth.
Chapter IX. treats of the essential diversity of the experience of faith in the case of different individuals, or
in different circumstances of the same individual's life;
Chapter X., of the personal conditions upon which
the thoughts of religious faith are attainable; and
Chapter XI., of the manner and designed result of the
discipline which the individual believer undergoes in

living his earthly life by "the faith of the Son of God."

In consequence of the reasoning being confined to the analytical form, the concentrated presentation of result which synthetic statement allows has had to be sacrificed, and the readier apprehension at different stages of the writer's whole meaning which that facilitates. It may be proper, therefore, to state here briefly the result arrived at. If the induction attempted be correct, that result is, that faith cannot be intelligibly defined by any of the conventional terms or short expressions generally used as sufficient in speaking of it, but can only be described by its experienced consciousness, and that man's religious faith is his habitual emotional thinking of the historical manifestations of God's love to him, associating these with the person of the Son of God in such a manner as to make his believing a life whose essence is union of affection and of conscious spiritual sympathy with Him.

If it be asked what the use is of presenting this description of faith in the form of a lengthened investigation, the answer is the author's reason for attempting the statement. Room seems to exist among writings on the subject of faith for a somewhat detailed representation of it in non-theological language from a natural-history point of view. Perhaps it is greatly a consequence of a compendious definition of faith being unattainable that religious teachers have presented it almost always in its connection with systems of doctrine, and have treated of the importance of faith, and the consequences attached to possessing or not possessing it, without such description of itself as would enable learners to recognise it in their own consciousness. The effect of this, however, is the prevalence of hurtfully indistinct notions respecting this great element of religious life. Very many religious persons have no definite thought of what faith is. Many have a kind of feeling that it is some mysterious possession which those who are in Christ have, and others have not, but which cannot be understood at all by them until they have it. Some are afraid to think upon the subject with the definiteness which they would strive after in any other inquiry. Others, in contrast to this modest but injurious diffidence, make presumptuous assumptions of a faith which is not described in the Word of God. The following pages are meant to be a contribution to that simplicity which belongs to the practice of religion—what we have to do to be saved—as certainly as mystery is to be recognised reverently by human minds in the theology contained in revealed truth.

CONTENTS.

CHAPTER I.

THE LIMITS OF MAN'S RELIGIOUS FAITH.

PAGE

1. Faith, the thoughts of man's particular connection with God, . 1
2. The connection revealed as a unique one, ... 2
3. Faith not investigated but instructed knowledge; and not the whole of revealed truth, but a certain history, . . . 3
4. Glimpses of truth revealed beyond the province of man's faith, . 3
   Note.—Man's limited place in creation.—Original preparation of the earth for man's fallen condition, . . . 4

CHAPTER II.

THE SUBJECT OF FAITH.

1. God's exceptional affection towards man, ... 6
2. Especially as shown in his salvation, ... 6
3. God's love to man revealed as a family affection; by two ways, . 7
4. First, by means of assuring family relationships, . . . 7
5. The form of pre-Christian faith, ... 8
6. Second, by manifestation in Jesus of Nazareth, . . . 9
7. The assuring metaphors realised in Him, ... 9
8. Historical form of the revelation—one necessary to human faith, . 10
9. True faith's thoughts of God historical from the first.—Antediluvian, Patriarchal, and Hebrew faiths, . . . 11
10. Convincing force of historical religion.—Different origin, character, and power of heathen creeds.—The Greek *philosophie positive.* —Failure of mythical and philosophical religions for human necessities, ... 12
11. Their fall before historical faiths—Nebuchadnezzar—Pharaoh— Felix—the Greeks, ... 14

12. Reasons of revealed truth's success.—The human mind's recognition of reality—effect on sceptical hypotheses, . . . 16
13. Avoidance of the historical statement of the truth by sceptical reasoners—the Mythists, &c., ... 17
14. Congruity of revealed truth to man's consciousness—his subjective religion, if objectively proved, ... 18
15. Historical form of religious truth suited to all capacities—its single argument giving to different degrees of perception equal fulness of happiness, ... 19
16. Expedient form of propagating the faith; historical not doctrinal, 20
17. Inherent effectiveness of Scripture language, . . . 22

CHAPTER III.

THE EDUCATION OF THE WORLD TO FAITH.

PART I.—THE PROGRESS OF REVELATION.

1. Power to appreciate religious truth lost by sinning, . . 23
2. Man's fall; and change by God from familiarity to rudimentary revelation, ... 23

Antediluvian Faith.

3. God the avenger—the common faith of heathens and professed infidels, ... 25
4. Hopes of His mercy towards man—early chosen names, . . 25

Hebrew Faith.

5. God's drawing nigh to man—selection for a purpose, . . 26
6. Progressive revelation and appreciation of God the purpose of the Hebrew discipline, ... 27
7. First progress of revealing names, positional, moral, and affectional— El—Elohim—Jehovah—The Holy One—Merciful and Gracious, 29
8. Appreciative faith localising thoughts of God—Jehovah-Jireh, Ma-hanaim, &c., ... 32
9. Historical advance of appreciative language from the beginning to the times of the psalmists, ... 33
10. Progress of revealing institutions.—Primary priestly guidance and protection superseded by salvation and government by means of kings—suggestive kinghoods of David, Uzziah, and Hezekiah, 35
11. Progress of religious thought under the kinghood—Solomon and Joash, ... 37
12. Contemporary appreciation of the religious thoughts of the Psalms; and subsequent fruit of preparation for new truth, . 39
13. Progress of institutions.—Prophetic government superseding the kingly—its history and final condition, . . . 40
14. Advance of teaching from positive to moral and Spiritual, . 41
15. Coincident extension of prophetic mission to the outer nations, 42
16. Popular appreciation of the prophetic authority ever after, . 42
17. Culmination of prophetic work—foretelling the salvation of the world—Joel—Amos—Micah—Isaiah, . . . 43

18. Contemporary advance of faith's thoughts—Habakkuk—Jeremiah and Ezekiel—Isaiah's hearers, ... 45
19. Progress of institutions.—The Scribes—the precursors of the Spiritual rule of the written Word, ... 48
20. Latest Jewish thoughts of the meaning of "the Word of the Lord," 49
21. Progressive revelations of God's love systematically timed to man's felt need and probable impressibility, ... 50
22. Days of salvation like the "due time," 53
23. Revelation of God's love of the world, uniformly as a holy love, 53
24. Anticipation of " The Flesh," 55
25. Mankind looking for "Him that should come," . . . 56

Christian Faith.

GOD MANIFEST IN FLESH.

26. The Manifestation.—The completion of God's drawing nigh to man, ... 56
27. The Incarnation.—God who originally gave man his own nature taking man's condition in bodily life, suffering, and death, . 57
28. Progress of identification of Himself with man—substitution, and the assurance it gives, ... 60
29. Peculiar human ancestry of Jesus—"made sin for us," . . 61
30. The Propitiation.—Philosophical difficulties from overdrawn analogy, ... 62
31. The sufferings of fatherhood because of sin predicated of God, the same as those historically experienced by His human children in the nature created in His likeness, ... 63
32. The extension of sin's inevitable suffering to the innocent also a perpetual lesson of history—religiously taught in the Hebrew worship—interpretation of the sacrificial "lamb," . . 65
33. The substitutionary suffering of Christ not merely assumed but unavoidable, because of His peculiar historical connection with man, ... 67
34. Identity of suffering revealed for faith's comfort, . . . 68
35. Expiation of guilt necessary to man's subjective feelings and his historical position, ... 68
36. Progressive thoughts of Christ in the four gospels.—The Jewish Messiah — the Almighty Deliverer — the Son of Man — the Word who was God, ... 70

THE COMFORTER.

37. Revelation of God as one with them that believe—dwelling with man and in him, ... 72
38. Progress of revealing names.—The Comforter; bringing man into a reciprocal union with God, ... 73
39. His comforting exhibition of the truth; and earnest of its assurances, ... 74

THE INHERITANCE.

40. Heaven the family reunion accomplished, ... 76
41. Realistic character of the life of heaven; one appreciable by man, 77

42. An eternal perfected human life, ... 79
43. Revelation of God to man—why so slow, ... 80

CHAPTER IV.

THE EDUCATION OF THE WORLD TO FAITH.

PART II.—THE DISSEMINATION OF THE TRUTH.

1. Indirect education of Gentile peoples by observation of revealed faith, ... 81
2. Geographical positions of revealed truth—Hebrew, Christian, and probably Antediluvian—always centres of publication to the world of the time, ... 81
3. Designed result—self-education aided by direct revelation, . 84
4. Selected line of revelation never exclusive—Israel's stewardship, . 85
5. Contact of patriarchal faith with Mesopotamian and Syrian kings—direct revelation to Pharaohs and kings of Gerar—fate of Rameses, ... 85
6. Israel in Palestine.—Reasonings of Rahab—the Gibeonites—the Midianites—the Philistines—self-education of Canaanites—divine help—wars of Saul and David—David's court and body-guard—Solomon's view of the mission of Israel—his wisdom compared with the wisdom of Egypt, &c.—Israel with Syria and Assyria and later Egypt, ... 89
7. Prophetic mission extended to heathen—Elijah in Tyre—Elisha in Syria—Jonah in Nineveh—objects and subjects of Isaiah's prophecies, ... 91
8. The Captivities.—Education of Mesopotamian universal monarchs —proclamations of Nebuchadnezzar, Darius, Cyrus, Darius Hystaspis, Artaxerxes, Xerxes, ... 92
9. Europe at the time of the second exodus—mingling of Persian and Greek civilisation—Cyrus and the Scribes, . . 96
10. Last Jewish age.—Circulation of the Hebrew sacred books, and their publication in the universal language of the time, . 97
11. The education of the heathen world—1. systematic, 2. by instruction of the ruling people of the time—peculiar distribution of the Jews among the ruling nations—results indicated by first Christian Pentecost, ... 97
12. Contact of Judaism and Christianity overlapped by an age of learning—dissemination of Hebrew Scriptures and people in Greek, Roman, Mesopotamian, and Egyptian countries—their local influence, ... 99
13. Secular civilisations not transmitted as a continuous education of the world — generally contrasted — distinct characters of Egyptian, Assyrian, Greek, Persian and Roman culture, . 100
14. Historical succession of compelled comparisons of heathen civilisation with the power of revealed truth—Rameses and Moses, wisdom of Egypt and Solomon—Assyrian kings, and Israel's

people and prophets — Greek wisdom and culture, and Paul's preaching—Asiatic reformers—Roman government and Christian faith, ... 102

15. Extent of faith in the earth—salvation of the heathen—Isaiah's boldness—comprehensiveness of the Scriptural expression "in Christ "—opinion as to the salvation of unknown peoples incompetent in the absence of knowledge—revealed *direction* of thought on the subject, ... 106

CHAPTER V.

REASON'S TASK IN RELIGIOUS FAITH.

1. Faith a co-operative result, ... 110
2. Human part of the work, ... 110
3. Observation not investigation, ... 110
4. Properly contemplation of the facts of God's love, . . 111
5. Incompetence of reason for investigating divine truth, . . 112
6. Theorising, instead of observation, the source of both over-wisdom and scepticism—the Pharisees and Mythists—the Anti-supernaturalists, ... 113
7. Familiarity with the history the cure for scepticism, . . 116
8. Reason's work of observation—1. to receive proof, 2. to familiarise, ... 117
9. Proof—testing by "signs "—self-consistency—and congruity with human nature, ... 117
10. Duty of private judgment—faith and creed, . . . 119
11. Risk to faith in religious reading—imitative orthodoxy or scepticism, ... 120
12. Chief work of reason in faith—to assimilate the truth, . . 122
13. Reasoning and revealed ways of thinking to be identical, . 122
14. How to be made so—"think on these things," . . . 123
15. The process of civilisation individual and national—Brahmin Christians—the British nation, ... 124
16. Scriptural examples of religious civilisation.—Samuel and Saul, David, the first Hebrews, Samson, Jephthah, Barak, &c.—unstable Jewish faith—the apostles—the early Christian Church, Gentile and Jewish—Timothy—late conversions, . . 126
17. Means and hindrances to knowledge becoming faith, . . 130
18. Co-operation of God put within man's practice of faith—help given in kind, ... 131

CHAPTER VI.

THE MENTAL EXPERIENCE OF FAITH.

1. Faith described in Scripture chiefly by its opposites, . . 134
2. Psychologically—constant thinking on the things believed in, . 135
3. Nature of faith's thinking: two conditions, quiescent and active, 135

4. Unconscious thinking of faith—illustrations — a child, a pupil, a patient, &c., ... 135
5. Unconscious thinking the deposit of much active thinking, . 136
6. Faith's thoughts normally quiescent, ... 137
7. Analogy of bodily unconsciousness, ... 138
8. Conscious faith prominently emotional—like family thoughts, . 139
9. " With the heart man believeth"—emotional meaning of intellectual terms in Scripture, ... 140
10. What are the emotions of faith ?—Conventional terms of Christian thought on the subject confined — all the emotions comprehended belonging to contemplation of the facts of God's love, . 143
11. Our Lord's cases of faith not describable by one definition—can only be historically studied—so also cases in Heb. xi., . 145
12. Common element.—Emotional contemplation of a person, . 147
13. Appreciable distributively in parts through experience of human relationships, ... 148
14. First use of the phrase " believed in," 149
15. Consciousness of union the fundamental idea in faith, . . 150
16. Reverie characteristic of faith's thinking—musical expression of faith—Hebrew poetry and music, ... 150
     Note.—Element distinguishing religious faith from that of science, politics, &c., ... 151
17. Normal and occasional states of faith's thinking, . . 151
18. A believer's knowledge of the history of his own believing, . 152
19. Subject of faith's thoughts suited to its manner of thinking, . 153
20. Spiritual result of the thinking of faith—a co-operative change of nature—a product of earnings and gifts, . . . 154

CHAPTER VII.

SCRIPTURAL FAITH—VERIFICATIONS.

1. Verification of foregoing reasoning by Scriptural descriptions, examples, and analogies, ... 156
2. Scriptural descriptions of faith, ... 156
3. Scriptural faith, historical not philosophical thinking, . 157
4. Its generalisations realistic; in the spirit of past facts—concentration of historical thought in memorial observances; and in names made call-words of bodies of facts, . . . 158
5. Analogy of "a little child's" faith—a heart belief—realistic—not slow to believe.—Reasoning of adult faith much a reasoning back over lost ground, ... 160
6. Childlike faith of the cloud of witnesses, . . . 162
7. Child-faith of personal connection—seen in same examples, . 163
8. Emotional element in Scriptural faith—the reasoning of the heart, 164
9. Examples of emotional faith.—The patriarchs—Abraham—Job—Moses.—The Psalms.—The Gospel instances—woman of Syrophœnicia—Martha and Mary, ... 165
10. New Testament description of full Christian faith, realistic, personal, and emotional—Paul—Peter—John, . . . 171

11. Verification of the process of believing in God, . . . 173
12. Arrested attention—signs and wonders, . . . 173
13. Thinking on distinct facts, ... 174
14. Impression, appreciation, recognition, subjective attraction, . 174
15. Thinking with the heart, ... 175
16. Faith not an act but a state of spirit, ... 175
17. Dealing with definite single thoughts and indefinite contemplations, ... 176
18. Diversity in matter and manner of thought, . . . 177
19. Divine operation in producing faith, ... 177
20. Consciousness of connection with a person believed in, . . 177

CHAPTER VIII.

THE OBJECT OF FAITH.

1. The same person contemplated by the faiths of all times, . . 180
2. Christ the Love of God, ... 181
3. Historical conspectus in Heb. i., ... 181
4. Human history embraced in the history of "the Son," . . 182
5. Proof of identity, declaratory and moral, . . . 183
6. Declaratory—Proverbs, chap. viii., compared with John i., Heb. i.,
&c., ... 184
7. Human appearances made at forepointing epochs, to Abraham,
Jacob, and Joshua ; and 184
8. Identified with the Angel, Jehovah, I AM, Jesus Christ, . . 185
9. Moral identification—recognised sameness of characteristic individuality, ... 187
10. Early facts comprehensible only by the light of Christian revelation, ... 188
11. The "cry" of Wisdom, of Jehovah, and of Jesus, . . 189
12. Foretastes of "the flesh" and its sympathies, . . 190
13. Eden and Cana—the seed of the woman and Abraham's seed, . 190
14. Distinctive mercies of Jehovah those of Jesus—the flood and the
towns of Galilee—Babel and Nazareth and Gethsemane, . 191
15. Abraham's object of faith — the humanity of Jehovah that of
Jesus the "friend of man"—El Khalil, . . . 191
16. Abraham foretasting Christian faith, in God's love "not sparing
His own Son," 193
17. Faith in Christian providence — the fishermen of Galilee anticipated by Abraham and Eliezer, ... 194
18. "Being found in fashion as a man He humbled Himself," . 195
19. "Help thou mine unbelief"—Moses—Gideon—Elijah, . . 195
20. The Saviour of Christian times proclaiming Himself on Sinai, . 196
21. Manner of the grace of Jesus in the experience of Moses, Eli,
Samuel, and David, ... 197
22. Footprints of Jesus in the Psalms and Prophetical writings, the
Son of Man sowing words to lay hold on faith in the fulness of
time, ... 198
23. Recognition of them by the New Testament writers, . . 200

24. Anachronisms of history in the Psalms and Prophets, . . 201
25. And of religious sentiment, ... 201
26. Designed fruit of words of faith thus sown for future recognition, 202
27. Christ present in all the Law—Himself the "Schoolmaster to bring to Christ"—old histories not types but parts of the love of Christ, ... 203
28. Recognition of Christ the object of faith's study of the word, . 204
29. The Gospel revelation the revelation of sonship, . . . 205
30. Declaration in Christ Jesus that God's love to man is to a son who is one with Himself, ... 205
31. Revelation in Christ Jesus of man's nature original and restored, 207
32. Importance attached to "faith in Christ, the Son of the living God," appreciable from the manner of God's revealing Himself, 209
33. "Christ formed in" the believer, ... 211
34. Faith's thoughts of Christ, thoughts of the historical Jehovah, Jesus, ... 211
35. The day of Christ—all human time, ... 213
36. The "rest that remaineth"—the joy of man's Lord; eternal salvation, ... 216

CHAPTER IX.

THE DIVERSITY OF FAITH.

1. Diversity in all emotional thinking normal, . . . 218
2. Imitation of Christ not uniform but diverse, . . . 219
3. Meaning of diversity of religious faith, ... 219
4. Human causes of difference in propensity of thought, . . 220
5. Diversity of chief matter of thought among the personal followers of Jesus—Peter, James, and John—John, Peter, and Paul—the four evangelists—Nathanael and Thomas—Nicodemus and Peter —Mary of Bethany and the woman which was a sinner— Jairus, Zaccheus, and the Syrophœnician mother — would have compiled diverse creeds, ... 221
6. Double source of diversity in faith's thoughts; the presentation of the truth, and the appreciation of it, ... 225
7. Diversity in the matter of thought presented to faith, and in the manner of exhibiting it in the sacred books, . . . 227
8. Diversity of thinking propensity from human causes; e.g., the temperaments.—Equal attraction by diverse lines of thought to the historical Christ, ... 228
9. Faith and creed different things—diversity in both normal, . 231
10. Diverse affinities to the teaching of faith.—"I am of Paul," "I of Cephas," 232
11. The unity of the faith—personal connection of all believers with Christ—a harmony in diversity, ... 233
12. To be attained by faith's characteristic contemplation of the One Lord, the object of all religious faith, ... 234
13. Correction of propensities—John—Peter, ... 235
14. Progress of perception—Paul's successive thoughts of Christ, . 239

15. Convergence of his faith with John's and Peter's—a continuation of the faith of Abraham, Moses, and David, . . . 241
16. The work of the means of grace, ... 242
17. Historical divergences of creeds, and their causes, political and ethnical — Eastern and Western Churches — descendants of Jacob and Esau — confining or leading effect of national languages, ... 242
18. Recognised diversity of thoughts of faith in the cloud of witnesses, 245

CHAPTER X.

THE CONDITIONS TO FAITH.

1. A normal subjective condition necessary to believing in the historical love of God, ... 247

Moral Conditions to Faith.

2. Faith and faithfulness reciprocal, ... 247
3. Subjective sources of unbelief all separating the soul from God, . 248
4. Indifference causing inattention, ... 249
5. Self-indulgent trifling—Pilate—Agrippa—the Athenians, . . 249
6. Retained prejudices—the disciples and Jewish Christians, . 250
7. A fleshly mind—obscured perception, ... 250
8. Antipathy—subjective repulsion, ... 251
9. Examples of reciprocity of faith and faithfulness—love and the knowledge of God — German scepticism — heathen blindness —Christian misbeliefs as to the Holy Spirit—belief in human goodness and in God's—charity and faith in God's love, . 252
10. The impossibilities of faith, ... 255
11. Judicial element in unbelief—its source in man's necessary union with God, ... 256
12. A part of God's moral government of all human thought and action exercised through man's created constitution, . . 257

Intellectual Conditions to Faith.

13. A normal state of capacity and health.—Mens sana in corpore sano, ... 258
14. Value of an opinion affected by the personal peculiarities of the opinion maker, ... 259
15. Judgment of posterity—why of value, ... 261
16. Importance of the biography of an opinion in an age of much reading—secret history of peculiar creeds, . . . 262
17. Worldliness of one historical class of creeds—the Pharisees—the Latter-Day Saints—the Judaising teachers opposed to Paul, . 263
18. Circumstances of councils producing famous creeds, . . 264

Social Conditions to Faith.

19. Freedom of spirit to think independently, ... 265

20. France in the 18th century—Hume and his English contemporaries
    —the education of the Encyclopædists, ... 265
21. Recent Romish perverts, ... 266
22. Sectarian and political confinement of thought—artificial codes of
    morals, ... 267
23. Heathen society preventing conversion, ... 268
24. Technical education confining perception, ... 268
25. Peace of heart—faiths of solitaries—conventual or desolate life, 269
26. Value of the subjective in defence of unbelief—how far a man is
    not accountable for his belief, ... 270
27. Human subjective ignored by Hume and Comte, . . . 272
28. The subjective plea a foretold phenomenon of religious history, . 273

CHAPTER XI.

THE LIVING BY FAITH; OR, THE EDUCATION OF THE INDIVIDUAL TO FAITH.

 1. Original and latest representation of faith—living in a person, . 275
 2. Training by contact of faith's thoughts with circumstances, . 276
 3. Phases of living by faith, and their appropriate helps, . . 276
 4. Unifying element in them all—"Occupy till I come," . . 276
 5. Analogy of living by interhuman faith, ... 277
 6. Office of Providence—diverse training to habitual feeling of per-
    sonal connection with Christ, ... 278
 7. Living by faith in Christ so described as uniting to Him, . . 279
 8. The fight of faith—"the whole armour of God," . . . 280
 9. The work of faith, ... 281
10. The patience of faith, ... 282
11. The race or walk of faith, ... 282
12. The obedience of faith, ... 283
13. The domestic life of faith—Hezekiah—the Bethany family—
    training purpose of family affections, ... 284
14. The word of faith—"occupying" the means of grace, . . 287
15. Spiritual discipline, ... 289
16. The resulting spiritual condition—LIFE—union with Christ Jesus, 290
17. Consciousness of union—union making oneness, . . . 291
18. The healed universe, ... 293
19. Agreement with preceding conclusions as to the nature of faith, 293
20. Spiritual death—Adam's death "in the day that he ate" of the
    tree, ... 294
21. God's impossibilities and man's omnipotence, . . . 294
22. Conditions to assurance of salvation, ... 295
23. Sceptical reasoning primarily disuniting, ... 296
24. Eternal life—united individualities, ... 297
25. The idea of future union appearing in heathen religions, . . 297

Conclusion.

Apparent present failure of the true faith a uniform historical phenomenon—its success the lesson of history, . . . 299

versally referred to as "human nature." This consciousness becomes, according to its extent, a concomitant test of the correctness of revealed information as to the combined subject of the nature of God and the connection we can have with Him; and, as we shall afterwards see, it always co-operates in the forming of any individual man's religious faith. In the mean time we have to keep in mind that, however discovered, the particular connection limits the subject of connectional or religious faith.

Relation unique.

2. Now our revealed information is, that man's connection with God is unique in the history of being. We are instructed that man was formed a designed exception to all other creatures. His appearance among living things was heralded by the signal announcement that the Creator had special thoughts with reference to him. "God said, Let us make man in our image, after our likeness: and let them have dominion over the fish of the sea, and over the fowl of the air, and over the cattle, and over all the earth, and over every living thing that moveth upon the earth" (Gen. i. 26). The race was thus created exceptional, ruling over all visible earthly life; and though made "a little lower than the angels," yet "crowned"—distinguished exceptionally—"with glory and honour" (Ps. viii. 5). They were to be God's children as well as His creatures, as the genealogist quoted by Luke expresses it, recording "Adam was the son of God" (Luke iii. 38). In the changed position of his self-seeking departure from God, man's connection with Him was still declared to be exceptional. God spared not the other creatures who sinned, "the angels which kept not their first estate," but He spared mankind (Jude 6). And the love which God bears to the human race is exceptional, even when compared with that shown to His sinless creatures. This truth, so strongly illustrative of man's peculiar position, appears in the revealed fact that "the angels desire to look into the things" which God's love has moved Him to do for man (1 Pet. i. 12). As if they understood not such love, they desire to comprehend it. As it "passeth the knowledge" of our race, it is exceptional even in their great knowledge of God's goodness, and in their perfectly blessed experience of it.

3. What limits, then, are set to the contemplations of man's Faith instructed, not investi-gated. religious faith by the exceptional character of his relationship to God? Evidently if that relationship is one that needed to be revealed, because it could not be investigated, his religious thoughts must be characteristically, though it may not be exclusively, instructed thoughts. He has to deal fundamentally with knowledge communicated by God, not with opinions investigated by man. The function of his reason must be, not to theorise concerning God, and so construct a system of thoughts which he will entertain of Him, but to contemplate a plainly-revealed being. But within his range of communicated knowledge man's faith is farther limited. He is not to concern himself equally with all knowledge of God that is open to him, but as his peculiar business to think upon the things which God has told him respecting his own connection with Him. And farther, his contemplation of that especially important part of communicated truth will take its *form* from the manner in which the truth has been communicated. He finds the particular manner of revelation adopted by God to be essentially not the announcement of a systematic religion, but a historical detail of His manifestations of affection, past and future, towards man. His faith will therefore be essentially an emotional contemplation of that history.

4. Glimpses are opened in some profound passages of Paul's Glimpses of outside truth. writings of a wide connection of all creation with the human race, in which all earthly things, because of man's present state, are "subject to vanity"—failure, inoperativeness, unsuccess—and are destined to, and are now universally yearning after and waiting for, deliverance from this "pain" when man's restitution shall be finished (Rom. viii. 20, 21); his restitution being associated in promise with a wider perfecting and restored union of all created things, expressed by the phrase that "all things, both things in heaven and things on earth," shall be "gathered together in one" in Christ when man's inheritance is attained (Eph. i. 10, 11). The light thus let in upon the universal system, of which man is represented by it much as a central part, exhibits the magnificence of that system—indefinitely, however, like the apocalyptic visions of the glorious

blessedness awaiting man at the end of his earthly dispensation; but though, like these, serving grandly for consolation
and impressiveness as to man's importance in the purposes of
God, it is a light that only the more shows the exceptional
position of the human race in these purposes, and the consequent necessity that they should be guided in their thoughts
of God and of themselves as connected with Him, not by their
own observation and reasoning on things around and within
them, but by thinking on the particular history of that connection, and interpreting all other things by the help of that history. In accordance with this is the Bible's representation of
the simplicity of the thoughts which are to belong to man's
religion. They are to be such as a wayfaring man, though
unwise in other learning, cannot err in.

NOTE.—The conclusion drawn from revelation, that man's place in the purposes
of God is exceptional, is in harmony with the conclusion, apparently unavoidable
from physical truths, that his place in material life is exceptional, and that
the being inhabiting this earth is unique, and exists nowhere else. It would
be the loosest speculation to take into account the possibility of there being
other worlds in the universe inhabited by beings of our nature, if it is demon-
strable that no such beings can be in any of the celestial bodies likest to our
own globe. And since it is certain that upon no one of the solar planets except the earth could a being of our bodily constitution exist, it is simply a
corollary that no being of our spiritual experience—that is, no "living soul"
whose conditions and consequent capacities are the same as ours—can be anywhere else in the planetary system. We altogether beg the question if we say
that it seems to detract from the glory of God to think that He extended our
moral life and the love declared in His Word over so limited a space as our
earth alone, and that He will people heaven with the race of Adam only. We
cannot assume to be judges of what is most for God's glory; and to some minds
a selected sphere for human life will present thoughts best agreeing with the
attributes which God seeks us chiefly to associate with Him as His glory.
These are not physical, but moral. "God is love" (1 John iv. 8). "His tender
mercies are over" (above, overruling) "all his works" (Ps. cxlv. 9). To one
thinking on this declared character of God, what would seem an appropriate
greatness or grand thing in the history of life? That God should have created
a race upon whom He was especially to pour forth the inexhaustible love which
is His being—whose life was to be an eternal going on to know the breadth and
length and depth and height of His love—in whose nature He was to reproduce
His own moral attributes—in whose history He was to make gloriously manifest to all the universe of intelligence His grief and hatred against sin, and His
unquenchable love and compassion for His creatures deceived into it, giving

Himself in sacrifice for their deliverance,—may well be more astounding, more gloriously impressive, than would be the creation and peopling of a thousand times the number of worlds that we can conceive now existing. Indeed, any craving after belief in a population of beings like ourselves dwelling in the countless orbs of our sky and of the universe around, seems to partake of that hankering after material rather than moral grandeur, which appears in most of man's aspirations after great thoughts. Moral grandeur, such as God's is revealed to be, is not dependent on physical limits; and to think of Him creating a race for Himself to show forth His praise and glory in His love, should be no more difficult for us than to think that one day is to Him as great a thing as a thousand years. And if God made man to be in a family relationship with Him, inferring family affections and exceptional family importance, which is exactly the position of man towards God declared in God's Word, man's place may well be exceptional in extent as in all other respects. The family circle should be a circumscribed one—one taken out of the world of life.

As to an appropriate original preparation of the earth for the habitation of man in his *present* religious condition of a being to be recovered from sin, see Bushnel's geological speculation in his 'Nature and the Supernatural,' chap. vii.

CHAPTER II.

THE SUBJECT OF FAITH.

JOHN iii. 16.—God so loved the world.

God's exceptional love

1. THE subject with which religious faith is to occupy itself as its peculiar business is a restricted one. It is God's exceptional affection towards mankind. What we may call the key-words of revelation, which all its histories, promises, and forms of assurance expound, are, "God so loved the world." Our religious thoughts are directed not to God's nature, but to the facts and assurances of His love to man; and what thoughts are given to us of His natural attributes are presented to us in connection with that, the essential contemplation of our religion—His love to man—enhancing to our feelings its sureness, or its extent, or its tenderness.

in man's salvation.

2. We do not know to what extent God revealed to our first parents, at their creation, His peculiar love for them of all the creatures to whom He had given life. Our condition is in one great respect different, and the peculiar subject of our faith in God is the affection He has since declared to fallen man. It is an important fact, in agreement with what the Bible says of the great change which came over man's powers by the entrance of sin, that God had to, or did, educate the world anew to faith in Him, as it were from the beginning, by "line upon line, precept upon precept, here a little and there a little." Through a period of at least forty centuries He slowly unveiled to mankind, as they were able to think of it, His holy nature and the nearness of His connection with them, and His corresponding love for them. His love, as it is fully

revealed, is the subject of Christian faith ; part only of the thoughts of which was possessed by the early patriarchs, and even by the father of the faithful—and part only, though a larger part, by the chosen people.

3. The character of our fully-revealed faith is one distinctly defined and intelligibly marked. It is to be faith in a family nearness to God into which He has taken us, and in a corresponding love assured to us—the exceptional relationship and affection which the manner of our creation indicated to be His purpose from the first as to our race. *A family love :*

There are two bodies of facts given us in the Word of God by which to exercise our thoughts to the habit of looking to Him as in a uniting relationship, inferring a peculiar manner of love.

4. *First*, He has all along the progress of revelation bidden man think of Him by the light of certain familiar relationships, gradually unveiling fullest family union. These are relationships inferring affectionate protection—as a paternal monarch, a shepherd, a teacher; relationships inferring power and wisdom put forth in watchful and most considerate help—as a physician, a forgiver, a captain of salvation, a comforter; relationships implying community of nature and union of life—as a father, a brother, a husband. In the last stage of revelation other figures were added conveying an idea of closer union than human relationships experience—that of a branch to the vine, the members of the body to the head. By these lines of thought He bids us draw near to Him and understand the manner of His love to us, and learn to appreciate it. The help is one necessary to our understanding and our comfort alike. We cannot by searching find out God. His eternal power and Godhead are clearly seen from His great creation ; and those who can look upon the heavens and the earth, and not glorify Him as God, are inexcusable. But the thought of His greatness is by itself an oppressive one, and beyond it reason can hardly penetrate, and from it hardly extract comfort. We can make little of thinking about such subjects as eternity, infinity, and omnipotence. When Christian philosophers think that they reason closely from these bare ideas, *revealed first by assumed relationships ;*

they are unconsciously finding as conclusions thoughts which are really lying in their minds already, the unnoticed teaching of revelation.   The heathen world by its unaided wisdom knew not God.   A help mighty to save from much erroneous reasoning is this form in which He comes near to us, and draws us near to Him.   "The full thunder of His power who can comprehend?" but who is there, the feeblest and most cast down, who cannot understand and value and take to his heart the love and care a father has for his little ones, the " comforting" a mother gives, the " closeness " of a brother's affection, the life of faith a wife has in her husband, and the close clinging happiness which binds the union of these relationships, the "life hid in them," the belief of the heart, which is their occupation ?   When we are bidden think by these names of the love of God and our dependence upon Him, which He desires, we are already exercised to discern the good in which we are invited to believe.

the form of pre-Christian faith;

5. By this way of illustrative and assuring relationships God instructed mankind in the earlier ages of faith to believe in His holy love to them, and by these to interpret His government of them in His providence, and His messages to them by His prophets.   All were not revealed from the first; nor was any of them revealed with equal fulness of significance to all the generations to whom they prepared the way for the coming of God manifest in the flesh.   Some of them were not among the enjoyed thoughts of the earliest believers.   Abraham had not them all.   The Psalms show that some early saints could ponder most of them in their hearts; and their responsive language, in which Jehovah is spoken of as their "portion," their "refuge," their " dwelling-place," shows much appreciation of the love assured in His chosen metaphors of nearness. It is by the light of another revelation that the fulness of times has come to apprehend all the comfort sent with these names to mankind.   It is since the *manifestation* of God was added to their *representations* of Him that the love of the Father has been with full appreciation proclaimed evermore to the race, and the light of His countenance has shined upon them evermore.

6. *Second*, In what God calls the fulness of times, He added to these suggestive names of relationship another completing revelation of His connection with man. He gave the race not merely to imagine His relationship to them by the help of similitudes, but to see it with their eyes, as a man could behold and know the face of his brother man. He became Himself " manifest in their flesh," bone of their bone, flesh of their flesh ; as much taking their likeness and making it his own, as He originally made them in His likeness and gave them His nature. " No man hath seen God at any time ; the only-begotten Son, which is in the bosom of the Father, He hath declared Him " (John i. 18). In the affections and conduct of Jesus of Nazareth mankind had opportunity to actually see the love of God to man, and thenceforth they could understand and appreciate it as well as they could understand and appreciate one another's love. From that time the nearness of God's declared, promised, assured connection with man became a thing that had been visible to the world, a distinct matter of human recollection, a fact exactly as well known as any recorded fact respecting any individual character of history. To the personal attendants of Jesus, and ever after to all " who should believe through their word," the moral nature of God and His saving love to mankind became, not things to be reasoned of, but facts to be remembered, facts living for ever in the records of personal memory, or of history, the memory of the race. The holiness of God, His goodness, His truth, His abhorrence of sin, His desire to save fallen mankind, His sympathy with man's troubles, His self-sacrifice for man's sake, became not merely doctrines demonstrated by clearest reasoning from God's Word, and fortified by His most solemn assurances, but facts of human knowledge, things seen, things experienced, recollected, narrated, and possessed by the mind, as largely and as surely as a child could recollect a father's moral habits, and his descendants could confidently read of them.

second, by manifestation in Jesus of Nazareth ;

7. The visible life of Jesus of Nazareth also, as has been noticed, perfected the force of persuasion conveyed by the metaphors of human relationship under which God of old and to the end bade mankind think of and appreciate His love.

realising the metaphors of relationship.

If the similitudes of a father, a mother, a husband, a brother, a nurse, a comforter, a teacher, a healer, a defender, &c., could have been thought of before as in any degree merely figurative expressions, setting forth the boundless largeness of His love, but not, perhaps, promising such correspondent sympathy and special helpfulness as the love given by the human relationships known by these names, then the reality of the human life of Jesus—His "manifest" partaking of all our nature, His visibly perfect fellow-feeling of our infirmities—gave assurance that the divine love promised in these names is the very kind of help and faithfulness, the same manner of goodness and loving-kindness, that is looked for by needy human beings from such nearest human friends, only perfected in tenderness and trustworthiness and power by the guarantee of God's perfectness. The father and husband and friend and helper become eternal, all-wise, all-powerful, unchangeable, but still near and united, as if he were only human.

The historical progress of God's unveiling His love to man will be the subject of the next chapter.

Manner of the revelation—a history.

8. Inseparable from the subject of thought revealed to religious faith is the MANNER OF THE REVELATION. The form employed by God of making His love known to mankind is essentially a HISTORY of what it has done, and in being so is in exact accordance with what He tells us, that His nature is above our investigation. The history of religion shows that, universally, mankind must have an object of worship that is visible, or conceivable in terms of visible things. Every known people, except those expressly taught by God himself not to do so, has worshipped Him by visible images, meant to be typically or actually representative. When He made the great historical provision for checking the down-going of mankind's thoughts respecting Him through their own imaginations of a visible likeness to Him, and placed among the nations in a central position a people who, under His guidance, should serve Him in their sight without misleading images of Him, He gave that people an object of thought which should be visible, though not to their eyes, yet to their most common habits of thinking, the eyes of their mind — that is, their faith. He

bade them think of Him not as God, but as a father, a shepherd, a healer, a rock of salvation, &c. When in the end, the fulness of times, He completed His designed help to their "seeing Him who is invisible," it was by becoming a distinct historical person who had dwelt among them, and whose glory they had been "eyewitnesses of, the glory of the only begotten of the Father, full of grace and truth." It corroborates this view of faith being recognised by God as needing a visible hold for its thoughts, to find that He helped the earliest faith by some recognisable "presence of the Lord" (Gen. iii. 8, iv. 16); and gave a similar support to the faith of the Hebrew Church by appropriate visible associations with His concealed presence—the pillar of cloud; the tabernacle, made after a pattern shown to Moses in the mount; the temple, afterwards built according to divine description; and in both the miraculous cloud visible to the high priest upon the mercy-seat in the holy place. Even in the "spiritual" (John iv. 24) worship of the Christian Church, the Lord's Supper continues the same kind of help to faith. Since "the night on which He was betrayed," certain visible symbols, congruous to the fact which they commemorate, have by His appointment been used by the Church as a continual help to "remember" a visible, recognisable, historical person who is to dwell in our hearts by that faith which "endures as seeing Him who is invisible." The most distant future to which faith is to look is one of equally recognisable features—those of home, communion with known persons, health from known ills, &c.

9. This historical manner of God's revealing Himself, associating man's religious thoughts of Him with objects visible or imaginable in terms of visible things, was pointedly the manner of revelation from the beginning. The revelation was of a person assuring them of His love, but a person declared not by attributes, but by actions; the description of whose love was not a philosophical connection of it with His essential nature, but a history of its manifested care over individuals or peoples. Antediluvian knowledge of God was knowledge not of attributes but of transactions. Abraham's faith was associated with a long series of sensible manifestations of God to

Historical form of faith's thoughts from the first.

him in visions, actions, and promises. The first faith of the
exodus was to be in the history of Abraham, Isaac, and Jacob.
That of the Church in the wilderness added the striking
history called up by the words, "I am the Lord thy God,
which have brought thee up out of the land of Egypt, out of
the house of bondage" (Ex. xx. 2). The Book of Deuteronomy, bringing down the history of Israel to the end of the
forty years' singular experience, and comprehending declarations of the attributes of Jehovah only as they were made
apparent in historical connection with His deliverance of His
people, was the larger creed dictated by Moses for the settled
Hebrew nation. In the condensed form of the Song of Moses,
its historical thoughts of Jehovah were to be perpetually a
part of the religious services of the Church. The later confessions of Hebrew faith, the Psalms, known to have been in
regular use as solemn confessions to the end, such as the Passover Psalms (Ps. cxiii.-cxviii.), guided the people to distinct
historical thinking; or where to generalisations approaching
what we would call attributes, to generalisations always immediately inferred from or explained by specified history. The
thought of specific transactions was the faith quoted of the
examples of believing, enumerated in Hebrews xi., examples
spread over all pre-Christian times. Entirely such was the
faith of the Hebrew Church after the captivity (Neh. ix.) In
the Christian Church the Messiah at His coming was to be
looked for, recognised, and thought of, by the signs of certain
definite proceedings (Luke iv. 18-21). To believers to the end
of time the name of Jesus is to be a word calling up not
attributes, but a specific history, the centre portion of which
is a human biography. Such a faith the apostles called Jews
and heathens alike to, and that by divine direction, their
argument being prescribed to them—"Jesus Christ, and Him
crucified."

Convincing
force of his-
torical
above that
of philoso-
phical
faiths.

10. The historical form of the truth contemplated by
religious faith carries most important consequences with it
into the questions of religious study and teaching. Looking for the natural or non-miraculous causes to which the
first successes of revealed faiths are to be attributed, and to

which we are to look for the future success of Christianity, the history of those successes obliges us to give the chief place to this that the patriarchal faith and Judaism and Christianity have all had as the matter of their thoughts and ground of their inferences, an actual history of God's holy love of man, a body of facts which every individual believer could bring as distinctly before his mind as he could his own family history, of which, indeed, in the case of some of the patriarchs, the facts of their faith formed a great part. The character of the heathen faiths over which revealed religion triumphed in the judgment of mankind was very distinctly a contrast to this. They consisted of opinions instead of knowledge. The highest philosophical systems of heathenism which have been preserved were purely theories as to what the nature of God might be, considering what the nature of man is, but comprehending in their reasonings no known fact respecting God's government of mankind, no history of any connection ever shown to exist between them. In recent technical phrase, their theology was purely subjective, a construction out of the heathen's spiritual consciousness including no objective facts known of God's nature or His disposition towards man. Having no objective known to them, they supplied the human necessity for a visible or imaginable subject of faith by imagining a history, or rather innumerable histories, expository of how their imagined divinities would or might act among themselves or towards man. They constructed myths properly so called, pictorial representations of their own intellectual powers and moral feelings and habits attributed to supposed overruling deities. Those heathen myths affiliate themselves unmistakably to a corrupt origin, the state of society in which they arose, by marks of which no trace can be found by modern sceptics in the grandly pure and true and exalted objective representations of revealed theology which they would assign to a like origin. In the most religious times of Greece the popular theology was purely a personification of the observed attributes of human life, bad and good alike—as love pure and impure, wrath just and unjust, beneficence and greed, intelligence, taste, &c. ; and of the observed

sources of man's good or ill fortune, the elements, the fertility
of the ground, the earth itself, the atmosphere, and so on.
It was a good example of the merely *materialistic* positivism
to which the *Philosophie Positive* would confine human knowledge ; and a fair example, because one isolated from the light
of revealed truth and morality which now might disturb the
Philosophie, of how powerless such positivism is to help man to
the knowledge of the spiritual, or to better his moral condition ; and of how powerful it is to release the superstitious
propensities which revelation enables him to subordinate to
intelligent faith. The ancient and genuine philosophical religion, getting no farther than to imagine a possible God, the
concentration of human excellences, but active or inactive
towards earthly things, as the philosophers might consider
most dignified in a great man's conduct towards the world,
and without any link to real observed existence, was a shifting
theory which sat upon those that thought of it in the lightest
possible manner, and had no moral influence to guide or
restrain or support them. The highest Greek speculators in
the field of theology are known by their writings to have been
as low morally as the gross believers in the sensual myths of
the popular faith. The Athenians of Paul's days were the
most eminent triflers with life ; their acute and widely-inquir-
ing intellect seeing nothing better to do under their empty
thoughts of the immaterial world than to make the most of the
material (1 Cor. xv. 32) in careless, easy, self-indulgent existence
from day to day while the only certain lasted. The serious
thoughts unavoidable by man's nature they could only do their
best to get over the uneasiness of by industrious husbanding of
passing trifles of enjoyment (Acts xvii. 21), and resisting the
feeling of care about subjects of which they had no certainty
(ver. 32); but they were hopeless in the presence of the evils
of life, and effortless, to a degree hardly appreciable by us,
towards alleviating the most intense social miseries of their
time.

Their fall
before
historical
faiths.

11. Such religions of imagination fell before the theology
of actual manifestation and known transactions; the reasoning
continually upon historical facts with which Paul went single-

handed into the very focus of subtle metaphysical scepticism, cultivated frivolity and seemingly invulnerable self-satisfaction. But the same had been the effect from the beginning where-ever the religions of human subjective hypothesis came into contact with the revealed religion of historical facts. The reality of Judaism seized hold upon the spirits of observant heathens brought into prolonged intercourse with the Hebrew people. Nothing in history is so striking as the awe, thor-oughly rational and self-possessed, with which Nebuchadnezzar, imagining himself, as his Assyrian remains show, an entire believer in the gods of his mythology, looked upon the reality of the God whom Daniel proclaimed to him as the giver of the vision he was "troubled" by. The same feeling, recog-nising reality in the revealed God, is evident over all the earlier history of the Hebrews. The nations which Israel passed through or by during their forty years' pilgrimage, the Philistines near whom they settled, the Egyptians from whose oppression they went forth with a high hand, trembled and stood in sharply-reasoning dread of the invisible being, mani-festly the ruler of all things, who protected that isolated people. Their professed fear of their own gods, and fancied belief in them, vanished before the unmistakable realities of Israel's history. The Jehovah of the Israelites was evidently the I AM that He called Himself, the one reality, the one existence. He was an invisible being, the facts surrounding whom made Him felt by the spirit of man as a living, true, undoubted power, its master and its judge. Pharaoh trembled before the patriarchal *knowledge* of God, the faith which Moses came before him to demand his submission to, as much as Felix did before the more perfect light of Paul's preaching. The case of Paul in the cities of Greece is more in point than has been noticed above, as showing the force of the historical truth to make itself recognised. To meet the subtlety, the rhetoric and practice in disputation, of the flower of heathen apologists, Paul, though capable of learned display, was per-mitted to speak only the simple story of God's so great love of the world completed in Christ and Him crucified. This story of the cross of Christ was at first sight foolishness to the learned Greeks ingenious in philosophising; but it was the power of God and the wisdom of God to seize upon their own minds and turn them away from all their beautiful interesting imaginations of possible truth to itself; as a reality which the soul of man recognised, as the eye practised in the human countenance will recognise a portrait among pictures, and set apart its real life as quite a different thing from all imaginary individuality inserted into an ideal painting.

The human mind's recognition of reality.

12. Success is said to have attended some attempts to construct an intricate fiction, so as to pass with good judges for a narrative of actual occurrences. The rule approaching at least to universality is, that a narrative of actual life commends itself as a real portrait does to the numerous testing points which human experience educates ready feeling to apply to any narrative of human life.

This has been the case with the Bible narratives, and especially with the unique religious narrative of human life, the history of Jesus. No ingenious hypothesis explaining away the actual occurrence of the things related in the Gospels has ever been more than a forced haze cast about one or other particular of the history. The whole picture soon forced itself upon fresh readers as a picture of real life. The scepticism never could be made general if the story was allowed to be read. It was such a labour to keep in mind the suggested doubts, which would not suggest themselves, that they were always soon let go. A sceptic fencing himself in his study from all corrective contact with the testing realities of the visible world, and the ways of human thinking and feeling and acting, confining himself alone with his own resolutely retained fancies, can compile ingenious theories of doubt concerning human things in the Bible, or out of it. If he go out of his guarded chamber into the world of men for a while, the world he has created for himself slips from his grasp. He finds himself, as Hume confessed in his own case, thinking very much as other men think. However it is to be explained, the language of fact forces itself upon men's recognition. Metaphysicians who are obliged to share a great deal in the business of the world, plunged daily into the bracing bath of human realities, do not fall into the follies of philosophising which so often encloud recluse thinkers. This is perhaps great part of the reason of difference between what is looked upon as English common-sense and German dreaminess ; as the same difference in kind is to be found between metaphysical writings coming out of busy life, and others coming out of studious cloister-life in England itself. There seems to be little possibility of holding anything like the mythical theory, or of doing anything but feel the historical reality of the Bible narratives when the reader travels in the locality which they claim. Commodore Lynch, in his narrative of his expedition to the Dead Sea, gives a case of entire disbelief of Moses' narrative, among several in-stances of scepticism, being converted into entire belief, in the case of some of his party of explorers during their few weeks' survey. The language of the Scriptural writers, casual as well as careful, especially the figurative language pervading the large proportion of the sacred books that is poetical, so perpetually reflects the unique scenery, terrestrial and atmospheric, of the region they speak of, as to assign itself to authorship certainly within the influence which that scenery would have upon men's customary thoughts. Even in the case of the parables of our Lord, some of them so reflect the topographical features of the spots where they were spoken, that to doubt their authenticity would be like doubting the details of a battle while standing amid peculiarities of the battle-field, which make these details almost a topographical necessity. To untravelled readers of such books of travel in Palestine as Dean Stanley's, even the attentive reading of his notes is enough to make unavoidable the acceptance as genuine of the narratives and the devotional language of the Bible which he illustrates.

13. A strong negative proof of the importance, if not neces-sity, that religious truth should be presented to man in the historical form, is that successful sceptical writers have always withdrawn the attention of their readers from the actual picture presented by the sacred books as a whole—the Metaphysical school wrenching aside the notice to the bold preliminary ques-tion, whether we could by possibility believe a man telling us that he had seen a miracle — the Mythists absorbing the

Scepticism avoiding historical truth.

thoughts in ingenious statements of alleged circumstances of all kinds, which might have made the writers frame parts of their stories to be figurative representations of non-religious truth, or fables clothing popular sentiments to suit the habits of thought of imaginative ages—the German critical school confusing the mind by a perpetually shifting onslaught on frequently misquoted details, which in the tumult of fault-finding ignores and would conceal the absence of consistency in their own criticism, as well as the presence of a grand whole in the narrative round which they are skirmishing.

Congruity of revealed truth to man's consciousness.

14. The revealed subject of faith which is to lay hold on man's spirit as *the truth*, has another essential feature besides its form of a promptly recognised history of a reality. It is a reality which *suits his religious condition*. A human religion must be one fitting itself to human nature. Its faith must be of facts which are recognisable by the bearers of that nature as of value to them. It is of no consequence to me what precise number of asteroids have been discovered in the vacant planetary orbit space, but it is of consequence to me to have a parent, or brother, or friend, whose love will make the vicissitudes of all other fortune easily borne. The facts of revelation are of this kind—human facts—which in all stages of revelation man has felt to be in *rapport* with his conscious condition, and which, therefore, have made themselves his proper faith. The history of God's love to man is a system into which he feels that his condition as to weakness, sinfulness, wish for sympathy, and need of help, strangely fits. It is evidently his subjective religion if it be objectively proved. And the practice of faith belonging to this revealed religion, as seen in the lives recorded in it, awakes his fellow-feeling. It is the feeling of the truth as he experiences it. This is the kind of evidence which must discharge the essential function of religious evidence—persuasion. Its force is different in kind from the chiefly forensic effect of external evidences which compel the intellect to see a divine Being standing near with a message in His hand. Within God's revealed Word the whole conscious human nature, not of logical reasoning powers only, but inarticulate cravings, sympathies, propensities of imagination and desire, meets

truth articulately declared or set forth in expressive action, amidst which it finds itself at home, surrounded by features recognisable as akin to itself. The Psalms exhibit to us a great amount of this recognition by human nature of a congruous nature in the divine love expressed in the Word—" joy in its testimonies," "the entrance of His words giving light," "His comforts delighting the soul in the multitude of its thoughts within itself." The subjective cleaving of the most spiritual psalmists' whole souls to Him who appeared to them in the Word, is expressed in one place in a phrase which might be set as a motto before the mass of their religious self-expression —" I said, Thou art my God." The words contain the *rationale* of all human acceptance of revealed truth. It is truth that is *the truth* to man—human truth—truth of which human nature is consciously a part.

15. The particular form of the word of faith—that it is a record of facts which are congruous to man's conscious state of relationships, familiar to all, and persuasive of a love consciously needed; and of expressions of love so widely varied, and finding an answering voice in one or other human consciousness—exactly fits the condition of human kind; putting faith, as it should be, within the grasp of all capacities. Every individual, however his ability to reason differs from another's, can take in, and keep habitually before his mind, as much of fact, of certain realities of God's deeds of love, as will fill his own power of enjoyment. That is the perfection of adaptation of the means of faith to the endless diversities of condition of soul found in the wreck of human nature. It is not necessary that all the facts which demonstrate or illustrate God's saving love should be remembered and understood. They all show forth one thing, only placing 'it in different lights—that " God so loved the world." Religious knowledge, analogous to family thought, is not by any means strictly analogous to scientific knowledge, as to range of subjects. In science, as yet, ultimate truth is not one and indivisible, but consists of a number of truths only partially or not at all connected with one another; and a number of scientific facts presented to a scientific man may

[margin note: Historical faith suited to differences of capacity.]

lead his thoughts to a diversity of theories or ultimate points of knowledge, or a new fact may be irreconcilable with any established theory, and compel the adoption of a new ultimate truth. The hope of physical science is to get, *by the progress of investigation, at one ultimate truth,* of which all the present ultimate truths shall be found to be members, and not merely head truths to their respective bodies of facts. That is not the state of the religious knowledge upon.which faith rests. It contains one simple ultimate truth—"God so loved the world." No intermediate barrier of propositions need stand in the way of any one thinking from the facts of religion, or from any fact of it, directly up to that head truth. Every fact directly illustrates that. And the fitness to man's condition of this revealed manner of instructing faith lies in the human circumstance that one fact may fill up one feeble soul's power of feeling and enjoying the love declared, as wholly as a large history does "the multitude of thoughts" which a stronger mind is capable of gathering happiness from. In human family life the full-grown son differs from the little child in the number of facts of family love he has whereon to muse, but we cannot say his enjoyment is differently full. In receiving the happiness of faith, the case is the same as in the giving of the widow's mite and the rich man's abundance. The smallest in human measurement may be the fullest in enjoyment — it needs only that the capacity be filled. Who would venture to say that there was any difference in the happiness felt by those four examples of faith who so differed as to the number and kind of facts they had to think of in order to feed their happy faith—the Syro-Phœnician mother, the woman who washed the feet of Jesus with her tears and wiped them with the hairs of her head, the disciple whom Jesus loved, and Paul the "persecutor and injurious," but the "chosen of Christ to be His apostle unto the Gentiles"?

Expedient form of propagating the faith. 16. The well-marked way in which faith in God's love has been *learned* by man—viz., in contemplation of that truth as it appears in the history of it—must determine much what manner of *teaching* is expedient in man's endeavours to extend the faith. The teaching should essentially be historical, as distinguished from doctrinal. It should be chiefly the facts and the expressions of the word of salvation—its own narratives of the facts which made God's holy love of mankind actually manifest to generation after generation—its own representations of the special relationships which He assumes towards man, which are the nearest possible representatives of the facts or well-understood habits of family love—and His peculiar language, the marked expressions He uses to influence us, which make a feature of the Word so definite and impressive that the Bible stands by itself among writings as a treasury of texts, maxims, terse expressions of wide truths, cumulative expressions of affection, and penetrative single words of persuasion. These facts and words of God's own representation of saving truth, and not doctrines logically arranged by man out of all the materials afforded by the Word, are the knowledge which faith feels its possession of, the effective help to the human soul to " have the Lord ever before it." Systems of doctrine do not carry the same life, the same conviction of reality, with them to man's recognition. Containing always a mixture of other language with the Bible's language of fact,—containing also, unavoidably perhaps, as history would seem to teach, a mixture of human theory with Scriptural facts—of necessity, too, breaking often the connection of facts, and of expressions arranged in the sacred writings to come home to human consciousness,—they fail in so coming home. They have a convincing power which only ranks between the living transactions of revealed religion and the metaphysical reasonings of philosophical faiths, which have not facts, but only opinions which one man may reason out, but another not recognise as of value to him. All creeds must, as they have done, fail from this cause of such ready and wide acceptance as the Bible's own language has met with. Whatever be the defect in merely human religious language, no explanation in other words than the Bible's, even of the Bible's own emotional inferences from the facts it narrates, finds the same thorough recognition by the inner man, understanding, feeling, and desires, that the Bible's own expression of the true human reasoning of mind and heart upon these facts commands.

Inherent
effective-
ness.

17. The Bible's language being the language of fact, and not of imagination or of theory—being the narrative of things actually done by God, exactly according with man's conscious needs, and of feelings experienced characteristic of the human life all readers are conscious of—abounding, too, in representations, which other language might distort, of states of heart which individual readers feel, but which they thought their own secret—faults, failings, needs, troubles, or pleasures not common to man, certainly not described in man's books—its perpetually suggestive and demonstrative phrases pierce to the dividing asunder of the very soul and spirit, discern the unspoken, perhaps, till thus discovered, unperceived, thoughts and intents of the heart, and so become an irresistible evidence themselves to man's inner feeling—his peculiar knowledge of himself, that the religion they belong to is the gift of man's proper God.

CHAPTER III.

THE EDUCATION OF THE WORLD TO FAITH.

PART FIRST.—THE PROGRESS OF REVELATION.

IsaIAH xxviii. 10.—Line upon line, line upon line; precept upon precept, precept upon precept; here a little, and there a little.

JOHN xvi. 12.—I have yet many things to say unto you, but ye cannot bear them now.

1. WE have no means of comparing the first pair's original ability to understand and appreciate the nature and love of God with the power their nearest descendants had, except the but slightly approximate comparison we can make between a very virtuous Christian's readiness of head and heart and the slowness or inability of greatly demoralised persons to realise spiritual truth, whatever their ability to discern and appreciate other knowledge. The sacred Scriptures, however, give expressive representations of the effect produced by continued sin upon the power both of reasoning and feeling as to religious truth. The "understanding is darkened," or "befooled;" the mind is "turned away from the life of God through the ignorance that is in it," brought on by "blindness" or "callousness" of the heart (Eph. iv. 18). The conscience becomes evil (Heb. x. 22). The mind is "fleshly," and not "capable of accepting the law"—the fully declared will of God (Rom. viii. 7). *Religious perception lost by sinning.*

2. In exact accordance with this picture of the effect of sinfulness upon the human nature is the manifest change which God immediately made in His manner of intercourse with mankind after the change which their new condition of sin- *Man's fall and rudimentary instruction.*

fulness made in them. That change is accurately spoken of as a fall of the race in capacity as well as position. The first pair's original capacity for knowing and enjoying God we can infer from their place before Him. They were as His children, made in His own likeness. He evidently held intercourse with them in a manner so appreciable by their powers of perception and familiarly sensible to them that they recognised His approach at once; and his visiting them in that manner is referred to in Genesis as a thing of ordinary occurrence would be. After their sin, as if the power of appreciating His nature and valuing His pleasure had gone from them in the first act of separative disobedience, they at once felt towards Him as a God afar off from them, and hid themselves from His approach. In terrible contrast to the near family communion of the garden eastward in Eden, He seems to have had, as it were, to begin to reveal Himself to the expelled race as if He had been unknown to them ; and what is most instructive as to their having fallen in spiritual capabilities, He began to teach them divine knowledge slowly from its very rudiments. The chronological progress of revelation is strikingly a progress in slowly unveiling the invisible God, "line upon line, here a little, and there a little ;" from the fundamental truths of His almighty power and Godhead gradually describing to mankind, and opening their eyes to recognise His holy love of them. Even to Adam, God had to renew the feeling that His will must be supreme and all-powerful over His child-creature. God's perfect son, so degraded in his own eyes in the very hour of his sin as to hide himself, had at the same time fallen so in intellect and conscience as to think he could say to Him, "The woman whom thou gavest to be with me, she gave me of the tree, and I did eat;" and to need a new revelation of his position towards his Father and Creator made to him in the terrible form of fallen man's first lesson in the holiness of God, "Because thou hast hearkened unto the voice of thy wife, and eaten of the tree of which I commanded thee, saying, Thou shalt not eat of it ; dust thou art, and unto dust thou shalt return." To Adam's first-born child, the first son of the fallen likeness, God had to teach even His omniscience. Cain

had no feeling of the truth that God is everywhere, beholding
all things, and thought he could conceal his brother's murder
even from Him.   These two examples illustrate how suddenly
come to and great were the ignorance and the blindness of
understanding and feeling into which human nature had fallen
by its sinning against God, and from how rudimentary a point
the education of the race to right habitual thoughts and feelings towards Him had to be begun.

Antediluvian Faith.

3. During the first strongly marked period of sinful man's God the
history, extending from the expulsion of Adam and Eve from Avenger.
Eden to the destruction of the corrupted human world by the
Flood, the chief knowledge that mankind had always before
their eyes of God's moral position towards them was His
condemnation of sin.   That was the great truth published by
the prominent facts of antediluvian history; the expulsion
and bitter degradation and death of Adam and Eve, the
fugitive life of Cain, the universal burden of labour and
sorrow, and in the end the hundred years of threatening of
a flood.   There is one record left of the thoughts which that
world of men had concerning God, in Lamech's address to his
two wives when he had slain a man.   His ruling thought of
God was evidently as of the judge and avenger.   Jude tells us
that that was the special subject of Enoch's preaching (Jude
14, 15).   That rudimentary thought of fallen mankind's faith
received impressiveness from the feeling of God's almighty
power and Godhead, which, as Paul notices (Rom. i. 20), the
race continued capable of from the beginning.   It is instructive to observe that this is the feeling that still animates the
indefinite dread of retribution for crime which all but makes
up the professed faiths of heathenism; and that this rudimentary religion is with the frequency of a rule betrayed as an
unprofessed superstition, hanging like a millstone about the
necks of professed infidels.

4. That the divine abhorrence was of sin, and not of mankind Hopes of
themselves, cropped out here and there during that long mercy.

rudimentary lesson, lasting for 1600 years. That truth appeared in God's partial protection of Cain; in His communion with Enoch, and taking him away without death; and in the preaching of Enoch and Noah, both probably, since Noah certainly was, messengers of merciful desires on God's part to men if they would understand and believe and repent. These facts indicated the presence of love in some form along with holy anger. The promise that the seed of the woman should bruise the serpent's head, having been given in immediate connection with the condemnation of the woman and her serpent tempter, must have been understood by the first sinners, with all its indistinctness, as a promise of a merciful kind; something set against and alleviating the condemnation of death which had just been passed upon man. Eve's exclamation on the birth of her first son shows that she regarded him as a gift, not of anger, but of goodness. And doubtless the promise joined to "her seed" would be handed down, a traditional invitation to trust in the Lord God's having merciful purposes towards His human creatures. That the antediluvian patriarchs were able to think of God with some thought of His being willing to receive them, is significantly indicated by the names which some of them gave to their children. Enoch, according to Dr Kitto, means " dedicated ;" Mahaleel, a Sethite name, is "praise of God;" Methusael, a Cainite one, "a man of God." The fact that the holy name appears in more of the Cainite than of the Sethite names, and that those now quoted indicative of feelings able to turn to God with other thoughts than those of fear, are found among the descendants of Cain as well as in the race of Adam's better son, is one that breaks the deepest darkness of that dispensation of fear with some streaks of light.

Hebrew Faith.

God draw-
ing nigh.   5. God's manner with mankind after the Flood shows a great unveiling of His purposes of grace to the penitent. It would perhaps be proximately accurate to say that in the old world *He suffered man to draw near to Him,* and in the new-

begun world, which was separated so essentially from the old, in that it was the descendants of one selected and only pre-served family of the old, *He drew near to them.* His selection of Noah to begin a new population of the earth, was the type or first example of His manner of dealing with mankind during the next great period of sinful man's history, that which continued until the fulness of time. That was a policy of selection—selection for one constant purpose of training mankind by example to appreciation of God's moral nature, and faith in His disposition of kindness towards them. The religious history of the whole period was shortly this, that God brought up a nation to be the instructor of the world, and placed it and moved it about among the nations of the world so as to be an effective light to them, making known His moral nature and His dispositions towards man. The fortunes of the chosen people, which were constantly declared to be visitations for their fidelity to or sins against their holy Jehovah, manifested historically the nature of Jehovah to the peoples among whom their triumphs or captivities brought them; and the exposition of the religious meaning of the history was completed by the revealed religious knowledge and worship of the Hebrew people being brought systemati-cally under the impressed observation of those nations. The same system of examples and active guides in faith—*i.e.*, in true habitual thoughts of God—we see in narrower circles in the Hebrew history. Abraham, the great example of faith, is an instance before the development of the teacher-nation, and David in the period of its greatness. The examples of faith recorded in Heb. xi. were all lights in contemporary circles of society, as well as to succeeding readers of their story.

6. To these examples, both the nation and the individuals, of how He wished mankind to know and enjoy Him, God drew nearer than He had done to former generations, and nearer as time went on; and the progress is observable as one in faith as well as revelation—the nearness recognised as well as declared. He who in the old world was practically known only " afar off " by His creating power, or His general government of man in the interests of holiness as the avenger of crime, became, in

Progress of revelation and appre-ciation.

the new, associated with persons and places. He was Jehovah and Jehovah-Jireh, the God of Abraham, and of Isaac, and of Jacob. At the beginning of Israel's nationality, the drawing near of God to mankind was marked thus clearly. It was the beginning of a most distinct and advancing unveiling of His nature and His affections towards men. He speaks at that time of making Himself practically " known " to the Egyptians and the Hebrews—" known" evidently in a nearer position, and more closely compelling recognition, than they had thought of before. To the Hebrews the message was, " I will be to you a God, and ye shall know that I am Jehovah your God, which bringeth you out from under the burdens of the Egyptians " (Ex. vi. 7). Of the Egyptians he says, " And the Egyptians shall know that I am Jehovah, when I have stretched forth my hand upon Egypt to bring out the children of Israel from amongst them " (Ex. vii. 5). The progress of revelation had to begin with a rudimentary lesson to the Hebrews in Egypt, sunk for generations in Egyptian bondage, and succumbing to its idolatries. Jehovah had to them, as to mankind after the Fall, to reveal Himself somewhat from the beginning as the " I AM "—the Sole Existence—the Eternal—the Only Living —before whom the gods of Egypt were nothing ; and also to recall to their thoughts the primitive religious knowledge of their race, that He was the God of their fathers, Abraham, and Isaac, and Jacob. A promise of much advanced faith accompanied that new revelation made through Moses (Ex. vi. 3). It was that they should know Him as even Abraham had not known Him ; that He would take them to be to Him for a people, and be to them a God. And the progress of that special relationship to become religiously " known," recognised as well as revealed, was rapid as the Hebrew separation advanced. He became thought of by them as *their* deliverer, with a mighty hand and a stretched-out arm, from Egypt. He was speedily known to the nations to whom they came in their consolidating life of the wilderness, as the " Jehovah of their hosts," the God of their battles. The characteristic revelation belonging to Hebrew historical faith was His commanding a dwelling-place to be made for Him in the midst of

the pilgrim tribes of Israel, and His teaching them definite
knowledge of the feelings and conduct they ought to have
towards Him, and the sins they would be in danger of. He
definitely revealed a particular way of obtaining His forgiveness, and prepared and enjoined on them an extensive and
minute religious discipline, to train them into a habit of
thinking of sin against· Him as the great Evil, and of thinking
of expiation and purification as absolutely necessary—an expiation by atonement, not without shedding of blood ; and a
purification by self-government, combined with seeking and
trusting in help from Him. Equally near to them in secular
and spiritual interests, marking these to be inseparable, He
was their King, guiding them by an open oracle, as well as by
a minute statute law of His own dictation ; and their God
dwelling in the midst of them, though declaring that no house
that they could build could suffice for His temple, whose
throne was the heavens and the whole earth but His footstool.
And in the course of the generations during which He trained
the nation to be ready to receive the coming Saviour, and
understand the need of such an atonement as was to be made,
and to be habituated to the thought and belief of God's having
so great love for man, He progressively called Himself by
names of nearer and nearer human relationships to them—
names more and more declaring love, compassion, saving help,
self-sacrifice for men's sake.

We may consider separately the names and the actual history by which God revealed His nature and His connection
with man.

7. The progress of revealing names given to God in sacred
history is chronologically distinct. The name of majesty—
"Elohim," Deity—is alone used at first, but is used also of
false gods. It expresses no relationship between Him and
man but the rudimentary one which seems to be the faith of
every human soul able to think—the existence of an invisible
Being who is supreme over man. When He first revealed His
design of raising up a people for Himself to make Him known
among the darkened nations of mankind, He made Himself
known to the father of the designed instructor-nation by a

Progress of
revealing
names.

proper name and certain attributes describing His position towards mankind. Instead of "Elohim"=Deity, He called Himself "El," a name never applied without explanation to false gods, but used as His own proper name, and afterwards shown to import absolute supremacy; being used to that effect in combination with the common term, as "El-elohim," God of gods. At the same time He associated certain attributes with the proper name in His servants' thoughts. Melchizedec speaks of Him to Abraham as the Most High El; and Abraham says to the king of Sodom, "I have lifted up mine hand to Jehovah, the Most High El, possessor of heaven and earth" (Gen. xiv.) After the attribute of supremacy, those of might and faithfulness were soon revealed. "When Abraham was ninety years old, the Lord appeared unto Abraham, and said, I am the Almighty God; and I will make my covenant with thee" (Gen. xvii. 1).

The next great unveiling of the nature and will of the Deity, God of gods, Most High God, possessor of heaven and earth, the Almighty God, was to Moses in preparation for His great drawing near to mankind in common, and not to individuals only; proximately inviting the faith of the whole race. The revelation consisted of two parts. He first declared His peculiar position as the object of faith to man; the object of contemplation and ever-present thought to the whole universe of intelligent being. He declared Himself the only self-existent Being, the only living and true God; "I AM THAT I AM: Thus shalt thou say to the children of Israel, I AM hath sent me unto you" (Ex. iii. 14). He next made known the special relationship by which He wished His people Israel to think of Him, which was to be represented by the name "Jehovah." The name itself had been known to Abraham their father, and yet more expressly the father of spiritual Israel—"all them that believe" (Gen. xiv. 22)—but not the riches of "holy and reverent" thought and trust to which the name was to invite the chosen people. They were to think of His selecting love evermore by that name, and rejoice in Him as their own near, holy, unchangeably loving Protector, "Jehovah of Israel," "the Holy One of Israel," "their Almighty King." Thenceforth

they were to look upon Him whom they worshipped not instructed by titles of greatness, power, and supremacy, but by a
name promising a near selecting relationship comprehending
special trust and special guidance. The revealed relationship
began immediately to be acted upon. The moral Decalogue,
and the religious, political, and social law, were given them as
the will of their Jehovah—His godly, kingly, fatherly discipline. And coincident with that declaration of special temporal
relationship assumed towards Israel by God as their Jehovah,
it is important to notice a revelation made to Moses of a yet
far-distant faith which mankind would have; a revelation of a
relationship not to that people and time, but to all peoples and
times of that world which the Prophet like unto Moses taught
that God so loved. At the second giving of the Ten Commandments on Sinai, when Moses, despairing because of Israel's so
speedy fall back into idolatry, and receiving comfort of faith
in Jehovah's forbearance, besought Him, saying, " Show me
thy glory," the Lord passed before Moses and proclaimed
Himself " The Lord, the Lord God merciful and gracious, long-
suffering, and abundant in goodness and truth, keeping mercy
for thousands, forgiving iniquity and transgressions and sin,
and that will by no means clear the guilty " (Ex. xxxiv. 6, 7).
That short bright unveiling of God as the Holy and Loving
One was an early example of what Hebrew revelation contained often afterwards — testimonies whose full meaning
appeared only in the fulness of times. The grace and truth,
the meeting of fullest love and holiest justice, here put in
words, came only by Jesus Christ, and was understood only
when His coming made God the just, yet justifier of sinners,
visibly known. The revelation made to Moses was a forelight
of Christ, one of many expressions and acts not comprehended
at the time they came forth, but which, looked back upon now
as they stand one behind another extending to the beginning
of God's merciful unveilings of Himself to mankind, form the
precious vista of faith's retrospect, through which it beholds
the Saviour, the same yesterday, to-day, and for ever, keeping
the same watch in all generations over the race He came in
the fulness of times to save.

We cannot trace in the same chronological manner all the affectional titles from time to time assumed by or attributed to Jehovah in the comforted faith of His servants. The needs which called these forth did not come chronologically upon man. Attributed as often as assumed, they have their great value as illustrations of the progress of *learning* the truth, the acquisition by the instructed people of faith's comforting thoughts. That progress is distinctly seen in Israel's history.

Apprecia-
tive faith
localising
thoughts of
truth.
8. We find the Israelites taking from the first a special means of indulging themselves and impressing their descendants with the thought of their Jehovah's nearness and peculiar relationship to them. They marked by the ".holy and reverend name" places and events in their history, to be thought of ever after as sacred to His praise. Abraham, their father in faith, had left them a suggestive example of this practice of self-instruction. The place to which he had been called to offer up his son Isaac for a burnt-offering, but where instead of that great affliction he had received an earnest of Jehovah's taking upon Himself the burdens of men, the patriarch had named "Jehovah-Jireh"—Jehovah the Provider; and the phrase had remained proverbial among his descendants, a seed of future thoughts of faith in Jehovah's "providing" which were to rise higher and higher through Israel's generations until the day came that Abraham saw afar off. Their immediate progenitor Jacob had left them another historical name which was a rallying-point to their faith in after times. The place where he met the angels of God on his return home with his children, the fathers of the tribes, he had called Mahanaim—"the hosts"—the Lord's hosts ; and it became the religious sanctuary of the trans-Jordanic tribes; and it was David's place of safety in Absalom's rebellion, doubtless not without consolation from its suggestions of faith in Jehovah under his sore affliction, one like Jacob's in character and in its burden of self-reproach. In this habit of thought Moses called the memorial altar which he built on the place of Israel's first victory in the wilderness " Jehovah-Nissi "— Jehovah my Banner (Ex. xvii. 15). Gideon localised another

memory of Jehovah's coming near for their help, giving the title of "Jehovah-Shalom"—Jehovah is Peace—to the altar he built after the divine appearance to him, appointing him the deliverer of Israel from the Midianites (Judg. vi. 24). The places thus named became perpetual instructors, sights, memorials for faith to rest itself upon; and their Provider, their Banner, their Peace-giver, became thus assured attributes of Jehovah in Israel's habitual thoughts. "Perez-Uzzah" and "Baal-Perazim" (2 Sam. v. 20, and vi. 8) memorialised graver thoughts of faith. We trace this principle of indulging and helping faith by names historically descriptive made use of in the thoughts of faith revealed to Israel's later periods. The city of the restoration which Ezekiel was commissioned to reveal to the Jews of the captivity, was to be thought of by them by the name, "The Lord is there" (Ezek. xlviii. 35), suggestive of the same comfort of faith as Christians have in the description of the city of their rest, when they think of it by the words, "The Lamb is in the midst thereof." In the Messiah's reign, to which Jeremiah was made to invite their faith, "this is the name whereby He shall be called, The Lord our Righteousness" (Jer. xxiii. 6), a name now historically, as then, in promise, productive of comforting thoughts of definite saving grace.

9. The progress of new thoughts by this and other means to become habitual emotional thoughts—the advance of the *learning* as well as of the *teaching* of faith—is distinctly seen in Israel's history. By the time of Eli, Israel in general must have become accustomed to think of Jehovah by the peculiar tie first revealed to Joshua, "the Lord of the whole earth, the Captain of the hosts of Israel." Samuel's mother in her prayer vowed unto "Jehovah Sabaoth"—Jehovah of their Hosts. By David's time the Jehovah Sabaoth, the Lord of Israel's hosts, was under that title thought of as the Lord of the hosts of heaven and earth, "the Lord of hosts, the King of glory" (Ps. xxiv.); the Ruler of the natural and moral world in one (Ps. xix. lxxxiv.), whose service and the purpose of His government is holiness (Ps. xv.), exercising a moral government, a holy providence. Jehovah, a "shield" to Abraham, and his "exceeding great reward"

Progress of appreciative language.

C

(Gen. xv. 1), appears in Moses' thoughts the "dwelling-place of His people in all generations" (Ps. xc. 1). By David's time the figures of confidence in His sure and widely-sufficing friendship are of great frequency and expressiveness. He is "their rock and fortress," the "portion of their inheritance, and their cup"—the past, present, future Keeper of their safety. He is their "Shepherd," who has "led them in green pastures and by the still waters," whose guidance they will follow without fear "through the valley of the shadow of death." In the devotional language of the Psalms, the law written on the heart rises above the earlier statutes of purification, the sacrifices of repentance above those of burnt-offerings. Even the Christian joy of faith, the dispensation of the Spirit, comes almost into sight. The thought of a personal Holy Spirit of God enlightening, healing, helping the human spirit, bringing a spirit of holiness into human life — the thought so much perfected by Joel and Jeremiah's prophecies long after—appears in the "last words of David" (2 Sam. xxiii. 2), and in his penitent supplication (Ps. li. 11, 12). The completing thought of faith's privileged contemplation of the Lord of heaven and earth, the Holy One—namely, the thought of His nearness of affection, assured by so close assumed relationship to man—was approached in the Psalms with a fulness similar to the appreciation they show of His government and His holiness of nature. The recorded advance is from the national to the personal God, from the temporal to the spiritual King, and, above all, from the God to be feared to the God to be loved—a progress of believers' habitual thoughts of God from the class of thoughts with which Cain regarded Him towards those with which the evangelists would behold Him with the bodily eye. He is their "Father," the "Guide of their youth," the "Father of the fatherless, and the Judge of the widow," one not above and overruling, but in, under, pervading, actuating, or substituting all human means of happiness. After-times were to hear Him seeking to be thought of as a husband to the wife of his youth, a husband beseeching the return of an erring spouse; and a father who could not punish as they deserved his erring children, could not destroy them, his repentings were kindled together, he would heal their back-slidings and forgive them freely (Hosea xiv. 4).

10. The Historical revealing of God by His inseparable spiritual and secular government of Israel, advanced through prominent dispensations superseding or absorbing each other, for the better declaring of His nature and designs. During the consolidating period, when the collection of emancipated Hebrew slaves of Egypt were to be taught the sentiment of a religious nationality, and separated from their heathen habits of thought by a confining law of worship and self-government, the prominent visible guide and help of religion was the PRIEST-HOOD, and their subordinates, the soldierly Levites, who were the immediate administrators of the separative confining dis-cipline. The supremacy which the lawgiver Moses occasion-ally exercised over the priesthood, the ordinary guides of the people, when the importance of Jehovah's moral above His positive commandments had to be asserted, was continued to Joshua; but in the times of the Judges this occasional supremacy passed into something of a permanent prominence as a new development of the divine government. Jehovah's representative during those three centuries was less the priest than the magistrate; rulers called out of no special tribe; com-missioned for the occasional or continued exercise of supreme authority; sometimes exercising the sacrificial office, which, by the ceremonial law, was confined to the priesthood; sometimes having the prophetic function, which was, some centuries after, to be Jehovah's instrument of government, superseding both priests and kings; but always having one char-acterising faith in their especial connection with and authority from Jehovah for their particular tasks; and all discharging one distinguishing function, the kingly one of government, defence, guidance in combined action, and judgment with authority. Samuel, the last of that transitional order of magistrates, and who, above all the others, united with the civil government the prophetic function, and at times the priestly one, uttered at the beginning of the permanent kingly dispensation the principle of religion, or man's connection with God, which contained the reason of this and succeeding

Progress of revealing institu-tions. The Priesthood and King-hood.

developments. It was the importance of righteousness, order, and obedience to God above ceremonial worship of Him. "Hath the Lord as great delight in burnt-offerings and sacrifices as in obeying the voice of the Lord? Behold, to obey is better than sacrifice, and to hearken than the fat of rams" (1 Sam. xv. 22). That was the first prophetic rebuke of the new kinghood, repeated often in after-times, and disregarded till Jehovah destroyed the abused ordinance, which He had appointed for His people's education in holiness. The KING-HOOD, however, before its corruption and fall, had discharged a large religious task in accustoming Israel's thoughts to a higher view of their Jehovah's nature, and richer expectations, though only gradually becoming definite, of His gracious purposes. The developed kinghood of David, like the large portion of the psalter which belongs to the same period, was a great development of men's designed religious thoughts of God. The kingly power superseding the priestly in the government, defence, and edification of the sacred nation—a secular monarchy made the great means of religious guidance and constraint, the head over all things to His church, assuming at will the distinctive priestly functions of sacrifice, intercession, and consulting the oracle, adding also the spiritual function of instruction—was a development of the kind of thoughts which were to recognise the divine Helper, the Messiah, when He came. The assumption by the kings of the priestly dignity was the beginning, also, of the breaking down of that idea of caste in religious functionaries into which human nature has always been ready to be misled, and which the New Testament completely removed from spiritual religion when it taught that we are to be all kings and priests to God. The lesson of a saving, blessing, edifying kinghood becoming the great ordinance of God's grace, combined with, or in part absorbing or superseding, the first ordinance of a priesthood, which was exhibited to the chosen people in warm attractive colours in David's reign, was not an isolated lesson in the historical education which they received to expect a kingly, priestly Saviour. It was repeated by the reign of Joash, the youthful restorer of the obscured worship of

Jehovah—by that of Uzziah—and, above all, by the bright reign of Hezekiah, himself perhaps the prophesied type of the Messiah, and said by tradition to have believed himself to be the expected One.. From his days, which were so speedily, by Manasseh's cruelty of heathenism, demonstrated not to have been the days of the Messiah, the thoughts of faith, so far forcibly released from strictly secular expectation, looked forward much to the times of a just and merciful King coming to the deliverance of His people. In the expressions of the prophets, whose visions occupied that era of Hebrew history, the metaphorical representations of the coming salvation rapidly condensed into distinct features of a personal Saviour; and expectation grew to the distinctness which, before the Messiah appeared, looked for His coming as the King of the Jews.

11. What was the progress of acquired faith under the religious teaching given by the idea of divine kinghood? The advance of the spiritual to dominate over the formal, the moral over the positive, in the common religious thought, which we see so much in David's religious writings, was well pronounced in the reign of his son. It was manifested then, even in distinct and authoritative superseding of established form and traditional sacredness, in the interests of true religiousness. Solomon, who recorded it as of his faith that "to do judgment and justice is more acceptable to the Lord than sacrifice" (Prov. xxi. 3), showed that great principle advanced beyond the position of a theoretical thought, and able to break through all merely superstitious barriers which religious constitutionalism might oppose to justice; not hesitating to depose a treasonable chief priest, and to disregard the right of sanctuary, in the hope of which Joab fled to the altar (1 Kings ii.) His thoughts of the glory of Jehovah, rising above all forms of worship, which even Jehovah Himself had directed Moses to observe in the tabernacle service in the infancy of Hebrew faith, were larger than those possessed centuries after by the formalist Pharisee Jews; who were so often reproved by the Messiah for not knowing the spirit of their own religion, and who seem to have had no freedom of thought as to the matter

Religious thought under the Kinghood.

or manner of Jehovah's service beyond their patristic commentaries on the letter of Moses' ceremonial law. As examples, note that king's use of steps in the ascent to the altar, a thing forbidden by Moses, and his employment of a number of candlesticks in the holy place instead of the single seven-branched one of the wilderness—innovations which were both resiled from in the second temple. Akin to these changes was his so un-Israelitish borrowing of the architecture of the temple from all nations around him in addition to the ideas of the primitive tabernacle, and not abstaining even from graphic ornamentation, no particle of which was allowed in the second more Jewishly correct edifice. In the material appointments of the worship of Him to whom he prayed as the hearer of supplications sent up to Him towards " this place " (2 Chron. vi.) of His earthly presence by men of all nations of the earth, Solomon freely gathered all that he knew of natural or artistic kind impressive to the human worshippers of One whom no outward things could fully correspond to. And, in the midst of the first and last, because never equally repeated magnificence which surrounded that inauguration of worship, in the feast of the dedication he uttered the grand truth of Jehovah's greatness which has never been surpassed in man's thoughts, and which was lost by the orthodox Jews of the last days: "But will God in very deed dwell on the earth? Behold, the heavens, and the heaven of heavens, cannot contain Thee; how much less this house which I have builded!" (1 Kings viii. 27). The century of general apostasy from Jehovah between the reigns of Solomon and Joash affords no light on Hebrew religious sentiment. The singular facts, however, of the revolution in favour of true religion which set the youthful Joash upon the throne, were significant of the supremacy of spirit over form which the faithful among the priesthood had come to believe in. That revolution, conducted by Jehoiada the chief priest, with all its carefully-planned details, and the forcible expulsion from the temple limits, and the execution immediately after of the idolatrous usurper Athaliah, took place on the Sabbath. The young king's round-handed correction afterwards of the shortcoming stewardship of Jehoiada and the priests; and the ground upon which the writer of the chronicle (2 Chron. xxiv. 22) condemns the king's long subsequent crime in putting to death Zechariah the priest for reproving him; which was not the sacred character of the priest, but his being the son of Jehoiada, the king's early and best friend; are, equally with Jehoiada's act, marked manifestations that not the positive but the moral was in the common sentiment, the essential matter in religion. It was a recognition by the common mind that their divine King ruled and reigned in righteousness.

12. The religious knowledge, the revealed wisdom of Solomon's time, like all sowings of the seeds of faith, failed of fruitfulness in the recognised ways (Matt. xiii. 19-22), and part of its fruit was to be reaped only many days after. We cannot hold that anything like the whole riches of thoughts of God, put on enduring record in the Psalms, was the common faith of the nation in the time of their authorship. Though three thousand years old, they contain much that is still up to or above the religious consciousness of the most of spiritually-minded Christians. They were the utterance of revealed as well as spontaneous thoughts, and anticipated as they were to lead the religious thinking of the sacred nation and of mankind. Yet their spiritual ways of thought were to a considerable extent possessed by the writers, who, without doubt, were not isolated saints; most of their devotional and moral language has the ring of well-appreciated words, expressive of thoughts that were familiar, and has not the strangeness of compelled unapprehended utterances, phrases not revealed to the speakers (1 Pet. i. 11), which had to stand waiting their recognised sufficient meaning until the fulness of times. The psalmists' language of near, confided-in relationship, if it was not the expression of thoughts familiar to the common mind of Israel at the time, was the seed of a fruit of such faith which we can see after it had received the providential cultivation of succeeding reigns. Long-continued thoughts of Jehovah as a "Father," a "Father the guide of youth," a "Father of the fatherless," became prepared to hear Isaiah speak of Him as the Everlasting Father as well as the Mighty

(margin note: Influence of the Psalms.)

God, the Wonderful, the Counsellor. Jehovah-Shalom, Gideon's Jehovah of Peace, was coming to be thought of as the " Prince of Peace," for higher than national interests; taking man's spiritual troubles upon Himself. David's Psalms concerning that King's (Jehovah's own King's) suffering for His people, as well as His protecting love of them, contained language which David's history only slightly expounded. It fructified, however, in the multitude of thoughts which, in succeeding dark times, God's servants were comforted to have within them, preparing the place for the evangelical prophet's thoughts, the completing thought of Jehovah's love as a suffering as well as a ruling, providing, preserving love. The reigns of several heavy-laden, righteous princes had passed ere then, and Hebrew faith had a large history to look back upon—from David to Hezekiah—of chastisements, and griefs, and self-devoting labours, in which the religious king was beheld, ever the central sufferer of anxiety and endurance, crying unto Jehovah and receiving strength from Him to toil and suffer on to struggling but triumphant success, to deliver his people from heathen oppression, or to heal their backslidings and bring them back to the pleasure of the Lord. And that teaching of their religious history had prepared the time for Isaiah's speaking, not wholly to ears dull of hearing, the anticipatory history of Immanuel, God with us. " Surely He hath borne our griefs, and carried our sorrows. The chastisement of our peace was laid upon Him. All we like sheep have gone astray; we have turned every one to his own way; and the Lord hath laid on Him the iniquity of us all. When thou shalt make His soul an offering for sin, He shall see His seed, He shall prolong His days, and the pleasure of the Lord shall prosper in His hand. He shall see of the travail of His soul, and shall be satisfied " (Isa. liii.)

Progress of institutions. The Prophets.

13. Isaiah's teaching of the thoughts of faith was, however, the brightness of the revelation of God's nature and His grace to man by a new dispensation, the PROPHETIC ORDER, which was sent forth to supersede the kingly in the religious government of the sacred people, in the same manner and degree as the kingly authority had superseded the early su-

premacy of the priesthood. Prophets had always been among
the means of faith ; inspiring or breaking through the forms
of ceremonial worship to teach the spirit of true religion. In
Samuel and the schools of the prophets known by his time,
they became something of an established institution for such
correction and instruction, even of the forms and ministers of
Jehovah's worship; and for general correction of public morals;
by opportune declarations of the will of Jehovah immediately
commissioned, like Samuel's messages to Eli in his childhood,
or spoken spontaneously in appearance like his reproof of
Saul, " Hath the Lord more delight in burnt-offerings than in
obeying the voice of the Lord? Behold, to obey is better than
sacrifice, and to hearken than the fat of rams." These teaching
prophets, resident at court, or in known dwelling-places, like
" Gad, David's seer," and Nathan, like Jeremiah and Daniel
of the captivity, and Haggai and Zechariah of the restoration,
or appearing suddenly, no one could tell whence, in times of
profligacy and dereliction of Jehovah's worship, like the awful
Elijah, the dread of Ahab, are the figures that draw the eye
after the disruption of the monarchy, far more than the kings
of that tumultuous period, and almost to the exclusion of the
priests, the primitive religious authority. They are the only
permanent lights that shine in the so frequently darkened
generations between fallen Solomon and the captivities; the
monitors, correctors, and scourges of the idolatrous kings; and
the mighty bulwarks of the courage of faithful monarchs,
when such arose to stem the tide of false worship and corrupt
morals which made the last two centuries of the kingdoms so
akin to the dark ages known to Christian faith.

14. The denunciations of these great teachers exhibit a Advance
much-developed moral thought, an ongoing unveiling of the teaching.
holiness of God. Were their words the only history of true
religion during their times, we would learn nothing of the
religious importance of the ceremonial law. Their mission
was to lift up the thoughts and consciences of the chosen
people higher than the forms which they had self-deceivingly
come to make serve as the essentials of Jehovah's will. Even
in the northern kingdom, the prophetic reproofs we find

directed, not against the heretical form of worship leading to idolatry established by Jeroboam in the reigns when that was the national worship of Israel, but against the oppression of the poor by the rich, the drunkenness of priests and prophets, the licentiousness of general morals—sins against the moral law, the service of holiness. And these they reproved and corrected, to the ignoring even of all the ceremonial life at first ordained, which the emancipated slaves of Pharaoh had needed to confine and shape their minds to right thoughts and guiding habits, and which the unspiritual, immoral religionists of the last Jewish days returned to confine religion to again. "Rend your hearts, and not your garments," is the tone of their calls to repentance. " Shall I come before the Lord with thousands of rams, or with ten thousands of rivers of oil? He hath showed thee, O man, what is good ; and what doth the Lord require of thee, but to do justly, and love mercy, and walk humbly with thy God?" (Micah vi. 7, 8 ; comp. Jer. vii. 22, 23.) " Behold, the days come, saith the Lord, that I will make a new covenant with the house of Israel, and with the house of Judah; not the covenant I made with their fathers, which they brake. I will put my law in their inward parts, and write it in their hearts" (Jer. xxxi. 33).

Coincident extension of field.

15. Coincident with this expansion of the prophetic teaching in the dark times of Hebrew history beyond the bounds of Moses' formal ordinances, sacred history shows an instructively congruous expansion of it beyond the bounds of the sacred people. Not only Israel and Judah, but Tyre on the west and Moab on the east knew the form of Elijah in the days of Ahab and his Tyrian queen. Elisha was the monitor of Benhadad and Hazael, as well as of Jehu. During the great empire of the second Jeroboam, Jonah's preaching of the holiness of the God of the whole earth was carried, by the tragical events of his history, to the farthest bounds of the Mediterranean. He carried it himself to the centre of Assyria.

Appreciation of prophetic authority.

16. The prophetic institution continued the divine agency for the education of the instructor-people to faith in God's holiness during the corrupt decay of the kingdoms, when the institutions of the priesthood and kinghood had fallen into

uselessness or hurtfulness to the truth; and throughout the captivities, when these regular means of faith were suspended. Upon the restoration, the prophets had much to do with the organising of the second temple service, and in the popular faith seem then at least to have been conjoined with the priests as oracles of religious guidance (Zech. vii. 3). The continuance of that faith seems indicated by Luke ii., and in the popular sentiment as to prophets in our Lord's days. The union of the kingly and priestly authority, which appears in Zechariah's vision (Zech. vi. 11, 12), a forelight of the Messiah, may be compared by us with the history of the Maccabees, and with the union of both the magisterial and prophetic functions with the priestly in Caiaphas at the close of Hebrew faith.

17. The long reign of Uzziah saw the culmination of the prophetic work, by the inspiration of a band of those teachers of contemporary religion to execute a new and permanent work —namely, to put in writing, for the whole world of nations destined to receive their writings by one channel or another, visions of the relation and designs of God towards man, which were to be unfolded in the fulness of times. The prophetic books mark a grand stage in that unveiling of the salvation of God, the progress of which is traceable in the subjects of the earlier writings of the Word. The religious history of the Pentateuch, long the source of faith's thoughts of the ways of God with man, might be read as the Jews of the fulness of times read it, so as to see nothing, or hardly anything, the object of Jehovah's loving care, beyond the boundary of Israel's seed. The writings of David and Solomon, and others of the middle period of the separation of a peculiar people of Jehovah, were books for human nature's religiousness, more than for Israel's national views of faith. In the prophetic books, future religious history is the subject; and a developed faith appears, thinking of a God well known, hiding Himself no more in clouds, unveiling His face to speak with His people as a man with his friend; and now Israel's fortunes are no more the whole system of religious history, as in the Pentateuch, but around them, on every hand, arises a mundane system, dis-

Culmination of prophecy—salvation to the world.

playing God's purposes with all the families of man. The earthly fortunes of the peculiar people, and of the nations, are gathered together in secular connection where it existed, but in universal human relationship more prominently; and the brightening religious future, the spiritual heritage of God's love and holy life is an earthly heaven, that spreads over them all—Jehovah's spiritual Israel all—His holy nation, His peculiar people all—" whosoever shall call upon His name."

Joel, the introductory speaker of the things that were to come, paints with an indefinite glory the grace of the latter days, the removal of all national limits to the people of God —" whosoever shall call on the name of the Lord shall be saved" (Joel ii. 32); and spiritual enlightenment of like fulness, unconfined by place, or order, or age; prophecy becoming the gift of old and young, of sons and daughters.

Amos finishes his denunciation of Judah, and yet more of Israel, for their drunkenness, their heartless worldliness, and abuse of the forms of religion, by the proclamation of Jehovah's holy judgment upon all sinful nations, a judgment suspended, or made not complete, only to Jacob; and by announcing the deliverance of Israel from universal dispersion, in a grandeur of tone that can be understood only of a spiritual Israel, one expressly including " the heathen called by my name" (Amos ix. 12).

The indefinite visions of a coming better time condensed, in Micah's foresight, into an historical picture; completing the panorama beheld by the prophet of Jehovah's love as it was shown to Abraham, to Jacob, and to Israel in the wilderness, by the sight of One coming from Bethlehem-Ephratah, who should be Ruler in Israel, " but whose goings forth had been of old, from everlasting" (Micah v. 2); the city of whose dominion should be the mountain of the house of the Lord established on the top of the mountains, and all nations should flow unto it; and under His judging and rebuking they should beat their swords into ploughshares and their spears into pruning-hooks, and learn war no more (Micah iv. 1-3).

Here and there in their assigned places, and occasions of present reproof and instruction in righteousness, in the capital on the mountains of Judah, in Bethel, in Tekoah, in the high places of Israel, those nearly contemporary prophets, Joel, Amos, and Micah, committed to writing their visions, which lighted up the path of believers with glorious though indefinite hope for hundreds of years, until the Sun of Righteousness arose, but visions which our own times have not yet seen fully come to pass.

The vision of the day of salvation grew in distinctness of feature during the long life of Isaiah, the greatest of that constellation of heavenly seers ; and while their seeings helped his comprehension of what was set before himself, he was made able to proclaim and put in historical position in the places and times of the world's future, a personal Saviour ; and to give distinct pictures of the world-wideness of His salvation, and the universal subject of His salvation—all temporal life in and surrounding the life of man, and the spiritual and endless life of man himself—all creation, as Paul afterwards measured the restoration by Christ Jesus.   His writings, in which the history-like distinctness of their prophecies of near Jewish events has tempted critics to imagine a second Isaiah late enough to have described them as really history, gave to the world in graphic history-like prophecies the mystery of the Messiah's earthly condition, insoluble to the Jews as prophecy, demonstrative of the truth of Jesus as history; the unique union to be seen in Him of power and suffering, eternal glory of Godhead and meanest sameness with man, unchangeable holiness, and association with crime, death for sin, and endless joyful life in the pleasure of the Lord.

18. If we try now shortly to trace the progress of faith during the peculiarly prophetic period, the growth of common religious sentiment respecting Jehovah's love, we can see that faith, while listening to the proclamations of a coming good time which completed the religious lesson of the prophet's denunciations of the corruptness around them, received some help to believe in, and realise it from contemporary sight, the help given so much as a rule by Him who knoweth our frame, to lessen the difficulties of faith in the unseen.   The gentle beginning of Uzziah's reign presented to their eyes the peaceful reign of good foretold.   The horse of Egypt and Assyria, the

Growth of common religious sentiment.

associate of war and proud pageantry, was not the royal beast of his reign, but the ass, as in the kingship of David. His reign also presented a new priesthood, one of moral power and no more the soldierly Levite; one able to rebuke, and so expel from the holy places a transgressing king. The bright reign of Hezekiah was even as it were a parable, showing to men a figure, and, it would appear, an earnest of the good that was to be. The happiness of his reign was extinguished in the infernal darkness of his son's earlier years; the wild violent abandonment with which king and nobles plunged into licentiousness and rapacity, and, when reproved by the prophets, into persecuting idolatry; returning like dogs to their vomit, when released from the restraining hand of their late master. Hezekiah's time was the last historical light which Israelite faith had whereby to walk a long time through the dark place that Judah became to religious eyes. But if the trouble of Manasseh's reign served, as is the rule of grace, to constrain faith to endure as seeing Him who is invisible, His words by the prophets of His great grace would be more intelligible for the recollection of the so lately past comforts of holiness. However it came, the next forthcoming of recorded faith was brighter than Hezekiah's own thoughts of the comforts of God. Habakkuk, the next notable messenger of Heaven, speaks in the reign of Manasseh in almost Christian language of the condition of man in Jehovah's providence. Hezekiah, the pupil of Isaiah, the hearer of his glorious language, "Come and let us reason together," &c., and himself the receiver of so bright present grace, yet, when on his supposed deathbed, mourned the coming of death as a prospect of unmingled darkness. Habakkuk's words declare a trust in Jehovah as boundless in the freedom of its looking into the unseen as a believer in Jesus could manifest. He does not speak of everlasting life, but he speaks of earthly troubles as a Christian believer would do whose soul is anchored on the sure hope within the veil. "Though the fig-tree shall not blossom," &c., "yet will I rejoice in Jehovah; I will joy in the God of my salvation. Jehovah God is my strength, and He will make my feet like hinds' feet, and He will make me walk on mine high places" (Hab. iii. 17-19).

No dark veil anywhere hangs over his forelooking. Worldly troubles cannot cloud his futurity. Sin alone is the calamity he sees, grace the consolation never obscured (i. 2-4, 12-13; ii. 18-12; iii. 2). But in Jeremiah and Ezekiel, the manner of love of the fulness of times comes as it were actually within grasp. Their familiar foresight of Jehovah's future gift of the thoughts and feelings that were to make up man's true full faith in Him—men looking evermore unto Him as their own, and as being His own; He enlightening and comforting their hearts to this union of salvation, by His own Spirit teaching them —was as like an anticipation of apostolic writing as Isaiah's foresight was of the Gospel history. The new covenant—not according to the old broken one—God's law written by Him in the hearts of men—He their God, and they His people—no more teaching, nor needing to teach, every man his neighbour, saying, "Know Jehovah," but all knowing Him, from the least to the greatest (Jer. xxxi., Ezek. xxxvi.); are pictures of the full times of the Comforter already familiarly looked upon by those men. It is in keeping with the appreciating manner of these contemplations to read in the same age the language of Isaiah, addressed not to prophetic times, but to contemporary hearers respecting the Hebrew commandment of fasts and the observance of the Sabbath. His 58th chapter calls for a sanctification of the ordinances that was beyond the practice, but evidently not beyond the ready comprehension, of his hearers; in which the fast should no more be a formal humility, the self-seeking service of a compensatory tribute of worship paid to Jehovah, but the self-denial undertaken to help and save His needy and outcast ones, the "poor whom they had always with them;" and the Sabbath rest should not be the restraint of law, binding the rebellious hands while the heart went after its covetousness, but a delight, a service that love constrains; the Lord's day, the day of the honoured Jehovah, in which it should be a delight to be His with all the service of the hands, and of the thoughts, and of the heart. The atmosphere of Christian spiritual service breathes from the whole message of which it is a part. The universal call of all peoples to be the Lord's Israel, sounds in it (lx.) the glad tidings to the

woes of God's human children (lxi.), which the Lord Himself,
in the fulness of times, opened the book to read in the Jewish
synagogue, and said, though to ears again dull of hearing,
" This day is this Scripture fulfilled in your ears."

Progress of
institu-
tions. The
Scribes.
19. The times foreseen by the prophets of the captivity,
when no man should any more teach his neighbour, saying,
" Know Jehovah," but all should know Him, from the least
even to the greatest, were to be prepared for by another institution than theirs. The prophetic voice was to die out in the
mean time, but not before the books of Moses and the Psalms, and
much of the historical and prophetic books now in the canon,
were come into the room of all living voice, and were taught
regularly by an order called SCRIBES, who should be the human
guides of faith for four centuries, until the fulness of times.
With these new teachers of the truths of Jehovah we associate no divine appointment of the kind which the priests,
the kings, and the prophets had received. It was an unpro-
nounced appointment, that of Jehovah's silent providence,
which now appoints nations and churches to be temporal
means of grace; and their great place in the teaching of faith
was *recognised* by God manifest in the flesh, though, like
the priests and kings of old, they had fallen into unfaithfulness. "The scribes," He said, "sit in Moses' seat. All,
therefore, whatsoever they bid you observe, observe and do;
but do not ye after their works, for they say and do not" (Matt.
xxiii. 2, 3). The scribes, like the earlier magisterial and
prophetic orders, had risen into notice gradually—the trans-
cribers originally, but naturally becoming readers and at times
explainers of the law. The necessities of the captivity, when
the priestly function was superseded and the prophets could
not teach the widely-scattered families of the Hebrews, called
these scribes into the place of general teachers of the law;
and when the restoration came, Ezra, a priest, as probably
many scribes were, but known to the Persian king not as a
priest but as "a scribe of the law of the God of heaven,"
organised a system of regularly teaching the returned people
the books of the law, himself collecting the Book of Psalms
for that use. It was the last step required to reach the

spiritual rule of the written Word in Christian times, when every believer for himself should search the Scriptures for the testimony of Jesus. Under the constant light of the written Word made thus to shine in Israel, the occasional light of the prophetic messengers was to cease; Malachi, apparently the last of them, proclaiming the future rising of the Sun of Righteousness, and the sending of Elias to prepare the way for the coming of Jehovah Himself to His temple.

20. Between the time of Malachi and the advent of Christ we have no means of tracing Jewish faith except the apocryphal books. A most remarkable circumstance appears, however, in the works which represent Jewish thought in the period containing the advent. In the Targum of Onkelos, the term The Word of the Lord is used in a personal sense, and given as the equivalent of Jehovah in historical passages of the Hebrew Scriptures, such as Gen. xxviii. 20, 21; Exod. xvi. 8; Deut. i. 30, v. 5, ix. 3, xviii. 19. This personification of The Word of the Lord does not appear except once in the Apocrypha, the date of which is about the middle of the period when revelation was silent, but Wisdom is used personally in Ecclesiasticus. In Philo Judæus, The Word, when used personally, is surrounded with attributes so like those conjoined with the Christ by John and Paul; such as creative power and wisdom, being the First-Begotten of God, a High Priest, a King, a Shepherd; that a Christian origin for these ideas would be sought, were that not excluded by both the matter and the date of the writings. The commentary of Onkelos was written probably late in the first century; Philo wrote apparently about the beginning of it. The former was a Jewish theologian, of course not disposed to favour Christianity; the other shows more of the Platonic philosopher than of the Jew in the religious import of his writings. He lived in Alexandria, where Greek philosophy and Jewish religion were in close contact, and he may have wished to show how much of the Logos of Plato's philosophy could be found in Hebrew theology. It would be interesting in the extreme, as part of the great question of how far God by supernatural aid made the Hebrew Scriptures a light to "the nations," to be able to investigate the origin of this later

Latest Jewish thought as to "The Word."

D

Jewish understanding of The Word of the Lord. The Logos of Philo was a contemporary Greek idea. Did the outer world get its notions of that divine personality from an advancing understanding which the Hebrews had of their own revelation, or did the subtle Greek mind have the distinction given to it of seeing more in the sacred books of the Jews than the Jews themselves saw? Certain it is, that thoughts of the early coming of a personal Redeemer, a divine Being descending to deliver the earth from its miseries, filled the atmosphere of the outer world as well as the land of Israel before the advent of Christ.

Revelation timed to man's necessity.

21. In reviewing the progress of the teaching and the learning of the thoughts of faith as God's education of the world, we see, along the stages of the development, a great principle, congenial to most fully enlightened Christian thought, unifying the whole history of the revelation of God's holy love of man—that man's necessity was always God's opportunity. It was in a time of need that every successive lifting of the veil from the light of God's countenance took place. Prefaced, so to speak, by the summary of all His designed grace, spoken in the first terrible day of need — "the seed of the woman shall bruise the serpent's head, and it shall bruise His heel" —the revelations which succeeded came alike opportune to special needs of them, and with the expressed combination of result; success and failure—the head of the oppressive evil bruised, the means of salvation smitten always in its efficacy in the end. The revelations of God's loving help came always to His servants in times of felt need and probable impressibility. The warmest showing to Abraham of Jehovah's human-hearted friendship was made in the human form and sympathies, when the patriarch was sorely tried by long solitary striving to believe the promise of seed; and again, in a less degree, but in the same manner, the same loving help came to Jacob and to Joshua at crises of their trials of faith —while even Abraham's and Jacob's biographies show that their bright and opportune lights of faith continued to enlighten their eyes to full seeing but for a season. Israel's history of belief and forgetfulness, epitomised as a type of all

faith of unstable mankind in the 78th, 105th, 106th, and 107th Psalms, shows both aspects of the constantly-revolving history. Crushed under the heel of the mighty Rameses, Jacob's children were in bitter need of the drawing nigh to them of the God of their fathers, the almighty I AM, when Moses came to them from Horeb. Their need braced their souls to a temporary faith, which safety beyond the Red Sea saw speedily relax again in part; and a permanent necessity brought immediately an abiding means of faith. Their minds, demoralised by long slavery, unaccustomed to self-guidance or self-restraint, were put under the strong confinement of the ceremonial law of sacrifices and meats and purifications. The soldier-priesthood and divinely-appointed leadership were a needed staff through the long pilgrimage, an impressive rule of religious sentiment, and a visible religious executive, while memory failed to keep the truth and conscience to enforce faithfulness to it. After "Joshua, and the elders that outlived Joshua," that support to faith ceased to manifest efficacy. The first Israelite dark age, like all succeeding ones, had its "Jehovah's hidden ones," a "seed to serve Him;" but that wild period of the Judges made the need always more and more felt of some new visible aid to faith so unsupported, burdened instead, by the demoralised state of the priesthood; which had become no more a guide, restraint, and support to religious life, but a stumbling-block and a covering of the eyes. Faith received its needed help in the supraposition of kingly authority to control and protect the nation as the people of Jehovah; bringing prominently out the idea of obedience to the divine King as more essentially the service to be given to Him than the performance of rites, and infusing into faith's expectations of salvation the thought of kingly power to defend and uphold and rule, in addition to the thought of the priestly power to atone and make peace. The Psalms, the product chiefly of the kingly period, record how, in faith's thoughts of Jehovah, the kingly idea was developed —the thought of a "King reigning in righteousness," a "King of glory," a "King for ever and ever," a "King commanding deliverances for Jacob," a "King of old working salvation "

—a thought which, expanding beyond whatever David's or Solomon's greatness could approach, went forth into faith's only region of full satisfaction — " things unseen," " things hoped for." Similarly timed came the prophetic institution, when the necessity was sorely felt by faith of new helps to endure as seeing God who was so invisible in the affairs of the world. It came when the kingly authority and help and constraint to religion was fallen, as the priestly had done before, into irreligiousness—when idolatry possessed the royal houses of both kingdoms oftener than the true worship, and punctilious formality in observing the sacrificial ceremonies was the dead representative of religion; while nobles and priests, ordinary religious teachers and common rulers and heads of the people, were universally filled with drunkenness and luxurious selfishness, and there " was no place clean." Then was the time when, to the hidden thousands of faithful, known only to Jehovah, in the dense kingdom of Baal and Moloch, and to the wild idolatrous masses and their wildly sinful leaders, " He sent His servants the prophets, rising up early and sending them ; " to chastise with scorpion words the criminal stewards of His law and His providence—to speak from Him withering scorn of the religious observances He Himself had commanded, and now had to abhor—to ignore, despise, and sweep aside priests and kings alike ; but to bid believers endure in the faith of a coming glory of moral greatness and service, and expect the advent of a kingly priestly Prophet of justice and righteousness and peace. It is from the midst of these bursts of remonstrance and threatening against present sinfulness that their promises and representations of future holiness and salvation are sent forth. It was to the freshness of Babylonian captivity that Jeremiah's richest consolations, contained in his 30th and 31st chapters, came. It was in the midst of the sufferings of that sore chastisement that Ezekiel's compassionate reproofs were spoken, and his revelations of Israel's union again to Jehovah—the loving union of care and help and comfort on the one side, and faithfulness and godly sorrow and new life on the other

—the dry bones of the house of Israel living again (chapters xxxvi., xxxvii.)

22. Those days of the Lord, days of salvation, greatest *Days of* advents of new light to faith, were thus systematically timed *the Lord.* to states of need, and of, consequently, not improbable onward looking for some heavenly help—even like the last perfecting manifestation of the "Desire of. all nations," the moral opportuneness of which has forced itself upon observers of history—the coming of the Son of God in that "due time" when ungodliness was evidently proved to be without strength to help human needs. The Messiah came when, again, a sumptuous ritual and a system of costly sacrifices and minute service of ceremony had been so vainly sought unto by the despiritualised chosen people; and the outer world had so exhausted the ingenuity of philosophy and cultivation of taste in aspirations after moral ameliorations; and yet vice alone had come to have dominion in both Jewish and Greek life. His words, "Come unto me, all ye that labour and are heavy laden," which reveal the state of heart to which His grace will be welcome in human life, express, what both before and since His manifestation in time of need has been the order of divine grace; tribulation, faith, and comfort, coming in succession.

23. Another principle unifies the very diverse revelations *Holy char-* of Jehovah to Hebrew faith. The great truth revealed was, *acter of* that "God so loved the world." The principle that made one *God's re-* revelation of all the mixed history of goodness and severity *love.* is, that His love was a holy love; a love seeking to save mankind from the ruin of sin, by forbearance, by chastisement, by kindness, by endurance,—in the end manifesting itself to be so great a love as not to withhold from giving up His only-begotten Son for their salvation. The first denunciation and the first reproof began the never-changed manner of this instruction of man's thoughts of God. God has condemned through all time as a Saviour, and reproved as a Holy One. The bodily part of the judgment, "In the day thou eatest thereof thou shalt surely die," was unrelentingly exe-

cuted, but executed not so as to destroy but to save; with
an unhasting forbearance which sought, between the doom
and its execution, to restore the moral life by repentance and
faith.   So a hundred years lay between the proclamation of
the Deluge and its terrible coming.   Ten righteous persons
would have turned aside the doom of Sodom, but nothing else
than some turning from sin would have stayed its awful
destruction.   The extirpation of the completely corrupted,
fatally infectious peoples of Canaan, when their cup was full of
sin ·done against their own conscience (Rom. i. 18-23), was the
first task given to Israel as the family and people of Jehovah
—a task impressive to them of His all-seeing wrath against
sin, and the fear His holy love had of their and manhood's
ruin thereby ; but their constant work was the congruous one
of being a light to all who would see His mercy and grace.
The task and the work were a perpetual proclamation to the
world by history of His revelation of Himself to Moses as merciful and gracious, but who will by no means clear the guilty
(Exod. xxxiv. 67).   His discipline of Israel itself was that of a
father's inexhaustible love, yet not a love self-indulgent and
blind, but much more a suffering love, saving through sorest self-
sacrifice.   The terrible penal laws of that discipline against any
sinning after the manner of the heathens around—its severity
upon backsliding as sure as its overflowing love awaiting repentance, and its lavish encouragement of faithfulness—its removal,
ever and ever more, of unfaithful stewards and failing ordinances—its perpetual watchfulness to teach the service of
holiness as the sole use of all that was conventionally holy in
ceremonies or places or persons—are the family-like history
of the whole anxious period from Egypt to Babylon.   His language to man all the time when He was exercising that discipline is full and overflowing with affection as can be ; full of
ever-varying terms of kindness, names of family endearment,
reveries of fondness, purposes of heart to crown His beloved
with tender mercies ; but again and again, all the time, as
intense in pain as the pain can be which a father's pity hath
over terribly sinful children upon whom he cannot execute
the fierceness of his anger, or the agony of a husband because

of the unfaithfulness and sure misery of an erring spouse (Hosea ii. 2). All the varied course of that holy love which was revealed to Moses in Horeb was a long forelight of that love which, visible to the eyes of men, themselves also trying and burdening it even unto death, looked, in the last days of Hebrew faith, from the side of Olivet upon the holy city, and wept over it, and said, "O Jerusalem, Jerusalem, thou that killest the prophets, and stonest them that are sent unto thee, how often would I have gathered thy children together, as a hen gathereth her chickens under her wings, and ye would not!"

24. On the threshold of the fulness of God's manifestation of Himself as the Saviour of man, when the riches of significant names and illustrative histories and suggestive visions of His holy saving love were to be gathered together in one great interpretation and realised sight in Christ Jesus, it seems in place to look back upon a very early anticipatory unveiling for a moment, a glimpse of sight, of the reality and not the name of what was to come in a day afar off. A cloud of witnesses from Moses to David and the Prophets had received the names suggestive of assuring faith to think of God by—father, shepherd, portion, dwelling-place, &c.—and they could make use of these names with deeply-comforting faith in the nearness of the love meant to shine through them upon man's desirous sight; and their faith had been helped by many experiences of the promised manner of Jehovah's grace. In meet superiority to them all, the experience of the father of the faithful stands out by itself the first and best in the history of faith. His religious title was shared by no other in name until the reality came in the homes of such as Lazarus and John and Peter. He was "the friend of God"— the title by which His memory lingers round Hebron to the present day. The *human face*, so to speak, of Jehovah's love to man once looked upon him, with the complete human sympathy which would make that love man's perfect portion. In the light of that marvellous reciprocity of friendship to which he was admitted at Mamre he foretasted the day of Jesus; when the seed of the woman, the seed of Abraham, was to become the first-born of many brethren, through such

Anticipation of "The Flesh."

desire to forgive and save as had that day allowed His "friend" to plead even for Sodom and Gomorrah until his courage of intercession failed, not the hearer's plenteousness of mercy—and through self-sacrifice such as His servant was afterwards compelled to all but experience.

Desire of all nations.

25. " How beautiful upon the mountains are the feet of Him that bringeth good-tidings, that publisheth peace ; that bringeth good tidings of good, that publisheth salvation; that saith unto Zion, Thy God reigneth !" (Isa. lii. 7.) Like dawn upon the mountains those mingling distinct and indistinct lights arising here and there during the four thousand years of the morning of salvation, each shining chief in its season till embraced by new arising brightness, gradually filled the atmosphere of the world with the expectation of the Sun of righteousness, the birth of One who came down from heaven to deliver from all human ills, to bring back the golden age ; and the eyes of the nations looked towards Judea as to the mountain of the Lord's house, ready to see His star and arise and follow wherever it should bring them, asking, " Where is He that is born King of the Jews ?"

Christian Faith.

" GOD MANIFEST IN FLESH."

The manifestation.

26. The progress of revelation—that is, of God's unveiling His own nature and His disposition towards man—was great between the generations of the old world, when He was characteristically a God afar off, and the times of Israel's many educating fortunes, during which He showed Himself characteristically a God at hand (Jer. xxiii. 23). But gloriously greater, gracious beyond anything that eye had seen, or ear heard, or it had entered into the heart of man to conceive, was His nearest closest showing of His love which had awaited the fulness of times, but waited manifestly " straitened " till it should uplift for ever the veil and bid His fallen creatures look upon His face and believe evermore. No wonder that the hearts of the prophets who prophesied of the grace that

should come, " inquired and searched diligently what the Spirit of Christ which was in them did signify when it testified beforehand of the sufferings of Christ and the glory that should follow " (1 Pet i. 10, 11) ; or that "the angels desired to look into " it as a mystery (ver. 12).   How could God come nearer in tender goodness to the poor objects of His love, His fallen children, the blinded sinning ones whom He followed with a yearning heart, than when He called Himself a "father" to them, a " husband," a " friend closer than a brother"?—how more assure them of His protecting guidance, His providing love, than when He was their " shepherd," their "king," the " leader and defender of His people"?—how better give them thoughts of unbroken safety and peace than in being their " dwelling-place," the "portion of their inheritance"?   Only by one strangely impressive approach to them, one which no creature, however highly exalted, instead of being so brought low, could ever have dared to think of the Creator descending to. It was to be by putting away all metaphors of nearness and affection, even the metaphors so filled with realities, the names that were continually surrounded with the acts bespoken by them ; and actually exchanging faith for sight, turning similitude into reality ; showing Himself to be man Himself, and becoming even in the earthly elements of man's nature " bone of his bone and flesh of his flesh."

27. In the fulness of times He who in holy sorrow, the " repentance" of God, had withdrawn Himself from the sin-polluted earth behind clouds and thick darkness ; but watched over fallen mankind unseen, and spoke to them in visions of the night, and made Himself known at long intervals to chosen servants whose hearts He had prepared to know Him and teach their brethren the things of God ; who returned to earth to a single chosen prepared people in the thunders and lightnings of Sinai ; who afterwards dwelt among them in a secret place, and spoke from a holy of holies to them by an oracle, and sent to them testimonies of His holiness and His purposes of grace towards them by prophets whom He called to be messengers to them from His invisible presence ; He who shadowed forth Himself to them in the love of their guiding

God's incarnation.

fathers, the government of their holy and yet sin-atoning priests, and their righteous and beneficent kings, and their heavenly-minded prophets; He in the fulness of times drew near to them as one of themselves could draw near to another. The so long obscured fact of their close connection with Him, that their nature was part of His nature, was unveiled at last to very sight and pledged by a bodily life. He came unto His own, and was born among them after their own manner of birth. Always their own, He became their own after the flesh, joined to them by the most dearly acknowledged ties of earthly kindred. "Forasmuch as the children were partakers of flesh and blood, He likewise Himself took part of the same" (Heb. ii. 14). How instructive in the light of this text is it that the earthly genealogy which records the Son of God taking rank in human families as the Son of man, should exhume the buried fact of man's unique place in life, and record the nearness, not a new-bestowed but a revealed one, a nearness which had always been; saying, "Adam was the son of God" (Luke iii. 38). Thus was the reality of Jehovah's declared *coming nigh* to mankind guaranteed. The reality of His *compassion and love* for them and the perfectness of His *sympathy* were made evident to sight in the same manner. In His assumed earthly life in their own flesh He took their position entirely, the position to which He had in all former time held forth His offers and assurances of loving-kindness and tender mercy, the condition of "a man of sorrows." "He was tempted in all points like as we are" (Heb. iv. 15). He completed the manifestation of His willing identity with the race whom He declared that He so loved, by submitting to their death. He did all this to persuade mankind of the one fact which all His revelations had been unveiling as fast as man could appreciate it—the one fact of which all the facts of religious history are parts—the fact to which all lines of religious thought are to bring the observant thinking soul—the fact which is to originate and sustain all religious affection and conduct—the fact He himself proclaimed in the day that He perfected it—"God so loved the world" (John iii. 16). So He directs us to read the meaning of His manifesting Himself in the flesh, and living our life, and dying our death. Already of our nature, He took our flesh, "that through death He might destroy him that had the power of death, that is, the devil; and deliver them who through fear of death were all their lifetime subject to bondage" (Heb. ii. 14, 15). "He suffered, being tempted, that He might succour those that are tempted" (Heb. ii. 18); and that we might know that "we have not an high priest which cannot be touched with the feeling of our infirmities, but was in all points tempted like as we are," and might "therefore come boldly unto the throne of grace, that we may obtain mercy, and find grace to help in time of need" (Heb. iv. 15, 16). It has been observed above (Chap. II. sect. 7) how the human life of God, the child of a human household, the intimate of human families, the equal associate of human labours, trials, griefs, and pleasures, made the long-used revealing names of father, husband, physician, shepherd, &c., no longer symbolical terms of indefinite though exceeding great love, but the representatives and assurances of degrees and manners of loving-kindness familiar, particular, definitely present to the thoughts, the coin of that manner of affection which is needed by and lived upon by man. The short life of Jesus of Nazareth engraved the reality of God's human love upon the imagination and the memory of man. The incarnation made the heavenly Father of prodigal man known and His love appreciable, familiarly understood, beyond all that believers previously could represent to themselves as the love of God's fatherhood; even as the meaning of His name Jehovah had been made "known" to Moses and Israel as even Abraham had not known it. John's words as to the Christian revelation remind us of that old advance of man to "know" Jehovah. "No man hath seen God at any time; the only-begotten Son, which is in the bosom of the Father, He hath declared Him" (John i. 18). Paul's words point out the greatness of that advance in faith's possessions : "Great is the mystery of godliness, who was manifested in the flesh, was justified in the Spirit, was seen of angels, was preached among the nations, was believed on in the world, was received up into glory " (1 Tim. iii. 16). It was looked back upon by those to whom it came as that which—" we have seen with our eyes, and have looked upon, and our hands have handled of the Word of life " (1 John i. 1); " no cunningly-devised fable of the power of the Lord Jesus ; " " we were eyewitnesses of His majesty, . . . when there came such a voice from the excellent glory, This is my beloved Son, in whom I am well pleased ; and this voice which came from heaven we heard, when we were with Him in the holy mount " (2 Pet. i. 16-18).

Progress of identification with man.

28. The nearness with which the incarnation brought God's love to the comprehension of mankind, like all preceding revelations of the great fact that " God so loved the world," advanced through progressive steps—His showing Himself theirs in nature—His making Himself one of them by their own family relationships—His taking their position in the troubles of their condition in every way that could assure them of His being one who could have a feeling of their infirmities. The last perfecting completing act of His incarnated love was so much in advance of all that had gone before, as to mark a new stage in God's coming nearer to mankind. It unveiled the perfectness of His taking His guilty offspring to Himself which faith needed to have for its peace. Human ways of thinking could come up to believe in great compassion, very tender love from so self-accommodating love as God had first declared under so expressive names, and then made actually visible in a human life ; but it may be doubted if human ways of thinking could get rid of fear on account of guilt. In man's experience even a parent's love cannot ward off retribution ; and penitence always needs more than compassion and sympathy ; it needs a salvation by restoration or deliverance. In the finishing act of the work of holy saving love to man which God had set before Himself faith was invited to look upon a new sight. In that act God advanced, as if passing over a great boundary, beyond all purely objective transitive love, all even His richly-furnished love of compassion, tenderness, even sympathy with man ; and became suffering guilty man Himself as much as one person could in these respects become another. He took man's place as Him-

self willingly the bearer of the consequences of his sin. He approached man more and more tenderly before to comfort and assure him ; He became one with him in the last otherwise impassable stage of his escape from his fallen state ; becoming " sin for us " (2 Cor. v. 21), " a curse for us," to redeem us from the law's curse (Gal. iii. 13). " As it is appointed unto man once to die, but after this the judgment, so Christ was once offered to bear the sins of many ; and unto them that wait for Him shall He appear the second time without sin unto salvation " (Heb. ix. 27, 28). " Christ hath once suffered for sins, the just for the unjust, that He might bring us to God " (1 Pet. iii. 18). In that going beyond all objective appearance of love, that perfectness of showing Himself one with the object of His saving grace, He was " lifted up so as to draw all men unto Him." The most guilty, fallen, frightened penitent could thenceforth think of the saving love he had to trust to as being as assured, as thoroughly protective to him, as if his father, healer, comforter, judge in one were loving, thinking for, suffering for, providing for no worm of the dust but for Himself. That substitutionary death passed through by God-man, and His rising again when the work given Him to do was finished, gave defined clearness and logical assurance of reality to the vision of faith unveiled by Him immediately before He went forth to that death : " Because I live ye shall live also " (John xiv. 19).

29. A strange but impressive illustration of this identifying Himself with sinful condemned man is presented to faith's thoughts by the particular human ancestry through which the Messiah appeared as the Son of man. In no way, perhaps, so fitted to satisfy our needed thought of His becoming one with us could He who " was made sin for us, though He knew no sin," have taken our fleshly state upon Himself. His bodily life was a link in a chain of human nature which contained the most illustrious cases of man's imperfect faith and holiness, but contained also the grossest human corruptions— viz., incest, adultery, and murder ; and the greatest human shortcoming in or sin against faith—viz., heathenism near religious light and apostasy from known truth. The Amorite

Peculiar human ancestry of Jesus.

Rahab, and the Moabite Ruth, the latter of a race debarred to the tenth generation from the congregation of Israel (Deut. xxiii. 3), were in the ancestry of His flesh as well as the mothers of Israel. The blood of Tamar and Bathsheba, as well as of Mary, of Ahaz as well as of Abraham, flowed in His veins. He was the son of Manasseh as well as of David, the descendant of Egypt and Canaan as well as of the chosen people. He came after the flesh through moral disgrace as well as honoured virtue; a representative of fallen human nature, universal as mankind could have wished for, but could not have dared to think of; yet perhaps only such as was needed to be the trust of the poor and needy, the sin-stained and despised—the substitute and elder brother of all ranks of earthly condition, and all diversities of moral estate in the " seed" which " He took up" or undertook for (Heb. ii. 16).

The Propitiation. Philosophical difficulties from overdrawn analogy.

30. Difficulties have been imported into the question of the propitiation oppressive to a good man's subjective notions of God's goodness, by an unphilosophical assumption of a distinction between the individuality of the heavenly Father and that of the only-begotten Son, such as would admit an element of antagonism so far as if a righteous father were exacting punitive satisfaction from an innocent son for the faults of guilty brethren. It is impossible to place the Father and the Son of Scripture language thus, two historical persons distinct in individuality as are the most united human father and son. Historically, the Father and the Son are one (John xiv.), and the Father is in fact suffering, in fact Himself meeting the penalty of His guilty children's sins; an idea which suggests no moral difficulties. We cannot explain to our human ways of thinking how the Father and the Son can be one, and yet make two so distinct ideas as Scripture presents to us ; but we are carefully taught to keep their unity in mind, and that fact obviates all obnoxious antagonisms. To our faith, to our power to think with comfort of our transgressions being blotted out by ample satisfaction, the assurance is given to be as great as if a father should lay on a willing son the unavoidable penalty incurred by a helpless one. Scripture speaks clearly as if the divine Father laid on His only divine Son the iniquities of us

His human children, who were without strength. We cannot understand the manner in which such action could be, as if it were between two separate identities; only the grace to us bringing salvation is to be as sure as if we could understand all, and we are to believe that love, and return to our waiting Father in penitence, and trust and believe, seeing in this how He "loved the world."

31. But if we study the saving love of God to man as it is historically set before us in the Word, the sufferings *arising* in the divine relationship because of man's sin, and those *undertaken* in it to make an end of man's sin, are things of a kind familiar to the comprehension of human love; and should be effectual in impressing their declared lesson upon human feelings—the impossibility of God simply ignoring sin, passing it by from mercy, even to those most beloved by Him. God's love to man, from His creation to His everlasting redemption of him, we are to think of as all being "in His Son," man's creator, providence, peacemaker, hope of glory, and judge; and God's education of the world to faith, presented from the beginning to mankind's thoughts, both through experience and revelation, this particular suffering because of sin—the sufferings of fatherhood. Historically, and in no metaphor, sin had cost Him bereavement of His created son, man, Adam and his seed, whom He had made in His own likeness to indulge His love unconfined upon him, His own nature placed in a home of its own—another heaven to the heavenly Father. And the peculiar suffering was set before man's eyes through all the course of his training to true thoughts, as human nature's (*i. e.*, the communicated nature's) most remarkable misery in connection with sin; while it arises, as if a thought inherent in that nature, into fearful prominence in man's own thoughts of expiation. The first pains of outward death which Adam reaped as the wages of his sin, was the violent death of a good son by the crime of a bad one. That blood of Abel, at the beginning of human history, was a writing which was to be brought into clear significance in the fulness of times, when the blood of God's own well-beloved Son, shed by His brethren, was to speak better things—words of forgiveness and congru-

[margin note: God's sufferings of fatherhood the same with man's experience.]

ous cure of the sin and death then so awfully inaugurating
their dominion (Heb. xii. 24). The first curse pronounced in
the new world, was degradation of a race for irreverence to a
father (Gen. ix. 25). That filial sin was a penal crime afterwards, under the divine government of Israel. Abraham's
training to fallen man's faith in Jehovah, included the giving
up to death for His will of his only promised son, the heir
of all the promises made to him. Jacob's characteristic grief
was bereavement of his well-beloved son by the hand of his
brethren. David's was the loss of a fallen but yearned-over
son by the punishment of rebellion, after dishonour of his
father and murder of a guilty brother. The completing plague
which made Egypt " know " the Jehovah of Israel and of man
was the death of the first-born. The passing over of the self-
same misery to Israel when, in obedient faith, they sprinkled
the blood of the innocent lamb on their door-posts, was their
great national fact, preserved in the characteristic commemorative service of their faith; and it was expounded afterwards
as only symbolical of man's deliverance by the substitutionary
death of the Lamb of God, " Christ our passover sacrificed for
us." Israel was to have the same thought of the sacrifice and
redemption of a son kept in their minds in a merciful form.
Every first-born son, throughout their generations, was to be
Jehovah's, and had to be redeemed by a substitutionary death.
We cannot put out of our sight, as having no connection with
the so wide appearance in revealed religion of the association
of this particular misery with sin, the other awful form in
which the same association is presented to us in fallen faiths
—viz., the fires of Moloch, and the question of the Mesopotamian Balaam, which was answered by him, but doubtless represented the oppressive sentiment of the peoples among whom
he dwelt. " Wherewithal shall I come before the Lord? . . .
Shall I give my first-born for my transgression, the fruit of my
body for the sin of my soul ?" (Micah vi. 6, 7). That is the dark, .
despairing side of the same truth, whose awful burden is represented in the revelation of love, not as taken away, but as
taken away from man to be borne by God Himself, while He
lays on mankind the merciful part of it only, that " they shall

look on Him whom they have pierced, and shall mourn and
be in bitterness as one that mourneth for an only son, as one
that is in bitterness for his first-born" (Zech. xii. 10). This
historical suffering inflicted by sin upon the human race is
the very suffering represented in the Old Testament as God's
agony over fallen man. "When Israel was a child, then I
loved him, and called my son out of Egypt. . . . I taught
Ephraim also to go, taking them by their arms. . . . I
drew them with the cords of a man, with bands of love. . . .
How shall I give thee up, Ephraim, abandon thee, Israel?
How shall I make thee as Admah, set thee as Zeboim? Mine
heart is turned within me ; my repentings are kindled together.
I will not execute the fierceness of mine anger, I will not return to destroy Ephraim" (Hosea xi.) In the New Testament
this misery is shown forth, as the reality of His pain, in both
man's sin and his redemption. He marks the nearness of
Adam to His heart—Adam, called in the fulness of times the
Son of God—by calling His well-beloved eternal Son the
second Adam ; and the suffering, the shame, the agony, which
the separation and fall of that created son caused Him, He
showed then in that second manifestation of His own nature
in human life—that second perfect Adam, perfect in holiness
and in the unbroken nobleness and lovableness and capacity
for happiness which should be human nature's portion—Him
made a spectacle to degraded mankind of scorn and hatred
as man should have been hated and scorned, suffering the
agony of sin's assaults as man should have felt them agony,
sorrowful even unto death as man should have been under the
horror of being forsaken by God.

32. The woe that sin carries forth beyond the sphere of the Suffering
sinner's own possible sufferings was also from the beginning a by others
than the
lesson of God's education of the world to faith. The ground guilty, an
historical
cursed for Adam's sake, and bringing forth briers and thorns, teaching.
starving the enjoyment, and burdening often the life, of all the
innocent creatures around him, was a humiliating reminder
continually to him of the change his sin had caused. In
Israel's history, the clearest writing of the truth which we have,
the lesson is emphatic. Why was the abhorrent work laid,

E

as their special task in the world, upon the Hebrews of destroying, woman and child as well as men, the corrupt tribes of
Canaan? Why was an Israelite, a child of Abraham Jehovah's
friend, a "little one" of Jacob His chosen, banished by Him
without ruth from His presence, and from the bounds of the
holy congregation, and from the communion of his own nearest
relatives, whenever any even chance taint of typical uncleanness came to him; and for him there was no coming near to
the tabernacle of Jehovah in thanksgiving or praise or supplication, and no intercourse with those who were bone of his
bone and flesh of his flesh for that lost day; but a washing of
his flesh and of his garment had to blot out, as it were, that
portion of time from his life? Such pain as accompanied these
horrible duties of Israel in Canaan, and such domestic privation
of happiness as burdened Israel's services of purification, guilt-
less sufferers universally meet in God's world—the penalty of
the sins of those dear to them. Israel's worship contained a
daily spectacle meant to teach man the same lesson. Why
was the sad sight before the eyes of the congregation at the
beginning and the end of every day, of the lamb slain for no
special, no known, sin of the night or of the day, but for the im-
pureness, always sinning, of even the beloved, the chosen people?
The never-ending spectacle of the most guileless, lovable, and
lifeful of living creatures put to a painful death, destroyed in
blood and burning, because the people were sinful more than
they thought of, was suited to beget, and continue, and inten-
sify the thought of every sin as bringing pain to some one
who should not suffer for it. Who had ever been in truth
the sore sufferer by mankind's sins, was unveiled in the end
of those daily sacrifices: a being of gentle goodness, of un-
complaining endurance, dumb as a sheep before her shearers,
"the Lamb of God," His well-beloved Son; the maker of the
human world; the bestower upon man of His original good and
perfect life; who had rejoiced in the habitable parts of the
earth, and had His delights with the sons of men, and looked
to an eternal heritage of joy in them. The sight of Him, the
inevitable sufferer by every sin of man's, yet yearning to suffer
all and save him, and the sight of God giving up His only-

begotten Son for man, are revealed as meant to be to all the
race who shall live for ever, the effectual motive to repentance and abhorrence of sin. With a congruous pain they shall
look on Him whom they have pierced, wounded in the house
of His friends; and they shall mourn and be in bitterness as
they would for an only child, their own first-born.

33. It is an historical teaching, also, that the substitution of
the sinless Adam for the sinful, as it was no metaphor merely,
was not an assumed substitution only. It was a voluntary
laying down by the shepherd of His life for the sheep. But
it was no purely forensic coming into man's place of one who
wished to take upon Himself, by arbitrary choice, the punishment of man's sins. That would have been an act which not
grief and shame, but only joy and exultation, might accompany. Man's redeemer was by historical union, a union never
broken, the inevitable fellow-sufferer with, though He was also
the willing substitute for, man in all his miseries; naturally
suffering as well as willingly. The second Adam who came
to be baptised in the consciousness of the first Adam's deserved
agonies of spirit, was the giver to that first Adam of his moral
and spiritual sensibilities—His own nature in which He had
created him; and He was never separate from that first Adam
and his race in actual as well as potential sympathy. So He
had rejoiced in the habitable parts of the earth at its creation.
So in its fallen state "He was afflicted in all man's afflictions;"
and had it as His desirous "joy set before Him," to deliver from
death that lost son of God, and bring him again into his first
union; one with God for ever then, and with new-added effectual
feelings of life in Him, because of the history of his salvation.

And does not the union, in the perfect manhood of Jesus,
of all the broken faculties and temperaments, all the perceptions and sensibilities which are but distributed over the
fragmentary humanity of the race now, give faith a painful
sight of how He did "taste death for every man," as every
diversity of human kind *should* feel that spiritual death which
he died daily—the contradiction of sinners, the disappointments of holy desires and efforts, the wounds in the house of
His friends, the shame of dishonour, the assaults of the enemy

Identification in suffering a fact of Christ's historical union with man.

of man, the horror of sin's foul associate, death, and the completing, destroying, agony—the hiding of God's countenance? If man's death be essentially separation from God, as man's everlasting life is union unto oneness with Him, the thought of Jesus possessing in Himself in completeness all the sensibilities of the human life, gives a forcible human meaning to the cry of the mysterious part of His sufferings in the hour of His bodily death, "My God, my God, why hast Thou forsaken me?" That was the cry of death in the very person of man, as well as because of man's sin; and it gives also a clear view of death and Him in the foretold human contact of the seed of the woman with the Tempter—the first promise of salvation—he that had the power of death bruising His heel, inflicting agony on Him in the same hour in which He made an end of death —that is, of man's separation from the source of his nature's life of holy blessedness, his Father in heaven. It was the last, the "finishing," earthly manifestation of that identification of Himself with man to save him, in which, having died for him, He would rise again for him also, giving him the faith thereby, "Because I live, ye shall live also."

Identity of suffering revealed for faith's comfort.

34. The divine suffering because of man; the self-sacrifice of God giving up His only-begotten Son, and the truly substitutionary manner of the Son's endurances—the man's agony which God endured for man—both foreshadowed in the history of human affection, unavoidably suffering with a suffering child, like Jacob's death in Joseph's (Gen. xxxvii. 35), and desirous to suffer for a prodigal son, like David for Absalom, "Would God I had died for Thee, O Absalom, my son, my son!"— God's human suffering for His human children, thus foreshadowed in His guidance of their training life, but manifested in the fulness of times—was a profound identification of the heavenly Father with man's misery, the contemplation of which is to constrain man to see in Him a Father of mercies, a God of consolations, in Christ Jesus.

Expiation of guilt necessary to man's subjective feelings and to

35. A writer of the school to which a punitive element in the sufferings of Christ is repulsive has remarked a difficulty, in the way of *excluding* the substitutionary idea, that if mankind are to be influenced by the thought of these sufferings,

they must be presented "in the language of the altar." That historical necessity is explained by what all profane history shows; that truth. human nature has a feeling that expiation by sacrifice must follow sin. The religion which is to command *man's* faith must contain that element; even such thoughts as mankind gathered from all pre-Christian revelation and history of God's love to man. And a faith that is to be possible to all men—the test of the true faith which the wayfaring man, though a simple one, could not err in—must have its thoughts of this historical character. Is it from the historical love of God, or from a philosophical conception of His love, that attractive theories of ultimate good are educed which seek to look upon God as enduring and employing suffering always to purify, as by a consuming fire, sin from the souls of men, and not at any time as a punishment of guilt? They have their attractiveness from their indefiniteness, which, unchecked, untested by historical or declaratory illustrations of God's ways, loves to see through a mysterious future of infinite love the likelihood of a process of long-continued elimination of moral evil, ending in entire purification of every soul from all that is not of God's nature, and, of course, the coming of universal blessedness. Out of such a constitution of divine love the necessity naturally drops of Christ's sufferings being substitutionary punishment of human guilt, and along therewith the " abhorrent idea" of God's being angry with His well-beloved Son—an idea " abhorrent" because of an erroneous contemplation of the divine relation of sonship, and the divine anger, as if they were like the human things of the same names. There lie, however, in the way of the indefinite imagination of universal welfare coming through God's infinitely suffering love, two definite difficulties belonging to the revealed historical character of His love as a holy love. One is, that all sanctification and holy union to God of the soul of man, by which alone the blessedness of human nature—essentially God's nature—is to be attained, has man's conscious faith indispensable to it. The other is, that the theory of ultimate universal blessedness contemplates the extinction of moral evil, from which suffering is inseparable. But neither the universality of faith nor the extinction of moral evil is a thought which history suggests. The termination of moral evil is not necessarily included in the deliverance, healing, and restitution of all things in heaven and earth associated in promise with the gathering of mankind to Himself by Christ. For the history of man and his " habitable earth" is exceptional, and the existence of evil is not mundane merely, but of wider extent. The language of the Bible, historically describing sin's future punishment, certainly does not contain any element suggesting a termination of it; and the punishment, not the mere cure, of moral evil, is the historical lesson taught by the destruction of the nations whose cup was full, the spared " destruction " of Ephraim (Hosea xi. 9), and the subjective expectation betrayed by the superstitions alike of heathens and modern sceptics.

Progress of faith's thoughts in the four gospels. 36. Let us here notice once more the progress of habits of thought—acquired faith—as it appears over the period of the writing of the four gospels, written with thirty and sixty years' after-thoughts of Jesus' manifestation.

Matthew's sight of the Lord, though not closely confined within Hebrew associations, is still a sight of Hebrew eyes characteristically. The things of Christ which he narrates remind him, far more frequently than any of the other evangelists, of " that which was spoken unto the fathers by the prophets." To him the Messiah is " the son of David, the son of Abraham " (i. 1); and though much of Jewish habit of thought must have been departed from by " Matthew the publican," his narrative of Him is marked with the exclusiveness of Jewish feeling regarding both the heathen and the Samaritans (xv. 24, and x. 5) in particulars noticeably omitted in the next gospel, though it was written in all likelihood under the eye of the apostle of the circumcision.

Mark's eyes turn most strongly to look upon the Saviour, not under any condition of national association, but as He was manifested mighty to save. His heart is set upon living pictures of Him travailing in the greatness of His strength, vivid details of His manifestations of power and wisdom, narratives of His healings of remarkable kinds or extent. If Mark wrote under the eye of Peter, the φιλοχριστος, whose writings characteristically contemplate the Saviour's office of salvation, we have to remember that before the writing of this gospel Peter,had much ceased to be a Jew of Jerusalem. The apostle of the circumcision had received the vision of Joppa, and had been much in interchange of thought with Gentile Christians, and, though still loyal to the institutions of Moses, was not a Jew only in his sympathies.

Luke, whose genealogy derives the human life of Christ not from Abraham, the fountain of Hebrew history, but from Adam, "the son of God," the beginning of human life, has his eyes characteristically drawn to contemplate the humanity of man's Saviour, His fellow-feeling with those around Him, and His power of sympathy over them. It is he that tells the stories of the widow of Nain, and the penitent in Simon's house (vii.), and of the thief on the cross. It is he alone who tells that it was the look of Jesus turned upon His unfaithful friend that made Peter go out and weep bitterly. Luke gives not so much his Master's authority-bearing discourses, as His discourses with His nearest friends. The stories of Emmaus and of the "standing in the midst" (xxviii.) are especially Luke's. Before he wrote, the revealed religion of Judaism had parted its hold on earthly nationality. Jerusalem was no more, and faith had to seek wider sympathy than was bounded by places; as upon the earlier destruction of the city of its solemnities, Judaism itself had been made to feel that it had a spirit which could and must live above and without the forms and ritual which had been deemed essential to it in Palestine.

In the latest gospel, John, looking back upon the utter ending of the grand dispensation of Moses thirty long years before by the destruction of the holy city—a change which to a Jew must have destroyed the importance of all other possible worldly changes—sees on both sides, beyond all Hebrew and all human time, Jesus the Creator, the Friend, the Saviour of man embracing all human duration in the history of His love. The φιλοιησους sees the person of "the Son" filling the glad tale of Fatherly love; from the joy of the past eternity; through the coming to His own unrecognised, to persuade them that "God so loved the world;" on to the gathering together into the Father's

house of many mansions into one with Himself, and His
Father and their Father, of the beloved, redeemed, human sons
and daughters of God, whosoever believed in His name.

God ONE
with them
that
believe.

37. After the work of incarnate love was finished, which
showed visibly to human sight, and prepared for record in
history — the world's memory — God's making Himself one
with fallen man to save him; the further progress of revelation
chiefly unveiled that saving union, so as to make familiar to
the thoughts of faith the practical results of that union on the
moral and spiritual state of man; its working, so to speak, now
from the opposite direction—that is, in raising man from his
fallen and guilty state to the holiness of God's likeness again,
and into union of affection and unison of spiritual sympathies
with God.

All the phraseology employed in the New Testament to
instruct our thoughts respecting the Holy Ghost the Comforter
is set round about this truth, to make it familiar to our
thoughts, that God is practically ONE with them that believe
in Him; and to make us understand the inseparableness of the
holy love we are to trust in, because of that union. "He
dwelleth with you, and shall be in you" (John xiv. 17), is the
new description of His connection with us. The necessary
moral human state of that connection is described,—"Know
ye not that ye are the temple of God, and the Spirit of God
dwelleth in you. If any man defile the temple of God, him
will God destroy; for the temple of God is holy, which
temple ye are (1 Cor. iii. 16, 17).

This connection of saving union is described in the terms
needed and sought by penitent sinners—a new appropriate
name under which God, after the manner of His revelation of
Himself from the beginning, invites men's faith in His design
and work by this indwelling union. He who was known by
so many names to the first races and the chosen people,—who
advanced, in the appropriated titles which He made His representatives, from Deity to Almighty, Eternal, Possessor of

Heaven and Earth, Most High—who, with selecting love, became Jehovah, Israel's Holy One, the Lord of their Hosts—who
came near to be a King to His people, their Shepherd and
Captain of Salvation—who came nearer to their homes, their
Father, Husband, Friend closer than a brother—who became
Jesus, partaker of their flesh, tempted in all points like as they
are, tasting death for every man to save His people from their
sins,—now dwells within them with a grace the nearness and
meet-help of which is named congruously to the nearness of
His presence. He is their Comforter. The dwelling-place of
His holiness, where they may worship Him, is no more the far-
off heavens ; nor even any nearer house of God built by adoring
hands ; but their own hearts : " Ye are the temple of the living
God ; as God hath said, I will dwell in them, and walk in
them " (2 Cor. vi. 16).

38. The peculiar title by which the dispensation of the Holy
Ghost was promised by "God manifest in the flesh " is another
development, or, accurately speaking, unveiling (revelation) of
the relationship of man to God designed in the salvation by
Christ Jesus. A union that is comforted and comforting ;
effected by a "Comforter" helping the infirmities of man to
come unto union with God—that is, with the Comforter Himself—in prayer, in desire, in realising of His love, in feeling
remembrance of His "things of Christ ;" is more than a formal
union, like the restoration given by forensic justification, or
the adoption known to human laws. It exhibits the union approaching from the other side also ; and makes it a union of two
lives mutually drawing each other close into one, each desired
by and desiring the other ; a union, so to speak, of reciprocal
complement of life. Jesus had in His personal teaching discovered to whoever could "bear" His words this design of
man's union to God by the way in which He used the language
of human relationship, which had all along the progress of
revelation been made the explanation to them of the nature
of the love of God. His expression, " My Father and your
Father," making one healed, comforted relationship, man's
sonship and His own, sent its flash of unifying meaning
through all the assuring metaphors of preceding revelation ;

Progress of revealing names.
The Comforter "helping" man's union to God

pointing them to indicate in richest fulness all the "comfort" which man's affectional nature was prepared to take from them ; if persuaded and helped to believe that so great a salvation of united life was within the purpose of the words. These all then became the "things of Christ" which faith could show to itself, and the Comforter would effectually show to faith, glorifying the Redeemer's love in its eyes thereby. For example, what comforts of Christ can the Comforter take and show to the appreciative recognition of believers interpreting by the words of Jesus, "My Father and your Father," the value of those earlier words of His—"Whosoever doeth the will of my Father which is in heaven, the same is my brother and sister and mother"? Are there not brothers and sisters who can appreciate the Comforter's words describing the communion of believers thus joined together to their Lord ; who know what it is to be "joined in one spirit," to "live not to themselves but to" one another, to have one another's "words abiding" in them, to feel it no self-denial but delight to serve one another's will; who have no humbling, but healing nursing "comfort," in feeling dependence upon one another's stronger arm, or wiser head, or sympathising heart?—brothers and sisters who know the uniting power and riches of these words, "My Father and your Father"? Is there not many a weakly child who has needed long past childhood's years a mother's watchfulness and care, or whom tribulation in maturer life has drawn to her for counsel or for comfort, who has known what is meant when a saving Comforter is said to be a "sure portion" to the afflicted, shrinking heart? what it is to have a wise and good and supporting counsellor, of whom it may be said that out of her fulness her needy child receives "grace for grace," receiving along with the mother's comforting her wisdom also, and her quiet spirit and her peace?

39. It is this "comfort" of salvation—not bare deliverance from death and sin—this comfort of salvation, from which the thought of guaranteeing saving union is inseparable—that the language of salvation was all along fitted to bring to man, and which the Comforter is to "help his infirmity," his "slowness of heart," to believe. In his teaching, the old metaphors of

by His comforting exhibition of the truth, and earnest of its assurances.

union advance in the assurance which they convey. Thus conjugal love, the highest human experience of rational and affectional union, which had been used in the Old Testament (Hosea
ii.) as illustrative of the great compassionateness of God's love,
the comfort of forgiveness, He brings into authoritative assurance of the comfort also of happiness, the revelation of completed life. The life of conjugal union, unique in created life,
in which two human beings are meant to be so joined in heart
and will and thought and life that they are spoken of as
become one, is now quoted as the manner of union of believers
to Jesus. The Church is the "bride," the Lamb's "wife"
(Eph. v. 32 ; Rev. xxi. 9) ; and the illustrative force of that
union is not fully perceived unless, as the Spirit the Comforter
bids us, we revert to the institution and first example of it.
The first pair whom God made one were not two originally
separate individuals made one by ordinance, but the woman
had her being from the very person of the man. She had been
a part of his body, of his flesh and of his bones, before her
separate existence ; as she became one flesh with him when
brought to him by their heavenly Father. The profound thought
suggested by this revealed parallel as to the connection of
human nature and life with God is the historical truth. The
connection is original oneness ; separation of individuality
(made for a time alienation of life by sin, and so needing the
long corrective discipline of salvation, as well as its propitiation) ; but to be characteristically a life-seeking union ; and
becoming oneness again. Another figure giving assurance
and explanation of the union that is to grow into oneness was
given by Jesus, but its form developed by the Comforter. It is
a human union which is hardly describable as a union of sep-
arates even now, but has a link of original unbrokenness—
the human union in which pure love and need and happy
dependence commingle—that of a little child to its parent.
Jesus had said, "Of such is the kingdom of heaven." The
child's-enjoyment and rest of the heavenly union is the teaching of the Comforter. As an infant nursling loves and hungers
for, and, resting in perfect peace, trusts to get the milk it lives
upon, so does He bid the little ones that believe in Jesus

desire the sincere milk of the Word, that they may grow
thereby (1 Pet. ii. 2). And, an earnest or pledge now of that
union or oneness of the life of heaven, the Comforter Himself is a helper of infirmities, a healer, a sanctifier, a guide, a
teacher, not even so little distant as a mother is from her babe;
not separated even by that least of all human separations; but
dwelling in man's own soul and heart, upholding every rising
effort after goodness, showing the penitent reader of saving
knowledge "the things of Christ," guiding his thoughts unto
all truth, helping his infirmities to pray for what are the soul's
needs and should be its desires, and inspiring desires unutter-
able by the words of man's fallen estate.

"THE INHERITANCE."

The family
reunion
accom-
plished.

40. The word of faith instructs us that this perfected earthly
drawing near of God in holy love to man under the name of
the Comforter is not the completion of His work of love—it is
"the earnest of our inheritance" (Eph. i. 14; 2 Cor. i. 22).
That inheritance being the subject of anticipatory faith, is,
after the manner of all God's revelations of things which we
are to look forward to, not described so definitely as the present
possessions of the Comforter's invisible love, which faith has to
think upon, and make more constant practical use of. The language of Scripture, however, concerning the everlasting life of
heaven, is clearly of the same idea of God's union with man;
or rather the other side of the same truth, man's union with
God—man taken by God into everlasting union of assured
life and holiness and blessedness with Himself. Man when
taken home (2 Cor. v.) out of the outer life of tribulation,
weakness, and danger where he has lived by faith of God's
near but invisible love—the faith of God dwelling in him, shall
then dwell in God, taken into His embosoming love, near, close,
one with Him. The nearness of saving love shall then be
quite unveiled. The Father in heaven shall no more comfort
His children by words, messages, assurances, tokens, names of
love, recollections of faithfulness. He shall Himself "wipe
away all tears from their eyes." He will uphold them no

more by secondary means of nurturing or gladdening efficacy; no more feed them daily with "food convenient for
them." "They shall hunger no more, neither thirst any
more." "The Lamb shall feed them, and lead them unto
living fountains of waters" (Rev. vii. 16, 17). No longer will
He uphold them with the nightly rest that here is so sweet a
present help in time of need, nor revive them with the light
of new days, and the sun that is so "pleasant for the eyes to
behold." "Their city shall have no need of the sun, neither of
the moon to shine in it, for the glory of God shall lighten it,
and the Lamb shall be the light thereof" (Rev. xxi. 23). "There
shall be no night there." In the present state of training the
exercise of and endeavour after fraternal union is the great
appointed practice, so to speak, for man's increase of union
with God Himself. No more will He exercise them by the
trial of faith in earthly relationships, the interchange of love,
and the self-devotion of gratefulness—the thoughts of parents'
counsels, the sight of brethren's good works, the provocations
of frowardness, the self-denials of charity. That work will be
over, and the enjoyment of finished work be come. The mutually training relatives and neighbours, the instructors by memory and by anticipation, the many fellow-helpers and fellow-
triers, whose imperfections caused separation often here, will
be gathered together to enjoy union evermore with Him and
with one another in the house of many mansions—the Father's
house made ready for all; the rest of each the rest of all; the
recollections of each the uniting of all; the harmony of
diversity, and unity of individualities perfected, of which
holy family life gives no little understanding and foretaste
on earth.

41. It does not seem out of place here to point out again *Realistic
revelation
of heaven:*
how the thoughts of faith are constantly invited to occupy
themselves with facts, distinct records of things done, or representations of things that are to be. Heaven is as definitely
described by elements fitted to make human happiness as the
incarnate manifestation of God's love was fitted to secure trust
for all forms of help needed by man. It is no Mohammedan
paradise of corporeal indulgence; but as distinctly pictured

as Mohammed's paradise are the essential elements of the happiness of the living soul, which are represented as making man's heaven; the human life reconciled and consciously united to its heavenly Father. Contrasted with the highest, purest, heathen notions of felicity after death—the misty thought of being absorbed into the torpid being of self-centred or even insentient Deity—the revealed heaven of the Bible is one not of lost existence, but of life new found ; a definite realisable life, full of means of happiness more or less familiar already to faith, or even to sight. Observe the distinctness of the features of the everlasting inheritance as the Epistle to the Hebrews sets them before our faith (Heb. xii. 22-24). These are—the religious happiness of everlasting nearness to God, such an enjoyment as nearest communions with Him on earth give a foretaste of : " Ye are come unto Mount Zion, and unto the city of the living God, the heavenly Jerusalem"—the new experience of happiness in beholding and knowing God's higher works of wisdom, power, and goodness ; the advance upon all thoughts and enjoyed emotions raised by mere earthly creation : " Ye are come to an innumerable company of angels " —the perfection of the happiness which human society yields ; communion attained with the great examples of the race, those unknown in the body, whom yet we realise by faith ; and communion with the former brethren of earthly life, the lost delight of the eyes, the helpers or cares of earthly days, parted from in frailty, or in clouded thoughts, rejoined in perfectness and everlasting honour : " Ye are come to the general assembly and church of the first-born which are written in heaven, and to the spirits of just men made perfect "—the best religious joy, that of gratefulness and indulged love, sitting evermore in the light of His countenance who loved us unto death : " Ye are come to Jesus, the Mediator of the new covenant, and to the blood of sprinkling, which speaketh better things than that of Abel." Nor are these spiritual affectional joys of the " rest remaining for the people of God " to be left by faith uncompleted by the contemplation of the bodily rest, which is a sorely-needed and secretly-cherished forelooking amidst much tribulation here ; the rest when corruption shall put on incorruption, and mortal shall put on immortality. "They shall hunger no more, neither thirst any more," is the apocalyptic prophet's summary of the rest awaiting the burdens of this flesh. The earlier prophet's words of the earthly day of salvation, the fulfilment of which Jesus bade the disciples of John see and hear (Matt. xi. 4), will be rightly read by many heavy-laden bearers of this death-stricken frame, with thoughts of the inheritance which is incorruptible and undefiled, and passeth not away : "Then the eyes of the blind shall be opened and the ears of the deaf shall be unstopped : then shall the lame men leap as an hart, and the tongue of the dumb shall sing" (Isa. xxxv. 5, 6).

42. The heaven offered to our faith's thoughts is an ever-lasting life of definite realities—an everlasting human life, in which the good already known is to be prolonged in a perfected condition ; and the things which are now the subject of faith's thoughts are to be the familiar objects of glorified senses. It is a home suited to human anticipation, thoroughly furnished for human desires ; a house of many mansions, having its many places prepared for mankind's necessary differences of anticipation—a home, not for the immortal spirit only, but for the "living soul" which man was created, man in a glorious body and a perfected spirit, like unto His glorious body who, "the first-born among many brethren," has gone to prepare a place for those He loved, the other children of His father and their father. The Christian's living faith is but taking its authorised comfort, when, walking in the valley of the shadow of death, sorrowing, but not as those without hope, it peoples for itself the house of the Father in heaven with the faces and forms of one and another of its well-remembered fellow-servants, as they have finished their work in the chambers of His earthly house. For, of the many comforts of the Father's discipline now, this is one, that every sanctified near relationship among His children in earthly life, when its cord of love is painfully unloosed, fastens a new band heavenwards upon the earth-abiding soul, to draw it by another uniting thought to that aye more and more familiar dwelling-place. And if man's heavenly home must, by the needs of his nature,

an eternal perfected human life.

contain active service of the holy object of his faith, as well as unassailable felicity in Him; that portion of the future of salvation is not of a kind, perhaps, which our present powers could realise; yet the words written of that spiritual fulness of times, " They shall serve Him day and night" (Rev. vii. 15), bid every strong uprising spirit take to itself the thought of boundless fields for the outgoings of the redeemed " soul, and strength, and mind."

Revelation of God to mankind— why so slow. 43. The question has often troubled sincere servants of God, " Why was God's revelation of Himself to mankind so slowly made, and so many generations allowed to live and die in so great comparative darkness; the full revelation of Him only coming when the world was four thousand years old?" It is the same question as the foretold question of Christian times, " Where is the promise of His coming?"—why is Christianity spreading so slowly? The answer is involved in the awful mystery of moral evil, which at once all but destroyed Adam's ability to think of God as he had known Him. The preceding pages endeavour to show a progress of unveiling God to mankind checked only by the human soul's ability to see what was unveiled; and always in advance of that ability, and evidently also accompanied, in man's consciousness, by help given to the ability. In every stage of the unveiling it was as with the personal disciples of Jesus, to whom He said, " I have many things to say unto you, but ye cannot bear them now." Is it not the same with the individual as with the race? The senses of every believer discern good and evil only progressively, as they are used to the discrimination. And as in the history of the individual, so in the history of the race, the progress of faith, " the knowledge of the Lord," has been a thing of flux and reflux, like " the waters covering the sea." The knowledge and faith of God is to be man's choice as well as God's gift; and the steady or the quick progress of that choice is interfered with in a manner that is theoretically inexplicable, if we entertain questions of *why* God permits it to be so, but plain as can be if we practically think only of *how* it comes to pass.

CHAPTER IV.

THE EDUCATION OF THE WORLD TO FAITH.

PART SECOND—THE DISSEMINATION OF THE TRUTH.

PSALM lxvii. 1, 2.—God be merciful unto us and bless us, and cause His face to shine upon us; that Thy way may be known upon earth, Thy saving health among all nations.

1. BEYOND the direct education of mankind to true thoughts of God through His revealing Himself by progressive steps, first to a selected line, then to a nation, there was always a simultaneous indirect education carried on by His providence, leading those peoples which surrounded the depositaries of revelation to instruct themselves by comparing the thoughts of their own religions with those of the revealed faith; and that self-education was helped by the task laid on Israel of making Jehovah known to surrounding peoples, and also by occasional revelation directly made to those peoples themselves.

Indirect education of heathen peoples by contact.

2. The geographical positions occupied from first to last by the people God "formed for Himself to show forth His praise" (Is. xliii. 21), are to the highest degree indicative of their having been chosen as commanding positions for that purpose. Ezekiel's language which he used of Jerusalem, the centre and example of true religion in the days of her power, was politically true of Israel through all their history, and of Palestine, the chief seat of revealed truth, during all ancient history. "I have set Jerusalem in the midst of the nations and countries that are round about her" (Ezek. v. 5). Indeed the prophet recognises that central position as one for the em-

Geographical positions of revealed truth centres of universal publication.

F

ployment of which Israel was responsible immediately charging them with unfaithfulness to their place. "And she hath changed my judgments into wickedness more than the nations, and my statutes more than the countries that are round about her" (ver. 6). "Palestine, though now at the very outskirts of that tide of civilisation which has swept far into the remotest west, was in Israel's time the vanguard of the eastern, and therefore of the civilised world; and, moreover, stood midway between the two great seats of ancient empire—Babylon and Egypt. It was the highroad from one to the other of those mighty powers, the prize for which they contended, the battle-field on which they fought, the lofty bridge over which they ascended and descended respectively, into the deep basins of the Nile and Euphrates." The first contact of sacred with profane history we read of was in Abraham's expedition against Chedorlaomer and his associates from Persia and Babylonia come to make war upon the southern kings of Palestine. "The battle in which the latest hero of the Jewish monarchy perished, was to check the advance of an Egyptian king on his way to contest the empire of the then known world with the King of Assyria at Carchemish." "The whole history of Palestine between the return from the captivity and the Christian era, is a contest between 'the kings of the north and the kings of the south,' the descendants of Seleucis and Ptolemy, for the possession of the country. And when at last the West begins to rise as a new power on the horizon, Palestine, as the nearest point of contact between the two worlds, becomes the scene of the chief conflicts of Rome with Asia. There is no other country in the world which could exhibit the same confluence of associations. In the ravines of Lebanon are to be seen the hieroglyphics of the great Rameses, the cuneiform characters of Sennacherib, and the Latin inscriptions of the Emperor Antoninus."—Stanley's 'Sinai and Palestine.' This choice of geographical centres for the publication of revealed truth designed to be the faith of the world, was strikingly exemplified in the Messiah's selecting the shores of the Sea of Galilee to be the scene of most of His teachings and manifestations of divine power. That region was to the

"Roman Palestine almost what the manufacturing districts are to England." "From no other centre could 'His fame' have gone 'throughout all Syria;' nowhere else could He have drawn around Him the vast multitudes who hung on His lips, 'from Galilee, from Decapolis, from Judæa, from beyond Jordan,' and 'ran through that whole region round about,' carrying in beds through its narrow but crowded plain 'those that were sick, wherever they heard He was;' and 'whithersoever He entered into any of the numerous villages or cities,' there 'they laid their sick in the market-places,' 'many coming and going so that He had not time so much as to eat.'"—(Idem.)

A position in this way influential may reasonably be presumed to have been occupied by the antediluvian line associated in history with God's revelations of Himself. Noah, the last of the line, was certainly in a prominent place among the whole contemporary race. Most of the others named would be the primogenital chiefs of their time and family; and the separation of the Cainite from the Sethite families seems not to have been one which prevented intercourse.

The geography of Israel's introductory bondage and subsequent captivities is very suggestive of a design to make them lights in the world. From their first Egyptian generations to their dispersion under the Romans, it was always among the ruling nations of the world that the Hebrews were scattered in families or settlements, and it was into positions fitted for their leavening those nations with the truth. In the peculiar character of ancient governments, those nations of the Nile, and Mesopotamia, and Greece, and Italy, were each in its season the world, having universal influence, wielding a centralised control over all existing generations. The result of that long missionary itineration of the civilised world by Hebrew truth, is indicated by the list of nations sending proselytes to Jerusalem at the Passover, which we have notice of at the famous Pentecost (Acts ii. 9-11). It comprehends the known Asiatic and African world of the period, and, in addition to the nearer Greek communities, whatever may be included in "strangers of Rome," which was at that time the capital of dominion, and the centre of civilisation, from the Atlantic to the Euphrates.

In the first century in which Christians were to be the propagators of revealed truth, this geographical provision for the education of the world to faith is a phase of the world's arrangement perhaps more remarkable than any period of history presents. Under the perfected condition of the Roman system of government, the wide region comprehending all that had been governed by all the earlier great monarchies, except the countries east of the Euphrates, was as united for all purposes of communication as a small modern kingdom is now. Over Europe, as far north as the Rhine, large cities were more frequent than has ever since been the case. So far as can be ascertained, the population was as dense as it is at present. Through the whole empire, lines of the famous Roman roads, well kept and protected, opened every region to every other. Greek philosophy, the concentration of all human thought and culture, had been disseminated among the wealthy Roman citizens to every corner of the vast dominion. Jewish populations, with their sacred books, were everywhere already resident and known, a foundation ready provided for the superstructure of Christian teaching. The result of such geographical facilities was the spread of Christian truth, and its acceptance in various degrees, so extensively, that, before all who had seen the apostles were dead, the Christians were almost dominant in influence. They outnumbered the whole legions of the empire, and were so numerous in every social rank, that one of their apologists said they had possession of every place in the community except the temples, and these were deserted.

Designed self-education aided by direct revelation.

3. This systematic choice of positions of widest influence for the home or the sojourn of the "keepers of the testimony," during the periods of the ancient universal monarchies, is a part of God's providence so peculiar as to oblige inquiry as to its purpose. When we have to add that the remarkable contact was no mere juxtaposition, but one producing excitement, generally opposition, and often persecution of the holders of the truth, must we not regard the result of the so-marked

arrangement as having been also the design of it—viz., to draw into self-education in the knowledge of the true God the families and nations who, by this sustained means, were invited or compelled to compare revealed religion with their own impure superstitions? This inference is strengthened much, or rather established, by another fact of Old Testament history— that God, with a frequency which we might also call systematic, all along interposed at times with direct revelation of Himself, to help the great heathen powers in this self-education.

4. Indeed we cannot regard the strongly-marked historical lines of revelation, wider and wider though they become during the Jewish times, as exclusive boundaries. God, who made Enoch and Noah preachers, and who universally in His laws given to Moses put under the responsible care of Israel the religious instruction of " the stranger within their gates," and " the nations that dwelt on their borders," was for ever Himself doing as He commanded, and giving gracious helps to those whom He directed His chosen servants to help. We may regard as an instance of this before the Deluge the protective mark set upon Cain, making those beholding the fugitive first-born of mankind think of God's mercy, while the sight of the fugitive's wandering life was continually an epistle seen and read of all men, making known His justice and His judgment against sin. Enoch walking with God set the life of faith before men's eyes, and his preaching proclaimed the retribution sin cannot escape from the holy God. But God Himself, at the same time, revealed to them the opposite blessedness awaiting every faithful one, when He translated Enoch; and men knew that the prophet was not because God had taken him.

Selected line of revelation never exclusive.

5. Among the second race of nations, the recorded instances were sufficiently numerous to be generalised by us into a method of God's dealing with the world. Passing over the historical lesson of faith bequeathed by Noah's family to all mankind, and found in the traditions of most nations, of the Almighty's taking vengeance on the sins of the world by a destroying flood; passing by, also, the lesson common to all races of the providential interference which originated the difference of languages upon the earth, and so defined the

Contacts of patriarchal faith.

separated families of men, the histories of the first Hebrew patriarchs give us instances of neighbouring kingdoms, visited by them during providential straits, being led through entanglements with the affairs of the patriarchs to most distinct practical recognition of the true God; and of those peoples being helped thereto by visions from Him of an educating kind. Chedorlaomer and his Mesopotamian allies may, more likely than may not, have known of Abraham's singular exodus from their already stirring country. It took place with deliberation. If Rawlinson's conjecture be correct that Ur was Mogheir, Abram's caravan, a large one, traversed the whole length of the region. It halted for some time at Haran, on the highway to Palestine. At any rate, Chedorlaomer's army could not ever forget the great Canaanite shepherd's pursuit of them, and the slaughter of all the four kings at his hands near Damascus, in the very enjoyment of their victory, when they were returning from reducing to subjection all their revolted tributaries along the Jordan (Gen. xiv.) The kings of the vale of Sodom did not profit by the neighbouring light of Abraham's faith, nor by his opportune testimony to Jehovah (ver. 22), but the testimony was given in their hearing. The irreclaimable pollution of life there was already ripe for the destruction which six hundred years later overtook the Canaanite peoples. It is in the story of that expedition that we meet with the most remarkable evidence that the patriarchal or any period affords of divine light extraneous to Hebrew limits—Melchizedec, king of Salem, "priest of the most high God," who blessed Abram, and received of him tithes of all his spoil taken from the four kings (ver. 18-20). That, however, was not a light derived from Abram, but a well enough understood divine agency, which will fall to be noticed later in this chapter. Of the self-education of contemporary persons, by observation of the patriarch's fortunes and divine revelation given in aid thereof, Pharaoh (Gen. xii. 17) is an example, and Abimelech of Gerar afterwards (xx. 6), both of whom received divine instruction, one in an understood affliction, the other in an articulately-speaking dream. Isaac afterwards received a direct acknowledgement of Jehovah from

another king of Gerar, because of his observation of the
Hebrew's fortunes (xxvi. 28). Abraham's and Isaac's eldest
sons both pass from sight out into the wilderness. Want of
history of them for long afterwards does not, however, infer
the improbable supposition that they left the light of their
fathers' instructions in the truth wholly behind them, and
gave none of it to their children. Jacob in Padan-aram, in
Canaan, and in Egypt was a light, the value of whose illumina-
tion we know not, but of the shining of which we read distinctly (Gen. xxix.-xxxi.), and of divine communication aiding
it (xxxi. 24). Egypt had, before Jacob's descent into it, pro-
fited in temporal things by the wisdom of his son; and that
wisdom was declared by Joseph and acknowledged by Pharaoh
with sufficient publicity to be the gift of the true God (Gen.
xli. 25, 28, 32, 38, and 39). .If a Pharaoh arose four hundred
years after who " knew not Joseph," the recording of *his* blindness indicates that Egypt had long had impressive remembrance of its great Hebrew saviour; and the last remarkable
fact of his history—" the commandment concerning his bones,"
preserved religiously in the traditional faith of the Hebrews—
was one peculiarly impressive to Egyptian habits of thought.
When the time came for that commandment to be executed,
its fulfilment was an incident in the most notable example history contains of that self-education of nations by Hebrew light
which was thenceforth to be the most remarkable element of
human history for a number of centuries. It seems to be
ascertained that the oppressor of Israel in Egypt, whose ob-
stinate resistance of the demands of Moses concentrated the
attention of Egypt upon the prophet and his miracles and the
words of God accompanying them, was the greatest of Egypt's
Pharaohs, Rameses or Sesostris; whose stupendous power in
the world of nations during his long reign fills so much of
ancient history, and whose gigantic statues, of the same proportions as those of the gods, ten times the size of ordinary
men, still identify the ruins of his capital—monuments for
four-and-thirty centuries of the awful greatness of that king's
power, and his still more magnificent self-esteem. His contest
with Moses; his grandly proud resistance of the Word of

Jehovah as an unwarrantable interference with his authority. (Exod. v. 2); his mightiest arrogance, taking to himself the prerogative of God, swearing by himself, " I am Pharaoh;" his impatience under the prophet's miracles; his repeatedly broken-down courage and fresh scorn of defeat; his final sub- mission, and then mad pursuit of the people, and the awful end of him and his daring warriors plunging into the miraculous opening of the sea; these made the terrible Rameses himself the central figure in the great lesson which that mighty peo- ple had to learn under the compulsion of the ten successive plagues.   That lesson was the omnipotence of Him alone whom their slaves had worshipped; and it was a strong and surely deeply-engraved instruction which was brought to fruit when the proud nobility of Egypt, soldiers, priests, and hus- bandmen, besought their so long humbled slaves to go from them, and loaded them with their own treasures, and thrust them out in the middle of the night.   The same assisted self- education in the true faith, the things mankind should think respecting God, is exemplified in the history of the forty years of the wilderness.   We see people after people comparing in their councils of war or of government the might of the Hebrews' Jehovah with all the might of other nations and their gods; and we see their reasonings assisted also by occasional miraculous manifestations to them of those attri- butes of the true God which they were thinking out for them- selves.   Balak's overruled counselling with the unfaithful prophet of Beor makes an eminent instance of both the self- teaching and the divine help interposed.   Balaam himself, a resident in Mesopotamia, is an example of an outlying light of truth far away from the chosen people.   At that crisis of Israel's need and the heathen's opportunity of learning the truth of God's government the prophet Micah shows Balaam uttering revelations, the spirit of which was in advance of what we know of contemporaneous Hebrew sight: " Where- withal shall I come before the Lord, and bow myself before the high God?   Shall I come before Him with burnt-offerings, with calves of a year old?   Will the Lord be pleased with thousand of rams, or with ten thousands of rivers of oil?

Shall I give my first-born for my transgression, the fruit of my body for the sin of my soul? He hath showed thee, O man, what is good; and what doth the Lord require of thee, but to do justly, and to love mercy, and to walk humbly with thy God" (Micah vi. 6-8).

6. In the times of the settlement in Canaan, the reasonings of the Gibeonites early introduced them into the sanctuary of the truth (Josh. ix.) Rahab's observation of the fortunes of the new people had earlier saved her and her father's house (Josh. ii.) The Midianite soldier's interpretation of his comrade's dream on the night of Gideon's onslaught (Judg. vii. 14), and the deliberations of the Philistine lords and priests after the fall of their god Dagon (1 Sam. vi. 1-6), were examples of compelled acknowledgment of Jehovah, however little it resulted in religious reception of the truth at the time. The battles of Saul and of David in the beginning of the monarchy, and the intercourse of David the fugitive, and afterwards of David the king, with surrounding peoples, must have called forth much of self-educating thought, the seeds of true thought concerning Jehovah. In the periods embraced by the reigns of David and Solomon, the kingdom became an empire of the rank of the great eastern monarchies, as wide in its dominion as the variable Assyrian empires; and Solomon's understanding of the design of Israel's position among the nations is clearly expressed in his great religious prayer (2 Chron. vi. 32). "The stranger coming from a far country for Thy name's sake" expresses exactly the education of the world to faith. The extent to which the Hebrew king contemplated that education follows in his prayer, "that all people of the earth may know Thy name, and fear Thee as doth Thy people Israel" (ver. 33). Glimpses of how, in those two reigns, the light may have shot out among the darkened races, are afforded in the names of some of David's, the religious king's, fastest friends—Uriah the Hittite, Ittai of Gath, and Hiram, king of Tyre. We can hardly conceive a believer of David's whole-heartedness not seeking to instruct in the truth the members of his body-guard, the Philistine Cherethites. A suggestive fact of the same period is the residence of the ark in the house of

[margin note: Israel in Palestine. Observation and propagation of the truth.]

Obed-edom the Gittite, and the Lord blessing the house of the alien because of it (1 Chron. xiii. 14). Heathen embassies seem to have attended the grand procession of the ark to the city of David (Ps. xlvii., lxviii.) The Arabian, or possibly Abyssinian, queen, attracted in her own person to Jerusalem by the fame of Solomon, and "all the earth seeking to him to hear his wisdom which God put in his heart" (1 Kings x. 24), give a high idea of the influence that must have been exercised in his reign by Hebrew affairs upon the thoughts of neighbouring peoples, with so many of whom he came to form those close connections which in turn ruined his own religious fidelity. A wide interchange of thought did evidently take place; the human philosophy, the "wisdom" of the Syrians, the Egyptians, and the Idumæan "children of the East," flowing into Israel, and "the exceeding much wisdom and understanding and largeness of heart God gave to Solomon" (1 Kings iv. 29-34) flowing out. The brilliant intercourse of high thought is commemorated in the names of the most famous contemporaries with whose wisdom Solomon's "excelling" wisdom was compared, "Ethan the Ezrahite, and Heman, and Chalcol, and Darda, the sons of Mahol," and Hiram, king of Tyre, whose interchange of questions, the form of philosophical discussion at the time, with Solomon, is noticed by the historians of his own country. The exercise of mutual influence between Israel and "the nations" we find repeated in later reigns continually. The process becomes perpetual of wide presentation of the light to those peoples who were in contact with the keepers of the oracles, though the reverse influence of idolatry, finding many in Israel to relish its corruptions, was too often a result of the intercourse. The Syrian Benhadad and Hazael, and the Jewish king Ahaz, are examples of both effects of the intercourse. Jehu, the appointed destroyer of Ahab's Baal-worship in Israel, is among the kings, his conflict with whom Sennacherib, the great Assyrian monarch, engraved in his inscriptions. An unavoidably impressive contact into which the same Assyrian king came with Hezekiah, the brightest witness to divine truth of all the kings of Judah, is narrated in the sacred history, and is suggestively omitted in any of the proud narratives of Sennacherib's own monuments yet discovered. The rising subordinate kingdom of Babylon, soon to become supreme under Nebuchadnezzar, seems to have sought the friendship of that Jewish king (2 Kings xx. 12). Jehu's near successor, the second Jeroboam, stretched the northern kingdom into an empire recalling the days of Solomon's wide dominion. Breaking the power of Benhadad's kingdom, he established Israel as the conterminous neighbour of the Mesopotamian power. The contact of the Hebrew kingdoms, occasional or frequent, with their most powerful neighbour, was soon to become the interfusion of the holy people among the nations of that mighty empire ; and by the captivities, Babylon, thenceforth for a century the dominant power of the world, became as it were the publishing house of the divine truth uttered by the prophets of the captive people. In itself and in its relations to the outer world, that all-influential state became, as it has been called, a second Palestine ; as did Lower Egypt from the same age, till it became the residence of a Jewish hierarchy and the place of a religious capital, and at last the fountain from which the Greek language carried Hebrew theology over the civilised world.

7. Besides these large secular causes of religious influence, there was added in the prophetic period, extending in rough outline from Rehoboam to Ezra, much of direct revelation of the truth to "the nations" extraneous to Abraham's seed. The prophetic institution has been noticed, as bringing a grand development of spiritual truth, rising above all positive appointments, filling with spirit, or superseding or rebuking, the formal ceremonies and priestly or kingly instruments of Jehovah's religious guidance of His own people. A kindred development of the influence of national contact, as has just been observed, took place in the same period, and an expansion too of the mission of the prophets beyond the boundaries of the sacred people. Elijah's range of prophetic travel embraced the east of the Jordan, the mountains of Moab, the southern desert, and the western state of Tyre and Sidon. It was there, indeed, into the very home of the idolatry of which he was the ordained enemy in Israel, unto a widow of Zarephath—

Prophetic missions to heathens.

though there were many widows in Israel, as the Lord bade the Jews observe (Luke iv. 25)—that the prophet was sent by Jehovah to receive protection during the famine in Ahab's reign. That was a remarkable breaking down of "the wall of partition"—one that brings up before the mind the healing visit made long after to the same coast to draw out "great faith" in one not " of the lost sheep of the house of Israel " (Mat. xv. 21), by Him whom this same Elijah, and Moses, His earlier and typical prophet, clothed in the glory of heaven, returned to meet on earth on the Mount of Transfiguration, to speak with Him of the death He was to accomplish at Jerusalem, not for Israel, but for the world. Elijah's commission to anoint Jehu to be king of Israel, and Elisha to be prophet in his own room, was also at the same time to anoint Hazael to be king of Syria. Elisha, the instructor as well as healer of Naaman the Syrian noble, went as a prophet to Damascus as well as to Samaria, and received embassies of inquiry into the future from the king of Syria as well from the king of Israel. Jonah, the prophet of Israel, is better known as the prophet of Nineveh. The Phœnician sailors of the Mediterranean would probably carry his impressive story to Spanish Tarsus, if not also to the tin-gatherers of Cornwall. It is from Isaiah, the foreteller of the dispensation of world-wide grace, that we know the contemporary roll of Israel's neighbour nations ; and we know it from his proclamations of the special providence revealed even then of Israel's Jehovah over those nations—a providence in which He appears governing them in the interests of holiness, putting them on the same platform of retributive regard as Israel, an equality of moral government the ultimate purpose of which the prophet discloses in his nineteenth chapter, by example : " In that day shall Israel be third with Egypt and with Assyria, a blessing in the midst of the land ; whom the Lord of Hosts shall bless, saying, Blessed be Egypt my people, and Assyria the work of my hands, and Israel mine inheritance."

The captivities. Education of Mesopo-   8. The imperial plain of Mesopotamia, the field of so much of the ancient world's history, which was the scene of the earliest of God's grand instructive lessons after the Flood,

making men or peoples of the earth know His all-ruling posi- tamian
tion, was the scene during the long captivity of a series of im- universal
monarchs.
pressively notable approaches of providence and revelation to
the great heads of the heathen world. Daniel's record of Nebuchadnezzar is essentially a record of this education of the
outer world of heathenism to the knowledge of the true God.
Three occasions or stages of progressive compelled feeling of
the truth of God are noted : *First*, We find, in the beginning
of the great king's reign, Daniel interpreting to him a dream,
in which " the great God hath made known to the king what
shall come to pass hereafter " (Dan. ii. 45); telling him what
the vision was that had gone from him, and declaring to him
the grand revelation which the image of gold, and silver, and
brass, and iron, and clay, and its destruction by the stone cut
without hands, was meant to give of the coming dominions of
the earth. How extremely instructive as to our present point
of consideration is this record of the revelation of a future, no
more Israelite but mundane—one announcing the connection in
which the dominion of the fulness of times should come in the
line of earthly dominions ; and of that revelation being made,
not to an Israelite, but, appropriately, to a Gentile monarch, the
head of the first of the succession of " kingdoms," the end of
which was to be the kingdom filling the whole earth." The
contemporary faith impressed on that head of the heathen world
by the interpreted vision, his grand compelled acknowledgment
of the true God, we have in Dan. ii. 47 : " The king answered
unto Daniel, and said, Of a truth it is, that your God is a God
of gods, and a Lord of kings, and a revealer of secrets, seeing
thou couldest reveal this secret." *Second*, After the deliverance from the fiery furnace of the three Hebrew youths whom
the monarch had been tricked into commanding to be thrown
into it for refusing to be idolaters, we read the much advanced
thought : " Nebuchadnezzar spake, and said, Blessed be the God
of Shadrach, Meshach, and Abed-nego, who hath sent His angel,
and delivered His servants that trusted in Him, and have changed
the king's word, and yielded their bodies, that they might not
serve nor worship any god except their own God. Therefore
I make a decree, That every people, nation, and language,

which speak anything amiss against the God of Shadrach, Meshach, and Abed-nego, shall be cut in pieces, and their houses shall be made a dunghill; because there is no other god that can deliver after this sort" (Dan. iii. 28, 29). *Third*, There was in store for the great heathen head of the world of his time a much higher faith still in Jehovah, which he made the subject of a solemn proclamation, "to all people, nations, and languages, that dwell in all the earth," of "the signs and wonders that the high God had wrought toward him." Daniel narrates the whole proclamation in his fourth chapter. It was the narrative of a warning vision vouchsafed to the prosperous king, not to forget "that the Most High ruleth in the kingdom of men, and giveth it to whomsoever He will," or for his compelled instruction in that truth, he would be driven from men, and they would give him his dwelling among the beasts of the field, and make him eat grass as oxen for a destined time ; and of the execution, after twelve months, of the unheeded warning, in an hour when he was proudly surveying his capital from the heights of his palace. A voice came from heaven repeating the doom; and madness, and all the threatened degradation, came in the same hour, till seven years passed over him. The proclamation was made when he was restored to reason and manhood again. "At the end of the days, I, Nebuchadnezzar, lifted up mine eyes unto heaven, and mine understanding returned unto me, and I blessed the Most High, and I praised and honoured Him that liveth for ever and ever, whose dominion is an everlasting dominion, and His kingdom from generation to generation. And all the inhabitants of the earth are reputed as nothing: and He doeth according to His will in the army of heaven and the inhabitants of the earth ; and none can stay His hand, or say to Him, What doest thou ?" " Now I, Nebuchadnezzar, praise and extol and honour the King of heaven, all whose works are truth, and his ways judgment : and those that walk in pride He is able to abase" (Dan. iv. 34, 35, 37). These three declarations of Nebuchadnezzar's thoughts of Israel's Jehovah are of peculiar value in the subject of this chapter, as they bear the form of copies of authentic proclamations by the king. The strange period of Babylonian history

to which Daniel's fourth chapter belongs, is referred to in the
inscriptions of Nebuchadnezzar's reign recently discovered, in
a manner largely instructive as to the impression made on the
public mind. The sole record is a confession, unique in Assyrian inscriptions; which are all of the successes and magnificence of the proud praisers of themselves, so well exemplified
in Dan. iv. 30—never of their failures or reverses—a confession
of a period in which "Nebuchadnezzar did not build high
places of power, nor lay up treasures, nor lay out in Babylon
buildings for the honour of himself or his kingdom. His kingdom did not rejoice his heart. He did not sing the praises of
Merodach, his god, the joy of his heart, nor furnish his altar
with victims, nor clear out the canals." The Chaldean historians speak of him as having been visited with a divine afflatus,
under which he foretold the destruction of Babylon by the
Medes and Persians, and then disappeared for ever. It is the
only case of prophecy being attributed by them to any of their
monarchs (Rawlinson's Bampton Lectures, 1859). To the important history of Nebuchadnezzar's education into so much
of true faith, are to be added the proclamations of Darius the
Mede, of his son-in-law and successor the great Cyrus, and of
Darius Hystaspis, and Artaxerxes, and the remarkable intro-
missions with Jewish affairs which fell to the lot of Ahasuerus,
the famous Xerxes of Grecian history. The contact of these
later Asiatic dominant powers of the world with the possessors
of revelation, and the thoughts of the true God which they
attained to in consequence, are preserved to us in the books of
Daniel, Ezra, and Nehemiah; in which the narrative brings
down the notice of God's special religious providence within
450 years of the end of Israel's custodiership of the oracles.
To what thoughts did those leaders of the Gentile world of
their time attain? What thoughts of Him did they, the practically absolute rulers of the ruling kingdom on the earth in
their days, circulate by proclamation in the nations under their
sway? Darius the Mede proclaims his faith in David's God,
that "He is the living God, and steadfast for ever, and His
kingdom that which shall not be destroyed, and His dominion
shall be even unto the end. He delivereth and rescueth, He

worketh signs and wonders in heaven and in earth" (Dan. vi. 26, 27). The decree of Cyrus, the king promised by Isaiah by name, whose "spirit the Lord stirred up," falls little behind the faith which an Israelite could have professed. He calls Him "Jehovah, the God of Israel, He is the God ;" and his decree is to restore the worship of Jehovah in Jerusalem at the cost of him, the Persian king, who held himself His servant for this end. "The Lord God of heaven hath given me all the king-doms of the earth ; and he hath charged me to build him an house at Jerusalem, which is in Judah" (Ezra i. 2). The de-crees of Darius the second and Artaxerxes (Ezra vi. 7) contain language which would be marvellous, did it not come after that of Nebuchadnezzar and Cyrus, but which extends their cases into an historical system of God's providence *calling* in the heathen world of that age, though He called so much in vain.

Europe at the time of the second exodus.

9. These remarkable records of Mesopotamian history bring us to a new phase in the world's history—the rise of European civilisation. The Homeric period of Greece was the golden age of Israel, the reign of Solomon. The Persian reigns now noticed lay side by side in time with the rising civilisation and power of the Greek communities. The decree of Cyrus (B.C. 560), ordaining the second exodus of Israel from a land of bondage into the land promised to Abraham's seed, was issued at the period which, Dean Stanley felicitously observes, marks the end of the ancient world, the beginning of the classical age, the close of the primal system of monarchy, the beginning of the new form of political civilisation, when Greece and Rome appear first in authentic history ; Pisistratus at Athens, Crœsus at Sardis, advancing to important political life ; Rome in its infancy under the Tarquins. Xenophon and the ten thousand were a chronological tie, whatever more they may have been, between the half-sacred Cyrus, the divinely-raised chief mind of the last ancient monarchy, and the tribes of Greek seekers after *wisdom*. Cyrus was himself nearer the position of a monarch of later times, than that of the old Pharaohs and Ne-buchadnezzars ; speaking a language not of the old world, but of Greece—the world-wide language to be ; head of the Persian people, a race as intolerant of idolatry as Israel had to be ;

less Asiatic than European in blood, being of the Aryan division—the children not of Shem but of Japheth—the blood of the future empires of Greece and Rome, and their Western successors. He was a fitting monarch for the new exodus of Israel—a willing Pharaoh now—the servant of Jehovah, to send His missionary people out into a new world of human history, into which they went out under a leadership new in name to Hebrew history, but in official character the type of the religious teachers of future European centuries, " Ezra a scribe of the law of the God of heaven."

10. We cannot, in the later times of Jewish national existence, point out the combination of occasional revelation of Himself by God coming in aid of self-education in true faith, of which Pharaoh and Nebuchadnezzar were so eminent examples. We have no sacred history of the last age of the Jewish Church. We know that the Jewish books got widely abroad, and we can in profane history trace, as much as we could have done in the profane history of earlier times, the world's self-education going on. The Macedonian monarchy, which would fain have served itself heir to the universal monarchy of its predecessors, was made heir to the same instructive contact with the religious light of the world. The Maccabeean history is the history of a very close and impressive contact, whatever its religious result may have been. The Egyptian part of the dispersion under the scribes produced the publication of the Hebrew Scriptures in the universal language of the first age of European learning — the Septuagint, the Bible of the Gentiles.

Last Jewish age. Circulation of Hebrew books. The Septuagint.

11. What effect may have accompanied these extensions of the opportunity of faith beyond the bounds of the people chosen to be the keepers of the oracles, we cannot say. Two points, however, deserve, or rather demand, notice. 1st, That degree of education of the heathen world to the true faith was *Systematic.* It is traceable over the whole time of Israel's existence (see, for example, Jer. xl. 2, 3). We have noticed but the prominent records of it. Nothing is clearer than that the chosen people were not, as the later Jews obstinately determined to think, chosen to the exclusion of other peoples from

Education of the heathen world, systematic instruction of the ruling nation.

G

God's saving regard, but with a view to their being gathered in. The whole spirit of Jehovah's language as to the designed work of Israel to "the stranger within their gates," and "the nations on their borders," and the proclamations of His being and will which the nations were to read in Israel's fortunes; the close intercommunion, impossible to be barren of religious results, which is indicated by the presence of Philistines, Hittites, Edomites—the formally-accursed nations—as members of the royal household; the distinct extension latterly of the mission of the prophets of Israel to neighbouring and distant heathen peoples;—these are features of the divinely-ruled history of Israel which give a comprehensiveness to our range of sight when we look back to see what the field of the world had always been which God's revealed grace recognised. It is a comprehensive view, which it is freedom to escape into, from the confined horizon within which the Jews of the age of "the traditions of their fathers," the fulness of times of darkness, determinedly shut themselves—not without much influence towards the same confinement of Christian thought, which has in so many things taken its impressions of true Hebrew theology and ecclesiology from that deteriorated phase of Judaism. The history of God's dealings with the peoples in contact with His "raised-up" people, from the time of Abraham's Pharaoh to that of Artaxerxes, exhibits an education of them to true faith which, though a contrast in extent to the education Israel received, was the same in kind. They had given to them a history of His dealings with them, and also direct revelations of His being and His will, whereon to think, and so impress themselves with the truth.

2d, It was always the *Ruling People* of the time that was in this degree enlightened in the truth. To instruct the terribly absolute monarchs of Egypt, Chaldæa, and Babylon, and the politically universal monarchs of Persia, and to cause them to issue their grand proclamations respecting the being and worship of the God of Israel, was really to influence the mass of their subjects in a degree which the most absolute monarchies of modern times do not know. And each of those great monarchies was in fact the world for the time, as Western powers

have never succeeded in being. Add to these considerations
the way in which the Hebrews in their foreign residences were
intentional or unintentional missionaries always of the revealed
truth. In the position, not of modern prisoners of war, but
like emigrant families or townships, their observance of their
religious customs became a light to innumerable neighbour-
hoods, which, in their chief and last captivity, the labours of
the new order of the scribes made gradually a most definite
guiding-light. That the result was a wide, though no doubt,
by proportion, meagrely fruitful, sowing of the living seed in
the outfield of the nations, is indicated by the account of the
gathering in Jerusalem on the day of Pentecost, of which
Peter's first audience was a part. Those strangers from every
known country must have been chiefly proselytes, and proselytes who, like the queen of Ethiopia's treasurer, could afford
to travel immense distances sometimes to worship the Lord
at Jerusalem. The " wise men from the East," not proselytes,
indicated a wider class impressed by the prophecies of the
Jewish faith at the time of our Lord's advent.

12. An age of learning, wielding the instrument of a uni- Age of
versal language, overlapped the meeting of Jewish and Chris- learning
tian times giving facilities, both before and after, unique in ping Juda-
the world's history, for the rapid diffusion and appreciation ism and
of thought. Under the decaying political consequence of the tianity.
small Greek communities, philosophy, which gave the Greeks
an acknowledged supremacy in intellectual empire, was intensely cultivated; and the powerful dominion of Rome, which
absorbed those divided commonwealths of Greece, protected
the freedom of thought with a toleration never excelled. The
way thus opened and kept open for the universal diffusion of
revealed truth was only opportunely ready for being occupied.
The Hebrew Scriptures were now in the Greek tongue, the
universal language of the learned. They were issued from
the centre of written learning in that age, Alexandria, and
their dissemination was accompanied and made utmost use
of by a dissemination of the Hebrews themselves, long
begun to that citizenship of the world towards which the fall
of Jerusalem only gave them their last impetus. The He-

brew race was, before that last dispersion, settled over the whole known world in an extent and manner which provided singularly for the freedom of the impulse which that dispersion of the Jews was to give to the discussion of Christian truth universally ; a discussion which, being inimical on their part as often as favourable, made sure of compelling Gentile attention to the offered faith.   Dean Stanley, compiling from various sources, shows the dissemination of the Hebrew people, in the time from the Babylonian captivity to the Christian era, to have been one of the most remarkable facts of history.   Only four of the twenty-four courses of priests returned to Palestine with Ezra.   Babylon remained the great home of the race. Three universities of Jewish study existed in Mesopotamia. Westward they formed a considerable proportion of the population of almost every province.   Alexandria was the great publishing centre of their Scriptures.   Numerous settlements of them pervaded Asia Minor.   In the Greek islands their force was such that in Cyprus, during an insurrection, they massacred 420,000 of the Greek inhabitants.   A little before the birth of Christ a large portion of the city of Rome was assigned to them. They had a native force associated with them everywhere of converts from heathenism, proselytes of righteousness or of the gate. In the decaying vigour of paganism and of the Roman empire, then becoming weak through over-extension and growth of luxury, the power of that one people, capable of so wide combination, and invigorated by their faith with strength of purpose, was an object of dread to their Roman rulers.   No part of the population of the empire could so command attention, and compliance with their demands.   Their synagogues were the only vigorous representatives of religion in the empire, and they were universal.   Paul found them in every Greek city in Greece and Asia Minor except Athens.

Secular civilisations not a continuous education of the world.   13. In reviewing the education of the world to revealed thoughts of God, and of man's relation to Him, discussion has naturally been omitted of any parallel education of the human race by transmitted civilisations, or the production of subjective capabilities and propensities of thought through the mixture of races.   These two elements undoubtedly enter into national civilisations, as the peculiarities of modern peoples exemplify, but they do not determine what is to be ; for elements causing distinction as certainly arise as those producing similarity.   Among nations, as among families, of which nations are the aggregates, the intellectual faculties, the different selections of taste, and perhaps the constitutional attraction to different departments of morals, are evidently distributed as much as educating influences are distributed.   Race manifestly comes into action in determining the matters of thought in which a people will take delight, or excel, or comparatively fail.   Writers on the subject of race even attempt to analyse the British character genealogically.   A historical comparison, however, of the civilisations of the successive dominant races of the world does not show any systematic connection making them one whole.   Progress has to be traced chiefly or nearly altogether in the fluctuating accumulation of objective knowledge, while the subjective characters of the races exhibit more of difference than of derivation.

The oldest empire exhibits, as its civilising element, a simple but earthly idea of God ruling all things—a divinity always in one stage visible.   Their Pharaohs were in their eyes only the youngest god reigning on earth until his bodily death, and then receiving worship at the hands of the next still earthly god.   All things in Egypt were regulated in connection with anticipated universal immortality.

The civilisation of the family of Chaldee dominions, partly contemporary with the Egyptian, and succeeded by the Persian empire, was essentially human and material.   The Assyrians had no thought of themselves as being in any way partakers in the divinity of their gods.   They were the subjects of the gods, and themselves essentially human, of the earth, earthly.   Unspeculative, they had physical knowledge of the observed kind, but apparently did not make much progress except in possessing what they knew minutely.   Their pictures are characterised by detail, like the pictures of the Dutch school.

The manly education of the Persian—to shoot the bow, to ride, and to speak the truth—had a higher theosophy, also, than the heavy Assyrian had constructed.   However preserved or derived, that people had thoughts of the unity and the government of Ormuzd, their divinity, which perhaps made the theology of the Hebrews, whom they found dispersed in Babylonia on their conquest of it, more quickly appreciable by them, so as to produce those high thoughts of Jehovah which are expressed in the decrees of Cyrus and his successors, preserved in the Old Testament. The Persian records now discovered show, it is said, uniformly that superior theology. As to the source of their knowledge of it, we have to bear in mind that those records are all of kings after the conquest of Babylon, written, therefore, after the time when Hebrew theology had access to the lively Persian mind directly, and may have been long reaching it before, through Assyrian intercourse; Babylonia having for long been growing into a second Palestine.

The next civilisation was a fourth distinct type, speculative in a unique degree, æsthetic in all materialistic studies and appetites, and superficial as to conscience. The Greek stands out from all historic races as the one which made the most enjoyment out of all mental and bodily capabilities, and carried itself freest from all moral cares that could restrain their highly cultivated and economised self-indulgence.

The Roman mind, æsthetically much inferior to the Greek, borrowing philosophy also as well as taste from Greece, had as its characteristic a moral greatness unknown to Greek history, as Greek speculation was to Persian or Assyrian. The science of order came naturally to that last great people, from whom the Western world has derived the great principles of law and government, and the benignity of authority extending its calm, tolerant, firm, fostering hand over all diversities of national life.

Historical succession of compelled comparisons with revealed education.

14. Those old-world ruling powers were thus more contrasted with one another than connected together. Connected by the link of succession or influence, their civilisations were not essentially derived from one another, but much more bear the character of separate facts in the history of mankind; unless we are to contemplate them in a historical connection which we can recognise in them. We can very clearly see in them a historical succession of compelled comparisons made of the world's different kinds of civilising theories with the power

for all man's moral needs which was claimed for the Hebrews' revealed religion in the prophet's proclamation: "All flesh is grass, and the glory of man is the flower of the grass. The grass withereth, and the flower thereof fadeth, and the grace of the fashion of it perisheth; but the word of the Lord endureth for ever" (Isa. xl. 6-8).

Egypt's theology was put to shame by the messenger of Jehovah, the God of Egypt's slaves. In that momentous contest in which the Egyptians were made to "know" the I AM, Egypt's man-god was the most stupendous approach to human almightiness which the world has ever known, the scornful Rameses, the Sesostris of whose universal conquering presence primeval history is so full. In later times Solomon's heaven-taught wisdom was compared with and excelled "the wisdom of all the children of the east country, and all the wisdom of Egypt."

The materialistic grandeur of Assyria was consciously rebuked over and over again by the unseen power of Israel's God; and the end of the long instruction—partly spoken as by Jonah, partly felt as by Sennacherib—was the great Nebuchadnezzar's experience, embodied in formal proclamations to his empire of the supremacy of the Hebrew's Jehovah.

Daniel's captivity saw that recognition followed by, if not developed into, the so Hebrew-like theology of the Persian rulers which we read now in the Scriptural extracts from Persian archives, and in the language of Persian records and inscriptions now available (Rawlinson's Bampton Lecture, 1859).

The bare narrative of the Book of Acts contains nothing of boastful or exulting reference to the triumph of the Christian truth; but no reader accustomed in historical reading to see the force of particular facts, can help seeing beneath the simple detail of Paul's doings in Athens, Ephesus, and Corinth—the three centres of Greek philosophy, religion, and cultivation of bodily felicity—an impressive picture of the far-famed Greek "wisdom" confessing itself a failure before the rudely-set truth spoken by the apostle.

The epoch of Greek philosophy contained a fact peculiar in the history of man's moral condition, an effort arising in all

civilised regions of the East after moral reformation, the entire
failure of which, for spiritual relief or regeneration, present
times can compare with the power unto salvation of revealed
truth, but as to which we have not any record of contemporaneous comparison like that of Paul's teaching with the Greek
" wisdom ; " though Christian traditions as to the travels of the
first - dispersed Christians indicate that the comparison may
have been made in all the regions in question. M. Guizot, in
his 'Meditations on the Essence of Christianity,' first series,
p. 57, gives the date of Confucius in China, 551 B.C. to 478 B.C.;
Zoroaster in Persia, 564 B.C. to 487 B.C., or 589 B.C. to 500 B.C.;
Buddha in India, 543 B.C. ; Pythagoras in Greece, 580 B.C. to
500 B.C.; and Socrates, 470 B.C. to 400 B.C. He adds: " Confucius was, above all, a practical moralist, skilled in observation, counsel, and discipline; Buddha, a dreamer, and a mysti-
cal and popular preacher; Zoroaster, a legislator, religious and
political; Pythagoras and Socrates, philosophers, bent upon
instructing the distinguished bands of disciples whom they
gathered around them. There is no doubt, notwithstanding
the trials of their life, that neither power nor glory amongst
their contemporaries was wanting to them. Confucius and Zoroaster were the favourites and councillors of kings. Buddha,
himself the son of a king, became the idol of innumerable multitudes. Pythagoras and Socrates formed schools and pupils
who were an honour to the human mind. By their personal
genius, and by the excellence of some of their ideas and actions,
these men have insured themselves the admiration of all posterity. Did they act up to their teachings, and accomplish
what they attempted ? Did they really change the moral and
social condition of nations ? Did they cause humanity to make
any progress, and open to it horizons which it had not before
known ? By no means. Whatever fame attaches to the names
of these men, whatever influence they may have exerted, whatever trace of their passage may have remained, they rather appeared to have power than really possessed it; they agitated
the surface far more than they stirred the depths; they did
not draw nations out of the beaten track in which they had
lived; they did not transform souls. Considering the facts at

large, and notwithstanding the political and material revolutions which they underwent, China after Confucius, India after Buddha, Persia after Zoroaster, Greece after Pythagoras and Socrates, followed the same ways, retained the same propensities, as before.   Still more, among these very different nations stagnation was only to be succeeded by decay."

The next great putting forth of the "glory of man," "the grace of the fashion" of his wisdom, for the relief of earth's moral and social needs, was that of human moral force impersonated in the grandly-sustained social order and protection of free thought and all philosophy which the Roman government gave to the civilised world.   Inheriting all that had been transmitted of experience and learning and philosophy by preceding forms of concentrated human influence, and able to utilise all by the advantage of thoroughly-established centralisation of authority and free communication of knowledge and liberty of sentiment, the world of Roman times ought to have been helped to a new life had the means been adequate.   From the Atlantic to the borders of Persia "national antipathies had been suppressed, and war had ceased, while the lives of men were regulated by an admirable code of laws. . . . Yet, except to court poets, that age did not seem golden to those who lived in it.   On the contrary, they said it was something worse than an iron age ; there was no metal from which they could name it. Never did men live under such a crushing sense of degradation ; never did they look back with more bitter regret ; never were the vices that spring out of despair so rife ; never was sensuality cultivated more methodically ; never did poetry curdle so readily into satire ; never was genius so much soured by cynicism ; and never was calumny so abundant, or so gross, or so easily believed" ('Ecce Homo'). It was that phase of human inventions that had to compare itself with Christian revelation. The comparison which took place was first to ignore the existence of anything special in the new religion ; then to acknowledge its peculiarity, and endeavour to crush the superiority to persecution which it showed ; at last to submit and yield the place of honour to it "as the power of God and the wisdom of God" for temporal salvation.   This last great struggle of earthly faiths with the revealed one was so amply provided for on the side of polytheism that it must be regarded as the pitched battle between all human inventions and the historical religion of the Bible. Rome, in the first Christian century, possessed all the philosophies of man's invention. From her perfect organisation the gathered speculations and the most effective teaching of them had facilities for universal diffusion. And a class educated to appreciate them was to be found everywhere from the Atlantic to the Euphrates, and over the now debased southern shore of the Mediterranean, all in perfect communication with each other. During that century the most philosophical toleration was understood and practised by a succession of emperors who are quoted in history as the world's examples of wisdom and benignity. It was a fair spiritual contest fought out under the eye of that whole world, and drawing every order of men into it personally. The hand of the state was kept aloof until the victory showed itself by unexpected effects—not the mere overthrow of philosophies, as in Greece before, but the discomfiture of the Roman empire's power to govern supremely ; the production by the new faith of a strength of purpose and power of enduring suffering which threatened to make the exercise of authority useless. The succeeding persecutions were a confession that the last perfection of human invention for the earth's salvation was put to nought, just as human religions and human philosophies had been, and that the power of social authority to secure the peace and usefulness of common life must in its turn yield the place of supremacy to the historical faith of the Christians.

Extent of faith.

15. The subject of faith being "God so loved the *world,*" perhaps calls for, at least it suggests thoughts of what education to faith the world has received beyond the limits to which Hebrew and Christian contact have carried part of the developed truth of the Word. It is the question of the salvation of the heathen that makes this an agitating matter of thought to readers of such Christian language as "there is none other name under heaven given among men whereby we can be saved but the name of Jesus only" (Acts iv. 12). Is the restriction that is often thought of in connection with these words a miscon-

ceived one; as the Jews misunderstood similar language of their
Scriptures when they read it as confining salvation to the Jews,
and so nationally, as it were, misunderstood it, that even Paul
characterises Isaiah's language as "very bold," in which he
breaks the bounds of the Hebrew Church to include in God's
Church of salvation them that were "no people"? Is not the
restriction of salvation which Christian Scriptures declare "to
as many as believe in Jesus," a restriction that is meant to be
read by those who know these *Christian* Scriptures, peculiarly
for their own warning; an example of that *judgment of self*
which the receiver of the ten talents was to exercise? It could
not be read so as to exclude pre-Christian times. The language
of salvation "in Christ" must have a wider meaning than any
that would make a knowledge of the history of Jesus of Nazareth a necessary condition, else that language would be inapplicable to all the Old Testament saints, including Moses, to whom
the Epistle to the Hebrews applies it, and Abraham and David,
to whom Jesus himself applied it. Is it only boldness of the
same kind as Paul attributed to Isaiah, to apply it to races
who knew less still of the knowledge of our sacred Scriptures?
Does not history invite the boldness of believing in a gracious
revelation beyond the limits of Hebrew revelation in early times,
when it tells us of Job, Melchizedek, Balaam, and the Pharaoh
and Abimelech of Abraham's history whom God's communi-
cations to themselves did not surprise, and of contemporaries
who certainly worshipped God by the name which Abraham
first knew Him by (Gen. xxxi. 53), "the God of Abraham, and
the God of Nahor, the God of their father"? It would be
falsehood to history to leave out of consideration what traditional theosophy may have descended from Noah, the reposi-
tory of all antediluvian knowledge of God, a preacher of
righteousness himself, and the receiver of a new covenant from
God. For it would be ignoring the widely if not universally
found traditions of the entrance of evil, and the destruction
of evil-doers by a flood. It would be ignoring the universal
ideas found among heathens of man's sonship to God, of retributive judgment, of sacrifice needed for sin, as well as
offered in thanksgiving, and of immortality secured by a son;

high religious thoughts as to which subjects—call them traditional thoughts, or call them subjective philosophy—have
been, to some surprise of Christians, disinterred by Max
Müller widely in the sacred books of Asiatic heathenism
written centuries before Christ. Keeping in view that the
language of salvation "in Christ," expounded so much by the
parallel phrase "in His Son," is to bring our thoughts to God's
unveiling to us our own sonship to Him—created, hidden
from our evil hearts, made credible to us through long revelations, at last manifested to sight—what is the meaning of the
New Testament including among believers "in Christ" believers in God's love living over a period of 2000 years before
Jesus was born? How much does it mean of a revelation of
their sonship to God having been made to their faith, a sonship
which they contemplated as to be consummated by some
divinely glorious exercise of salvation? How much may such
a knowledge of God, communicated by the Father of spirits to
the spirits of His human children, have extended beyond the
geographical limits of Hebrew light? The cases of Job,
Balaam, and Melchizedek show that the knowledge of the
full historical revelation of God to man was not indispensable
to faith at any period of historical revelation. Upon our
ignorance of the extent to which faith will at last be found to
have existed we cannot build any form of knowledge in the
shape of argument; we must even deny ourselves to forming
opinions which we are to use for sad thoughts of the fate of
the heathen. But though without knowledge and without
opinion, we are not without very decided indications in God's
Word, pointing the opposite *direction,* for our thoughts of Him
and of our unknown brethren of mankind to look forth in.
What is the meaning in this connection of God's having
"winked at the times of ignorance" (Acts xvii. 30), yet not
leaving Himself without a witness? (xiv. 15-17.) What the
meaning of Jesus' own comparisons of Sodom and Gomorrah,
and Tyre and Sidon, with the cities which had heard Him, and
His distinct declaration, that in the day of judgment it will be
more tolerable for those heathen cities than for the enlightened
towns of Palestine? And what the meaning of the glimpse

given us by Paul of God's principle of judgment, discriminat-
ing between those who, "without law, are a law unto themselves,"
and those that "sin in the law" (Rom. ii. 12-16), following his
history of God's judgments on the heathen when unfaithful to
the light which they had? (Rom. i. 18-32.) Without any knowledge, let it be repeated, as to the future of relatively darkened
races, opinion is incompetent; but the line of our thoughts believing in God's "so great love"—the love we find proved in our
own case—is directed by these things not to stop short of
believing in His love beyond historical limits; but to believe
that, however Christian minds may be perplexed or grieved at
times in thinking of whole regions of the earth, and many
generations in other regions, which have never known the
blessed light of the truth that alone has made dwellers in
Christian lands so free as they are, yet, when the end of God's
government of the world shall make His ways known from
the beginning, nothing will be seen in those ways disappointing to the thoughts which a good man loves to cherish concerning God's grace. Looking from the times of Christianity
across the heathen world, it may be only patches of glimmer-
ing light that we see; but twilight as surely testifies of the
sun as the growing morning does. It may be like the darkness of night that we look upon, but it is a darkness in which
there are stars.

CHAPTER V.

REASON'S TASK IN RELIGIOUS FAITH.

Ps. xxvi. 3.—Thy loving-kindness is before mine eyes ; and I have walked in Thy truth.

Phil. iv. 8.—Think on these things.

Deut. vi. 6, 7.—These words, which I command thee, shall be in thine heart : and thou shalt teach them diligently to thy children. Thou shalt talk of them when thou sittest in thine house, and when thou walkest by the way, and when thou liest down, and when thou risest up.

Faith a co-operative result. 1. The use that is to be made by man of the historical revelation of God's " so loving the world " is the subject of this chapter. The human and the divine operations by which faith in God's love is produced are not separated in practice. They are a co-operation. In describing, however, the practice of faith, the work which man himself does may be separately contemplated with advantage.

Human part of the work : 2. David describes practically the origin of his habit of living in God's faithfulness of love ; " Thy loving-kindness is before mine eyes, and [as a consequence] I have walked in Thy truth." The human origin of faith is the believer's own thinking upon the reasons he has for believing in God's love. These reasons are chiefly revealed in the Word of God, or set in authoritative connection there ; and accordingly we are taught " faith cometh by hearing, and hearing by the word of God." Some of the reasons are matter for man's own observation, and all must be set before his mind by man himself, and so the direction is also given to us, " My son, give me thine heart, and let thine eyes observe my ways." " Believe me for the works' sake."

3. It has been already seen (Chapter II.) that the reasons for

believing that "God so loved the world" are definitely marked *not study of doctrines,* and pointed out as historical reasons. They are God's "ways" which man's own eyes can observe, or which he can learn from "the Word of God." The subject of faith is the facts of God's love recorded along the world's history—the facts or doings spread over His works of creation and providence, and the assurances of His love, which are given in His Word historically by means of pledging facts and assumed relationships to man —relationships which, to our habits of thought, have the form and force of familiarly understood facts of human life. It is not God's attributes, but God's ways, that are the study of faith —not generalisations, doctrinal propositions logically collected, but the events and relationships themselves, both historical and anticipated, from which doctrines of theology would be collected.

4. This settled point, that observation and not speculation *but contemplation of the facts of God's love.* is the domain of faith's characteristic thoughts, prepares us so far to deal with a question which meets us at the threshold of any inquiry into man's part of the co-operative work—viz., What is the proper business of human reason in matters of faith ? In the case of all facts that are to produce emotion, which is the essential character of the facts of religious knowledge, the work required is to set the facts in the most impressive light by contrast and illustration, and to make their reality felt also by proof where that is left to be done. This, then, is to be the aim of man's reasoning in religious knowledge. The subject is one of definite facts, and the relative emotions they should excite ; which are often also so far settled, being described in God's Word in connection with the facts. The work of discovering entirely new truth, investigating theories from known facts so as to open up separate subjects of inquiry, which is reason's occupation in unrevealed knowledge, is not left to it in the definite subject of man's thoughts and interests revealed for his religious contemplation. Revealed religion does not contain theories in the sense which the word has in physical or metaphysical science. Its subject is simply demands of affection upon the consideration of facts of affection, after the manner of the example already quoted, "My son, give me thine heart, and let thine eyes observe my ways." Where theories of God-

head and manhood, and their necessary relations and possible contact, are in human creeds, they are importations from metaphysical studies. And they bear a distinctive mark of their having a different origin from the line of thought given to religion in God's Word. They do not bear fruit in emotions, like the *things, facts, ways, deeds of love,* which the Word bids mankind think upon.

Is reason competent to investigate in the case?

5. With reference to the propriety of human reason being barred from its common function of theorising, in the case of revealed religion, it is of importance to consider its competence for investigation in such a subject. Does it run with such accuracy upon the scent of truth in familiar fields as to warrant its entering boldly, as it has always wished to do, into that awfully unknown one? With all history before him, does man reason conclusively upon political science? Is it the case, even in experimental philosophy, that his advance is only a slow groping process, making but a step or two in a generation? Is the science of the human mind still without any generalisation deserving the name of a comprehensive theory—a generalisation bearing practical inferences—still a collection of facts which have almost held their place of ultimate facts from long before the birth of physical science? Is, then, the faculty which is yet so baffled in this department of mind competent to investigate the manner of the Divine mind, and establish principles which must or ought to regulate His working? Even in physics the unity of the great "forces" is yet but guessed at in the midst of every means of experimenting so as to make them declare themselves. Is the reason which can get so little below the surface of visible things able to investigate the unity in diversity of the Father, Son, and Holy Ghost? No one will be slow to answer the question after reading the confused and confusing manipulations of words, making a form of knowledge, which stopped all progress of reasoning in obscurity, and shunted religious energy on to the line of polemical zeal, in the metaphysical age of the Greek Church, when so many of the terms were invented which have been used since in the contests of theological speculation, and used as if the words really represented perfectly understood definite things.

6. History teaches us that the wanderings of reason, either to the side of scepticism or of over-wisdom, have arisen, as a rule, out of departures from considering Christianity (revealed religion) as a religion of observation—one habitually contemplating a certain history. The state of mind which seeks to be wise above what is written, and ends in knowing nothing as it ought to be known, is that self-conceit which in all ages has come, in its mischievous progress, to substitute critical discussion of theories for emotional thinking of recorded deeds of saving love—tempted, by the gratification of intellectual triumphs, away from the humble enjoyment of thinking upon the distinct promises and relationships and expressive forms of assurance of love which surround, and are to be associated in our thoughts with, such names as " the Father," " the Son," and " the Holy Ghost"—names given for historical, and not for philosophical, thinking. Successful scepticism has to the same effect seduced the mind away from thinking of the separate facts or whole history of revealed love, to look at something else. The Pharisees, by boldly asserting that Jesus cast out devils by Beelzebub, drew away the attention of their hearers from the deeds they saw done to that startling theory on the subject, to think of how that might be the case, and reason on that question, and shut their eyes to Him. Had their minds not once gone off on that hunt after a tempting exciting theory—had they stayed to look in the face of the facts of Jesus' healing the possessed—they would have seen and felt that the health and peace and new life which His healing gave to Satan's victims could be no work of Satan's will. Like the blind man who could not be reasoned out of feeling the greatness of the fact of his own deliverance, they would have laughed to scorn the theories which would assign such works to any but God. Yet Jesus had to bring them that saw the miracles back even to that plain reasoning once they let themselves be led away from it. The doctrine of myths is a modern example of the same kind. When the thoughts are busied with considerations of how universally mankind have had beliefs in supernatural beings and arts—such as fairies, magic, &c.—the reason forgets what manner of supernatural

Source of over-wisdom and scepticism—theorising instead of observing.

H

beings the Scripture histories record, and that they have nothing in common with the fanciful creations which the ancient world and our great-grandmothers' world were full of, except their uncommonness; and when mythical philosophers boldly assert or quietly take for granted that they were much the same, an unaccustomed thinker, confused by the confident representation, has no clear recollection of the Scriptural wonders in his mind to compare with the ghost stories, fairy legends, and witcheries of unscientific times. Once, however, he reads the stories of the Bible again, the uselessness of such explanations appears, and the myth vanishes before the actual personages, the human beings and earthly life that fill all the Bible anecdotes, as the fairies of twilight always disappeared from the beholder when he had an opportunity of seeing also a being of flesh and blood. It has been already noticed (Chapter II.) how sceptical thinkers have found that the myths which seek to assign the professed histories of Scripture to the exigencies of religious theory or to non-historical legend, signally fail to keep hold on the thoughts in the presence of the scenes of Scripture narrative. If the sacred stories be read amidst the topography of Palestine—in sight of its mountains and deserts, its wells and rocks, its cities walled up to heaven, its diversity of climate and vegetation—then Abraham and his journeyings, Moses and Aaron and the forty years of the wilderness, the life that fills the Book of Judges, above all, the days of the Gospels, arise into inevitable reality. Untravelled readers experience something of the same rectifying of mythical visions in reading graphic descriptions of the places associated with the Scripture histories. Persons who accustom themselves to realise and make familiar to their imagination all the minute details of those old pictures of intense human life do not need such rectifying. They, however—the readers most accustomed to look, as it were, on the familiar countenance of Scripture story—appreciate most the filling up of the life-pictures which such books as Dean Stanley's furnish. To them such books summon up innumerable promptly-recognised features of reality, when they set in the light of local features of the country phrases of the narratives whose value was unknown before for want of such illustration. Bushnel sets aside narrative for philosophical meaning in his attempt to explain the sufferings of Christ as the pains, not of sacrifice instead of man, but, of love's unavoidable anguish over the sins and sorrows of those He came to save. He confesses himself that his mythical kind of theory is altogether inoperative on human hearts, and that if the sufferings of Christ are to be made influential over men, they must be presented to them in the historical light of altar-sacrifices. The history is congruous to something which mankind feel concerning themselves, and the nerve of spiritual consciousness will not awake to the touch of anything else.

The logical scepticisms of Hume, and afterwards of Strauss and Comte, have had their practical effect in the same way as the attempts of the Pharisees and mythists. They lead the mind away from looking at the miracles of the New Testament themselves into thinking chiefly about the mental process by which we could deal with such things as miracles at all. The rulers of the Jews, who had not the advantage of being eighteen hundred years distant from Jesus and the apostles, could not escape believing human testimony as to their miracles, however much they wished it. Their language was, "We cannot deny it." Hume's question of the credibility of testimony in the case is simply a part of the wider sceptical question of the credibility of testimony by our own senses—the question of how we can know that we see or hear or feel any particular thing, or only have some inner imagination at work that we are seeing, hearing, or touching. Any unexpected sensation—the rough handling of a tender part of the body of the subjective reasoner, or the dropping of a glass of cold water on his head—will summon his faith to the outside immediately, and he will have no doubt of there being real things for his senses to deal with. So familiarity of the thoughts with the peculiarities of the Bible miracles brushes aside the difficulties about human testimony. What we must have seen to be miracles had we witnessed them, we can very well believe on the testimony which satisfies us for any historical fact. Suppose the testi-

mony of predecessors not to be trustworthy; let us then stand
in the place of our predecessors, and suppose that we ourselves
saw the things testified to.   If we saw a maimed body made
complete again by a word, or two or three loaves of bread
become enough for thousands of hungry persons, leaving
numerous basketfuls of broken pieces, we might not be able
to say how we felt sure that that was a work of divine power,
but not the slightest doubt would be on our minds about its
being such.   If it will not do to make the testimony of history
as to the miracles untrustworthy on moral grounds, since
enemies to Christianity bore witness to its miracles as well as
friends—nor upon defects in the historical transmission of the
evidence, since that is equal to or better than what we accept
for any ancient history,—then the credibility of these miracles has hardly to do with human testimony at all, but with
the question, Whether we could believe a miracle if we saw
it? and of that in the case of Jesus' miracles in general there
is no doubt.

Cure for
scepticism
—familiar-
ity with
the history. 7. The practical cure for scepticism has been familiarity
with the history of God's love, as the want of that familiarity
allows doubt to be insinuated. The case is analogous to the
progress and the cure of family distrust.   Only in absence
from his father's house can distrust of his father's affection be
with great facility sown in the mind of a son.   Return to daily
communion with his father heals his failing faith; his fancied
conclusions are dissipated day by day if he allow the presence
of his parent to exercise unresisted the influence on his
thoughts which it will have.   His own sight and hearing and
touch of his father rebuke his understanding for having
doubted; in the Hebrew phrase, he "believes with his heart."
So, as has been pointed out above (Chapter II.), the recognition
of *reality* is accompanied by the recognition of *congruity* when
the thinker is brought face to face with the things of the
Bible.   They are in so close harmony with man's consciously-
felt nature that he takes hold of them as of the same spiritual
life with himself.   They are such facts as were needed to suit
him as the facts of God's love for him.   They are suitable
and indispensable to human religion.   He can recognise and

believe in them as he believes in bread to be his food or water to be the relief of his thirst.   His conscious nature knows them as things fitted to be its own portion.   The miraculous healings and comfortings and deliverances are so much the very manner of things which he feels that he needs, that, though miracles, they are not wonders to him; and though they may be extraordinary things for human testimony to have to add to its common testimony of ordinary facts, they do not look at all extraordinary things for human nature to receive from Him who brought them; but they are the very things to be recognised as His proper gifts, considering who He said He was.   They are true in character to the connection in which we read them, as certain conduct would be true to the relationship of a parent.   The argument was a good one: "Never man spake like this man."   "Come, see a man that told me all things that ever I did: is not this the Christ?"   "Did not our hearts burn within us when He talked to us by the way, and when He opened to us the Scriptures?"

8. What, then, has reason to do in matters of faith, if it is to deal almost entirely with the recorded facts of God's love, and confine itself to drawing inferences from them in lines pointed out by God's Word, because it is not to be trusted with the venture of investigating in other lines?   The work prescribed to our reason is appropriate to its capability, and amply sufficient also, as it is an unceasing one.   First, it has to judge of the evidence upon which the history of God's love is to be believed; secondly, its longer, its endless work is to familiarise the mind and the heart, the thoughts and the affections, with the facts recorded. *Task of observation.*

9. First, God has set the proving work of human reason at the beginning of every man's belief of His revelations.   The *liberty* and the *duty* of private judgment are placed by Him at the door, to give entrance to all real faith into the soul.   The first appeal which the Most High has always made to mankind has been to their own understanding, to consider what was laid before them, and convince themselves of it; God accepting the habitual human question, "What sign showest Thou?"   Abraham, when he was about to receive for himself and his *First, To recognise matter of faith.*

family the offered covenant with Jehovah, asked for evidence which should convince his own reason that it was Jehovah that was speaking to him; and the evidence was immediately given. When Moses was sent by the Lord to His chosen people, the prophet asked, and his request was freely granted, signs which would convince the Hebrews that Jehovah had sent him. In the same way did our Lord seek acceptance for His revelations for His "works' sake." Jehovah's ready compliance with Gideon's request for a double evidence is a marked instance. It has only been false teachers who have sought to lord it over reason, and demanded faith without evidence, and made perdition the penalty of refusing the bold assumption of authority.

In the cases in which God himself spoke directly to man a doctrine or a duty, reason needed only evidence that it was God who spoke. Faith, then, man's conscious connection of subordination with God, received the religious truth, seeking nothing more than the authority, "Thus said the Lord," or, "Verily I say unto you." When truth has to be received at the mouth of human messengers of revelation, reason has a farther commission, to watch against the danger of mistaken faith. It has not only to examine the facts which accredit the professed agent of revelation, but also to compare his message with truth previously revealed by God, to "try the spirits whether they be of God." If truth thus revealed pass in the learner's mind through the state of knowledge to that of faith, reason has a farther work—that of recognising its agreement with the attributes and condition of human kind. For if much of religious truth must be, as it were, objective at first, new to man, outside his common thoughts, beyond his power to discover, all religious truth which becomes faith must be discovered to be subjective also—that is, it must be recognised as being in thorough harmony with the believer's consciously-felt nature. And any individual, as he increases in his faith—his continual emotional thinking of, his perpetual beholding of, revealed truth—must experience this fact, that his growing feeling of it is fed as well from within as from without; his own consciousness, as well as the

facts of God's other dealings, making the truth both credible
and necessary to him. When the Word of God, directing men
how to recognise truth, bids them "try the spirits whether
they be of God," "know them by their fruits," "prove all things,
and hold fast that which is good," it gives them not only previous revelation for a test to compare new truth with, as the
Bereans tried Paul's teaching, and to reject "any other gospel,"
anything not according to the law and the testimony—it gives
them also this other test, of comparing new truth with felt
human nature, declaring that a dutiful state of heart is prepared to be a judge of religious truth, and that the heart must
be exercised to sensitiveness in this function. "He that doeth
the will of God shall know of the doctrine whether it be of
God." "Have your senses exercised by reason of use to
discern good and evil.

10. This requirement of the Revealer, that His revelations Duty of
shall be tested in prescribed adequate ways, points out that if judgment.
the liberty of private judgment must be at the beginning of all
real faith, the duty of private judgment as certainly must be
there. The liberty of private judgment is not to be abused
into the licence of refusing to consider the matters set by God
before man's observation. That abuse is the common source
and form of infidelity; which is mostly not reasoning disbelief,
but carelessness or unwillingness to consider. Whether a man
is accountable for his belief or not, he is undoubtedly accountable for the pains he has taken to know the truth. The duty
of receiving religious truth, when it is proved to be truth, must
as little be interpreted into relieving the hearer from judging
whether "these things are so." That avoidance of personal
inquiry gives birth to credulity instead of faith. A man may
have a *creed* which he has suffered to be imposed upon him
without his taking the liberty of thinking for himself, or
which he has adopted at second-hand without having taken
the trouble of thinking for himself; but in neither case has he
a *faith* as well as a *creed*. As the unbelief is little worthy of
respect which arises from mere carelessness of attending to the
things of revelation, so the fancied faith is worthless that is
not thought out by the believer himself, with God's Word and

his own consciousness of human needs before him to test and
value the new instruction which he adopts. If faith be missed
by the carelessness or distaste which lets the living seeds of it
fall as "by the wayside," such belief is rootless and without
fruit, as the seeds that fall " upon a rock and forthwith spring
up." The "word" which results in faith is heard and attended to with an "honest and good heart;" and the fruit of the
consideration is " patiently brought forth " in abiding thought,
in some " an hundredfold," in " some but thirty," according to
different capacities for seeing much or little in a truth contemplated.

Risk to faith in religious reading. 11. The great risk to faith in an age of much religious
reading, whether of popular or profounder writings, is, that
this necessary condition to real faith—the exercise of personal consideration — will be neglected. Though at first
sight that risk seems an improbable result of the thoughts
being more solicited to religious matters, yet it is found to
exist; and the fact is, that an age of much reading of human
books on religious topics may be an age of unstable faith. The
reason is simple, and obviously sufficient. The reading of the
" effectual " Word is extensively superseded by the perusal of
feebler human writings; and besides, whatever the subordinate value of these may be, the thoughts of all but a few readers
are sure to go no further than the words of their chosen
writers, often missing the fulness of even their thoughts.
Hence great part of what is heard in the talk of the present
day about " the development of truth," " the opinions of thinking men," " advanced views," &c., is only jargon—words which
do not represent definite thoughts belonging to the speakers or
imitative writers. It is balanced by a cant of the same value,
what, by a denomination equally unrepresentative of actual
thought, is called " evangelical truth," " orthodox views." Both
are chiefly borrowed views, or rather nothing more respectable
than borrowed phraseology, and likely to give place to any other
strong " wind of doctrine " (Eph. iv. 14) that may blow over the
undutiful avoiders of religious painstaking. The cure for such
dissipated looseness of thoughts on religion is familiarity with
its facts and the inferences connected therewith as they are writ-

ten, examples of true reasoning, for man's guidance in the words of God Himself. If " advanced views " of religious truth do not take along with them all the facts and their appended lessons which make religious truth, they have not advanced in the truth, but run away from it. On the other hand, no "orthodox" handling of point after point, or—what has been, under every famous creed as yet, the character of human writings—a selection of points of the emotional truths of revealed religion, can give to the mind and heart confident hold of them, like the divinely-appointed and divinely-fitted description in which the Word sets them before us truly connected; truly balanced, so often shown to us in the form of life-pictures, the histories of real men's real intercourse with God. Whatever theories or difficulties may be about " verbal inspiration," the expressions of the Bible and its collocations of thoughts come home to man's convictions as no human choice of different language, and no other logic, ever comes near to doing. The neglect of God's own Word, then, for any professed assertion or discussion of its contents, is a most illogical disregard of the actual merits of the case to be judged; for that case is the offered facts and their offered evidence presented by the Offerer in the connection which He says is true. The disbeliever who has not examined these for himself has no disbelief — he merely can repeat the words of professed disbelievers. The believer who has not examined these for himself, who does not think on these things for his faith, has no faith in them; he is merely quite willing to believe them, but as yet he only believes in the man whose opinion he has copied with such a saving of trouble to himself. No shortcoming in the practice of faith is less defensible than the neglect of private judgment. The command is distinct to " search the Scriptures," "try the spirits," " prove all things, and hold fast the good," " be ready to give to every one that asketh you a reason of the hope that is in you." The religion that is required of us is not a thing that can be made up of indolent well-meanings, or fond or slight imaginations and credulous beliefs. It must be the loving work of heart and soul and mind and strength; and its faith must grow out of deliberate consideration, diligent thinking on God's own statements of the truth, convictions made our own by much thinking, and comparing His words with the histories of His love and with our own conscious condition. So much is this the case, that even those most distinctly revealed truths which God's authority is to be enough for our accepting, we do not believe as we have to believe them until we also, by considering them from every side, in every connection with our consciousness, commend them to our feelings as things true for us, as well as divinely declared to be truth— truths subjectively true for man, necessary parts of man's absolutely-needed religion, as well as given him by the Revealer of all truth. A man has that possession of religious truth which we call faith only in so far as he feels it fitting him, and consequently " ever before him." Any other portion of truth laid up in his mind may *become* religious truth to him, and is in the way of preparation for becoming such, but it is not religious truth or faith *to him as yet*. From this arises the necessity of—

Second, To assimilate recognised truth.

12. The second work of reason in acquiring faith—a work also commanded. It is, that we shall not only examine and satisfy ourselves of the evidence of revealed truth, but shall then go on to familiarise our minds with the proven truth, making it habitually present to our feelings. After " proving all things," we are to " hold fast " that which is good. " Whatsoever we see to be true, seemly, just, pure, lovely, of good report—whatever excellingly virtuous or worthy of praise " —we are, after knowing them, seeing them to be so, to go on " to think on these things." This is the human proceeding by which truth that is known is to become in any man what the Scriptures mean by *faith*.

Reasoning and revealed truth to coincide.

13. Indeed so thoroughly does religion require that its revealed truths and the habitual thoughts of our reason should be brought into most satisfied union, naturally at home with each other—so entirely are these truths to possess our minds habitually, that our reason and our religion are meant to be really one, different names only for practically one guide of life; so that when we think on any religious matter, we shall be thinking as our own reason spontaneously guides us,

and when we reason on any matter of worldly life, our reason shall of itself bring up the very principles and maxims of revealed religion. There is no unacknowledged error of thought that so dislocates the facts of man's condition here, or which should be so universally corrected by the logic of human feeling, as the prevalent habit of speaking, and consequently so far thinking, as if a man's religion were a different thing from his life—corrective of it, or otherwise related to it, but only related. The only true feeling, the only good logic, in the matter is, that a man's religion *is* his life and his life is his religion. Nothing else comes up to the needs of human nature, every faculty and propensity of which is in need of being healed, savingly controlled, or helped. The objective religion taught us by God and the subjective religion (connection with God) felt by us must be one and the same. The second department of the work of reason in connection with revealed faith is the lifelong one of bringing this to pass by accustoming the soul to feel as well as know the truths of revealed faith. Having satisfied the mind of the truth of the great assurances of God's love, and of the reasonableness of the requirements of human love and service to Him which these imply and have appended to them, the reasoning faculty has next, by setting the precious instructions in all their lights before the soul, to bring it to love and take them to itself, and assimilate them, feeding its natural life of emotional thought and activity upon them as its needed and sure food.

14. What is the process of this appropriation? It is described and enjoined in the Word itself: "Think on these things;" "Abide in me, and let my words abide in you;" "Thy word have I hid in my heart;" "Thy testimonies have been my songs in the house of my pilgrimage;" "Thy lovingkindness is before mine eyes, and I have walked in Thy truth." In the fact that this is the appointed process of assimilating religious truth into being the soul's own habitual thoughts and feelings, we have the explanation of how faith is so far from being coextensive with knowledge of the truth—a coextension which religionists are apt to assume. It is not the

Process of assimilation.

truths which a man knows that form his characteristic ways of mind and heart, but only such of them as he habitually thinks of; not the knowledge which he possesses, but that part of it which, as it were, possesses him—which is in the way of coming unbidden into his thoughts, and mixing itself irresistibly up with all his judgments of other things, so forming his ways of thinking. The knowledge of a human parent's affection does not abide in a child's mind in the form of know-ledge, in which a stranger might possess it as largely, but in the form of perpetual thought—not always conscious thought, not often purposed thought perhaps, but thought that is ever going out and in in the chambers of emotion, intermeddling with all the other life of the heart and all the activity of the mind. Our faith is to be thus dominant over our whole being; but no truth merely known to be true is that.

The process of all civi-lisation. 15. The sanctification of an individual through education in the truth is like what has always been seen in the civilisation of a people. Both keep pace not with the acquired know-ledge of purifying, elevating truth, but with the acquired habits of thinking on such truth. A person may acquire in a short time, according to the quickness of his intellect, the knowledge of a number of higher, more refined principles of feeling and conduct. These new and better laws he may feel the truth of forcibly whenever he is led to turn his mind to them. But still that which will be found most to rule his manners, his feelings, and his actings, will be his old accustomed thoughts, which, without needing to be called up, place themselves before him always when he does not intentionally supersede them by the new. When he is on his guard, the rules he has learned may guide him; but when, under surprise or other disturbance, he is not watching himself, his accustomed thoughts will most naturally slip into the guidance of his conduct. His new-learn-ed, but not yet habituated, principles do not show their power so as to purify the heart, to overcome the world, to bring down high thoughts, self-exalting imaginations, into captivity to the obedience of Christ—that is, his knowledge is not yet faith. It is merely in the way to become faith, to which end the man must *abide* in Christ and keep His words *abiding* in him,—

familiar to him, made his own, his natural thoughts, ever before
him.   In every country, general civilisation, whether religious
or non-religious, has never taken place but during the passing
of successive generations.   No people has been raised from
barbarism, taught gentle manners, habits of self-denying kindness, respect for laws, &c., in place of rude ways and strong coarse
selfishness and turbulence, except by the slow process of accustoming them to new habits of thought.   Men and women,
taught in mature life the knowledge of better things, may
preoccupy the minds of their children with these better principles which they have learned, and by restraining themselves
before their children, may accustom them chiefly to hear and
speak, and so think, of *these* things ; and the children being
thus in a greater degree than their parents habituated to the
new thoughts, will be under their sway also in a greater degree,
and may in their turn help their children to a similar advance-
ment upon their habitual thinking of and feeling these new
things.   But the old, who learned the new truths only in their
grown - up years, will, in spite of their knowing better, be
over and over again caught and impelled by their former accustomed thoughts and feelings.   Veracious accounts of missions
to the heathen give exactly this picture of the Christianity
which is fresh from heathenism.   Dr Ogilvie of the Church
of Scotland mission in Bengal, in an account of some converts,
describes the Brahminical pride of caste and the heathen sav-
ageness of revenge as coming in fits at times upon men whose
conduct in general is worthy of comparison with the worthi-
est Christians, and the men have to summon up hastily the
thought that they have become Christians.   In our own land,
many generations ago, the best educated, though they knew
and inculcated right principles of conduct, were, upon interested and even upon unguarded occasions, habitually guilty of
most unprincipled conduct, chargeable with acts and manners
of which any class of persons except criminals would now be
ashamed. · What habitual sway religious reasons have now
over the common thoughts of the nation, bringing forth habits
of truth and righteousness, has been the slow growth of centuries.   The ground was gained only as one generation of new

minds after another presented a less and less blotted page for
somewhat more of renewing knowledge to be written perma-
nently on the memory, ready to suggest habitual thoughts.   The
seclusion of the written Word of God from general use, of
course, impeded greatly the progress which oral teaching could
make in diffusing knowledge of its true ways of thinking.
But when the Bible was set free, the same rule of human nature
still kept habitual life lagging much behind general knowledge ; and it has only been as matter from the Bible's store-
house of endlessly-diversified treasure of thought was everywhere exhibited by teachers and independently seized upon by
individual minds, under the influence of sympathy or other
connecting cause, that the inner life of the nation, the people's accustomed ways of thinking and looking at things, has
become leavened with the honour and purity and peaceable-
ness which make the general disposition of the community so
different now from its state in long-past times.   An instructive comparison with other peoples in a different condition, as
to the means of being thus leavened with Scriptural truth and
relative sentiment, is possible to us now by the extensive
knowledge which nations in the present time have of each
other's general morals, both political and social.   The British
people stands in distinct contrast with the leading Continental
nations as to reverence for the Bible and familiarity with its
direct teaching, and its matter suggestive of moral sentiment ;
but so also is the difference a marked one that there is, in
respect of political truthfulness and social purity, between this
country and nations which do not read the Bible, but substitute
books of piety, or, reading it, do not conserve its authority.

Examples
from
Scripture
history.

16. Both the Jewish and the Christian Scriptures abound in
illustrations of this law of human nature, that knowledge takes
time to become coextensive faith ; that a new thought only
by degrees attains to habitual emotional dominion, so' as to
stand the test of faith that it works by love, purifies the heart,
and overcomes the world.   Samuel, trained up from a child in
the way of the Lord, and Saul, brought under special religious
teaching out of a very wild state of society only in manhood,
exhibited very different, almost contrasted, states of faith.   The

prophet's history manifests him having the Lord always before him. It seems his nature to turn always into the true way of His service. The king, as was the case with the first of Christian monarchs, Constantine, called, like him, in confirmed years, exhibited to the end a mixed character—his knowledge of Jehovah never well assimilated and become dominant thought and feeling. Features of true religion and of heathenism commingle perpetually in him. We see him at times following the commands of Jehovah with all-compelling zeal, by-and-by not having Him in all his thoughts ; naming one child, Jonathan, " the gift of God;" a second, Melchishua, " the help of Moloch ;" another, Esh-Baal, " the man of Baal ;" re-naming him, in an access of deep repentance, Ish-Bosheth, " the man of shame :" at one time slaying the wizards, at another turning for aid to their forbidden arts,—never able to learn habitual obedience to the word of the Lord. His successor David's life is a record of broken lights, mingled masses of character—pure and impure, tender and savage, spiritual and sensual. David was only the introducer of much of the so greatly-advanced thought and feelings in which his Psalms abound. His youth grew up in an atmosphere of thought and feeling of a coarser, grosser, spiritually-darker kind—viz., the court of Saul and the Philistine oppression ; and his Psalms were not his habitual life even in his mature years. They but record the heaven-bestowed impulses of sight and feeling which carried on his sanctification. And some of them depict the mixed character which was the subject of those divine influences, such as his biography depicts him. The earliest advances of divine revelation to leaven the habitual thoughts of the chosen people—even by those truths of God's nature and will which were taught them with the impressive accompaniments of the plagues, the Passover night, the passage of the Red Sea, and the giving of the Law—were slow in the generation which Egypt had habituated to different thoughts. Some of the characters which appeared among them in later periods —such as those of Jephthah and Samson, who are cited by Paul among his instances of faith, recognised servants of God, who endured and did great duties of appointed work, beholding

Him as their strength—are hardly conceivable in our state of society, but, doubtless, could be extensively paralleled by modern Christian missionaries, as they could be from the earliest Christian history of our own land. The first Hebrew king was, in religious character, a type of the whole Hebrew race. Under the dominant intellectual and social influence of the Egyptians during four centuries, they had lost the thoughts of monotheism which were natural to Abraham, and had become possessed by those of polytheism. They were recovered to true habits of thinking only by a thousand years of direct teaching, enforced by long periods of severe compulsion to attend to the true knowledge revealed to them. It was only the end of the seventy years' captivity that saw the re-establishment of monotheistic sentiment in natural sway over them. In the generation which first knew the truth as it is in Jesus the same difference presents itself between truth learned and truth assimilated. We know so little of the habitual Christian thoughts and feelings of the apostles, except from their writings, that it might be as erroneous to depict minutely the personal character of John and Peter and James, by filling up unhistorical features of it in exact accordance with their writings, as we know it would be to construct a character of David from his Psalms alone. But those apostles' habits of thought were evidently diverse from one another, not equally nor similarly new-formed by their equal possession of formal Christian knowledge; and in the course of their education to faith under the personal teaching of their and our Master, their apparent progress was a wavering one, exhibiting slowness of heart to believe and a provoking for-gettings of things which one would think no one could have forgotten. They drew from Him who knew human nature so as to allow for its common weakness such complaints as, " O ye of little faith !" "O fools, and slow of heart to believe !" " O faithless generation, how long shall I suffer you ?" The Comforter when He came healed much of that breach between knowledge and feeling in the case of the eleven, and brought to their minds the mass of their Master's forgotten lessons, and guided their thoughts thereon unto all truth ; yet with differ-

ences of chief sights and feelings which perpetuate their faith
as examples of all human faith—a faith not the equal companion of knowledge.   The mass of their near followers, the
first generation of Christians, were too evidently a parallel case
to the first generations of Israel.   Among those converted in
mature life from heathenism, habits of seeing and feeling
Christian truth constrainingly were attained slowly and with
many fluctuations.   The profanation of the holy table at
Corinth to an occasion of excess, the toleration of an incestuous
person in the communion of the church, and their strife and
envy, biting and devouring one another, complained of by Paul,
showed how far the assent of the intellect to the truth was
from being immediately followed by life-compelling thoughtfulness and habitual emotional contemplation of that truth.
Religious knowledge had not ripened into much of religious
sentiment or taste.   In the Jewish section of the first Christian
Church the crime of Ananias and Sapphira was an equally impressive illustration of the difference between knowledge and
the faith that overcomes the world.   They knew the truth of
the Holy Ghost's omniscience, but they acted as if they had
not known anything of it.   No thought of it had come to have
constraining power over their minds.   Their fate, like that of
the Egyptian generation of the Hebrew Church, became, and
perhaps was needed to be, a lesson to their successors in the
Church, upon whom great fear fell in consequence of it.   The
great trouble of Paul's ministry among the Gentiles, in places
where there were Hebrew Christians, arose from the extreme slowness of the converted Jews to quit the thoughts of
Judaism, which Christian thoughts had superseded.   The
person whose religious character he dwells upon with most
unbroken affection and happiness, while he has to complain of
or mourn over so many, Timothy, was a Gentile Jew in his
education, probably always hearing the Jewish peculiarities
less made of ; but he was also a believer whose unfeigned faith
had been nurtured upon knowledge of the Holy Scriptures
from a child, and that by the most leavening teaching, the
emotional teaching a woman would try with a child when the
woman was the child's mother, or her own more indulgent

I

and more experienced mother. Does the same state of matters
present itself now? Does conversion in mature life from
confirmed habits of evil kind, or from carelessness to feeling
of religious truth, often or ever result in the same natural-like
feeling—the same inartificial, unassumed thoughtfulness of
all religious things—the same easy, constraining influence of
them over the life, which seems no constraint, as is seen in one
who has from early years been growing into habits of spiritual
life? Do the late convert's convictions blend with his moral
nature like congenial elements, not joined together but become
one? How much of habitual faith or spiritual "wisdom" has
been produced by "revivals"?

Means and hindrances to knowledge becoming faith. 17. If we look now at some of the representations which
the Word of God gives of the means of and hindrances to sanc-
tification, we shall see that faith, the source of all sanctification,
all purifying of the heart, and all overcoming of the world, is
described in accordance with the above deductions as being
the accustomed thoughts, the things always before the mind—
not the things learned, accepted, held as incontestably proved,
undoubtedly true, but the things habitually thought of. The
human means to be taken to produce all the religion of faith
are so described in the beginning: "These words which I command thee shall be in thine heart, and thou shalt teach them
diligently to thy children; thou shalt talk of them when thou
sittest in thine house, and when thou walkest by the way, and
when thou liest down, and when thou risest up; and thou
shalt bind them for a sign upon thine hand, and they shall be
as frontlets between thine eyes, and thou shalt write them
upon the posts of thy house and on thy gates" (Deut. vi. 6-9);
"Train up a child in the way he should go, and when he is
old he will not depart from it" (Prov. xxii. 6); "Keep thy
heart with all diligence, for out of it are the issues of life"
(Prov. iv. 23). Again it is from the accustomed, the besetting,
dominant thoughts that the chief hindrance to the Word of
God arises. The "cares of life, the deceitfulness of riches, and
the lusts of other things, choke" the growth of the thoughts
produced by the Word (Matt. xiii. 22). The description of
missed faith, "By hearing ye shall hear and shall not under-

stand, and seeing ye shall see and shall not perceive" (Matt.
xiii. 14), is the very description of a mind preoccupied—so full
of other thoughts habitually that truths the most evident,
tidings the most important, pass before it, and are seen and
heard, but leave no trace behind them.   And how more exactly
could the same cause of loss of sanctification through the
truth—thoughts habitually bound to other things—be described than thus: "They come before Thee as the people
cometh, and they sit before Thee as my people, and they hear
Thy words but they will not do them; for with their mouth
they show much love, but their *heart goeth after their covetousness;* and lo Thou art unto them as the very lovely song of
one that hath a pleasant voice, and can play well on an instrument, for they hear Thy words but they do them not"
(Ezek. xxxiii. 31, 32).   In the Gospels the abiding nature of
the thoughts with which faith occupies itself is set forth on
another side.   They are thoughts which give pleasure, the
sure indication that they are habitual because cherished
thoughts.   "He that doeth truth"—the description of a man
living by faith, by constant constraint of the truth—"cometh
to the light" (John iii. 21).   He seeks communion with revealed truth; he is attracted to it by the pleasure he enjoys
of knowing thereby that "his deeds" of heart and life are
approved by God, are such as "are wrought in God."   "He
that doeth evil," by the same emotional law, "hateth the
light."   He will not come to it; he avoids letting his thoughts
have to do with it, "lest he be reproved."

18. In a treatise confined to the practice of faith, if we speak Divine co-
of the human origin of faith it must be of what man can do to operation
put within
produce faith.   Primarily, that must consist of things within his man's practice of
own power—his own learning of revealed matters of thought faith.
—his own reasoning himself into strong feeling of their truth
in themselves, and their truth in relation to him—his own
assimilating the thoughts and feelings so acquired into being
the habit of his mind and heart.   But inseparable from this
purely human work in the ways of God's grace, coincident,
co-operating, working in an indivisible work, is the divine
origin of faith.   That is God's "teaching savingly and to profit,"

—His "putting His law into the heart" and "writing His commandment on the mind," and "causing the man to walk in His statutes and keep His judgments and do them "—His "pouring out of His Spirit" upon the fleshly learner to "help his infirmities," to "teach him what to pray for as he ought," to "raise desires" within him, to "recall to his mind the words of the Saviour," to "take of the things of the Saviour and show to him," "to enlighten the eyes of his understanding" to know, and to "strengthen the inner man with might to comprehend and go on to know the love of Christ." Is then this divine work in producing faith in any way comprehended in as well as inseparable from man's *practice* of faith? Is the divine as well as the human operation practically in his power? It is so. Man has to practise the *seeking* and *obtaining* of the coincident help of God toward believing. By the uniting means of prayer, every portion of the divine help is linked to man's own practice. The measure of that help is regulated by man's own practical husbanding of the portions of it dealt out to him. And, further, if we are to learn anything beyond the lesson of man's responsibility from the parable of the talents, it seems to teach that God working in us both will and ability, *helps in kind.* He enlightens the looking eyes to see. He opens the listening ear to hear. He gives the hungry soul more desire as well as fulfilling. He guides the actual suppliant to pray as he ought. "Thou hast heard the desire of the humble, Thou wilt prepare their heart, Thou wilt cause their ear to hear" (Ps. x. 17). "The preparation of the heart in man is from the Lord," but the man "has his senses exercised by reason of his own use of them to discern good and evil." "My son, if thou wilt receive my words, and hide my commandments with thee; so that thou incline thine ear unto wisdom, and apply thine heart to understanding; yea, if thou criest after knowledge, and liftest up thy voice for understanding; if thou seekest her as silver, and searchest for her as for hid treasures; then shalt thou understand the fear of the Lord, and find the knowledge of God. For the Lord giveth wisdom, and out of His mouth cometh knowledge and understanding" (Prov. ii. 1-6). The co-operation of the believer's loving thoughts and

God's help given to think is expressively set forth in Paul's prayer for the Ephesian Church, in language which commends itself to man's conscious desires and needs. " I bow my knees unto the Father of our Lord Jesus Christ, of whom the whole family in heaven and earth is named, that He would grant you, according to the riches of His glory, to be strengthened with might by His Spirit in the inner man, that Christ may dwell in your hearts by faith; that ye, being rooted and grounded in love, may be able to comprehend with all saints what is the breadth, and length, and depth, and height ; and to know the love of Christ, which passeth knowledge, that ye might be filled with all the fulness of God " (Eph. iii. 14-19.)

CHAPTER VI.

THE MENTAL EXPERIENCE OF FAITH.

PSALM xciv. 10.—In the multitude of my thoughts within me Thy comforts delight my soul.

ISAIAH xxvi. 3.—Thou wilt keep him in perfect peace whose mind is stayed on Thee.

Faith chiefly described by its opposites. 1. IN the Scriptures we have faith more directly described by negatives than by positives. The wicked "have not God in all their thoughts;" "they like not to retain Him in their knowledge;" they have "an evil heart of unbelief, departing from the living God." Failings in faith are described, that they who fail "are blind, and cannot see afar off, and forget that they are purged from their old sins." The sustaining cause of unbelief, producing occasionally strong or constantly increasing departure from the living God, is besetting sins, habitual thoughts and desires "going after" different things from God's will and His love, "cares of this world," "deceitfulness of riches," a "law of sin in the members" overcoming the better law or habit of the mind, fleshly desires "warring against" the spiritual propensities of the soul—no alarming single attacks of evil, or overpowering trials coming at a time, but the common habits of the earthly or sensual soul, the law of indulgence it has allowed itself—Judas's encroaching covetousness, Demas's love of this present world. The *opposite* of faith is thus exhibited to us as a want of thought, a dislike, an inability to think of or remember the things of God, a "departure" of the heart, through whatever combination or progress of evil causes, "from the living God."

2. Faith, then, the result to be produced by the reasoning of faith, the intentional study of the things given us to believe, is to be a habit of "thinking on these things" of God. In making a natural history of faith, the most comprehensive generic feature to be set down is, that the believer is *constantly thinking* of the things in which he believes. ^{Psycho-logically—continual thinking.}

3. What is included in this thinking or constant contact of the believer's spirit with the matter of his faith it is easier and more useful to illustrate than to describe, because terms accurately descriptive are perhaps not to be found; and, indeed, terms comprehensive enough to embrace the diversities of experience in such a department of consciousness are not reasonably to be looked for in human language, which can describe only individual experience. ^{Manners of thinking.}

Two states of mind belong to faith's "thinking"—a quiescent and an active state.

4. Unconscious thinking is an inaccurate-like combination of words, but it suggests itself as the true description of a great part of the practice of faith. Unnoticed thinking, or thoughts not individualised, would perhaps be a better phrase. To "endure as seeing Him who is invisible," to "have the Lord continually before us," does not imply unbroken consciousness of thinking about Him, but must comprehend much that lies between occasions of formal thinking, in intervals which are not void of communion of the soul with God, but filled with it. The authoritative analogy of human relationships, which is expository of the kind of truths that make up man's religious knowledge and thoughts concerning God, is as profitably expository of the manner in which that knowledge is present to his mind. Only parts of a child's knowledge of the best-loved parent are individualised thoughts; yet, along with all his formal noticed remembered thoughts upon whatever moves his young mind, his parent is in *all* his thoughts. A pupil in school is consciously occupied only with a succession of more or less engrossing mental exercises; but the presence and authority and wise help of his master, though but now and then distinctly thought of, are continually surrounding his spirit, and constraining and sustaining it. A sick ^{Unconscious thinking}

person may be able to think much or little consciously about his physician, but he is never in a state of having forgotten all about him. If he should do so at any time, he would awaken from his forgetfulness with some perhaps uneasy surprise at the state of mind. A soldier on perilous service may never see the general on whose guidance the success or safety of the army may chiefly depend; but if he knows much about him of soldierly qualities, and has thought much on his deeds of generalship, which are his followers' ground of faith in him, he will, while giving active conscious thoughts to the things and persons he is immediately in contact with, have underneath, and more of value to his courage and confidence, an undefined and undescribed comfort of mind relative to his believed-in leader. A writer enamoured of a model writes with a constant but not always realised propensity to express himself after the same manner. These examples seem to explain sufficiently what may be named unconscious thinking. They show us also that this degree of thought is the most common condition of faith with reference to its really fundamental subjects of thought. It may seem paradoxical to say that a believer is, as a rule, not consciously thinking of what really is the chief matter of his thoughts—viz., the affection and guidance and healing and protection of his Father, Saviour, Master, Teacher, Physician, Captain of Salvation, Friend closer than a brother. But the fact is so; and the explanation of it is religiously satisfactory in the highest degree.

the deposit of much active thinking.

5. It is, that this unconscious thinking is the result of a great deal of formal, sustained, desirous, self-instructing thinking upon the facts of God's holy saving love. It is knowledge which, having been searched after in the Word, and shown to the mind by the supplicated Spirit, is assimilated knowledge and thought now, possessed and enjoyed henceforth in the form of added strength of mind and healthiness of feelings, like the unconscious readiness of the body for more exercise and enjoyment of its functions which comes after the partly-conscious assimilation of its convenient food. The unconscious or unindividualised mass of thoughts are the quiescent deposit of many long-agitated thoughts of a distinct, formal,

logically-arranged kind.   Such a state of quiescent knowledge unconsciously used is a familiar thing to the experience of the human mind.   A skilled workman's readiness of
resource, and a reasoner's facility in appropriating the relevant
and important out of a mass of matter set before him upon any
subject, are equally the result of the man's having on his mind
a mass of deposited facts and truths, the individual presence of
which has by degrees ceased to force itself upon his notice, as
one by one, by frequent turning over in his mind, they have,
from being new, become quite familiar to him.   These so
familiar facts and general truths, lying quiescent together, not
individualised, are yet perpetually living truths within him,
and ready to present themselves long or briefly, but in full
prominence, to his thoughts as they are needed ; for with little
of accompanying consciousness, or none at all, they keep the
thinker on the shortest and truest road to the conclusion
which has logically to be reached.   Anything will break the
deadlike, but most essentially living, mass of accustomed entirely familiar thoughts, and bring any part of it into full
vigorous activity.

6. The normal condition of most of the thoughts which
faith enjoys must be thus, as it were, quiescent ; and the mind
most thoroughly furnished with matters of joyful faith, and
ablest to appreciate and enjoy and make use of any strongly
influential thought of a fact or an utterance of God's love as it
may arise, cannot but have likewise the greatest amount of the
unconscious unindividualising thinking of faith.   The state of
spirit that is to " rejoice evermore " and " pray without ceasing " is possible only to a faith which thus lives and moves and
has its being in the Saviour, Father, Guide, Comforter, even
when it seems to be asleep to sensible or conscious communion
with Him.   That is a faith of which the things that onlookers
see—viz., its zeal and fervour, its earnest supplication, its rejoicing outbursts of praise, called forth by particular occasions or
contemplations, are but the occasional things of its life—a
faith whose great mass of life is lying " hid " from mortal eyes
" with Christ in God "—Christ dwelling in its heart, His
words and deeds abiding within its ever-living united affec-

Faith's thoughts normally quiescent.

tions—the thoughts and affections of the heart, gathered together again, looking continually in quiet peace and daily comfort unto Him. It is in such a state of heart that the thoughts of Him may be a "multitude," and indistinct as their multitudinousness would imply, but "united to fear His name;" and so, as is promised to faith, restful and healing, making His "comforts delight the soul." The rejoicing evermore, the prayer without ceasing, are not quite fulfilled by a mere constant readiness of the soul to be called into joy and childlike supplication at any time. They are not merely possible conditions of the believer's spirit—they are actual; and when not also noticeably active conditions, the intervals are not blank of joy in God and of drawing near to Him, but full of those comforts of communion with Him—comforts which can hardly be conceived separable from a state of union with Him. They are states not of possible but actual faith and faith's comforts, and they are enjoyed as the little child's unindividualised happy continuous hours of joy and trust in his loving mother are :

> " Like some sweet beguiling melody—
> So sweet we know not we are listening to it."

Analogous to bodily health. 7. The term "unconscious" fails to express the real state of such living faith, because we associate unconsciousness, speaking roughly, with total inactivity of feeling; which is not correct even with respect to healthy physical unconsciousness, in which absence of observed sensation is sometimes all that is meant. Forces latent when *in equilibrio* show themselves to be in full action if the completeness of the balance be ever so little disturbed. But bodily unconsciousness furnishes a closer illustration of what we mean by unconscious faith. A person in full health lying in a state of entire rest is unconscious of the individual bodily feelings which, in mass and in connection, produce his state of comfort. But it is simply the universal healthfulness and full harmonious action of all his innumerable bodily sensations that is making him unobservant of any single one of them. Even individual perceptions may thus become latent. In a state of absolute quiescence, lay the most sensitive organs of touch, the points of the fingers upon any part of the body, and the perception of what is touched, and even the consciousness of that particular contact, will not continue for any time individualised, even though the mind feel after it seeking to regain the perception, and the quiescence will have to be broken by some motion of the body altering the pressure of the touch. Yet doubtless that particular touch becomes unfelt merely through its becoming a normal condition —part of what makes the body's general rest at the time. And the breaking of that particular unconsciousness of contact will bring out into felt life not that touch alone, but general bodily consciousness.

So far as to the relatively unconscious condition of faith.

8. When the thinking of faith becomes distinctly, promi- *Conscious* nently conscious, not quiescent but active—when it individu- *faith pro-minently* alises any particular subject of religious thought—the charac- *emotional.* teristic attribute of all faith, quiescent or active, becomes also prominent — viz., emotion. For the thinking of faith is a thinking of facts which make human happiness, and the contemplation of which excites the pleasures or the pains of that peculiar happiness. Its subject is the facts and assurances which show to mankind generally, or to any individual child of God, that "God so loved the world." Man's thoughts thereon, besides, turned to whatever points of our revealed knowledge of God, must have that particular character which belongs to the thoughts of family relationship ; and these are never purely intellectual, but the feeling of the family love, or its memories, accompanies all their thinking, and directs the lines it takes. Indeed, no real thinking upon the moral things of God can be without emotion. The apostle James adduces a terrible illustration of this—"The devils believe and tremble." Even the contemplation of God's almighty power and Godhead manifested in creation, mankind should not find to be a purely intellectual process. Emotion should arise in it (Rom. i. 21), compelling the thinker to give Him honour and gratefulness. And right emotion is missed by mankind in the intellectual contemplation of nature, as Paul further teaches (ver. 28), simply because wrong emotion shuts God out of their thoughts in connection with the outer world—the thinkers " not liking to

retain Him in their knowledge." The thought of faith bestowed
or restored by revealed religion, which brings intellectual study
of the great things of nature in among the things which produce moral emotions, is that expressed by the Christian poet—
" My Father made them all." To mankind who believe the
Word, the whole world is their Father's house, prepared for
their dwelling with Him in blessedness when they were innocent—preserved and again fitted for them to dwell with Him
under discipline when they fell—made sacred to them by marvellous transactions of His redeeming love culminating in the
coming of His only-begotten Son to die for them—and filled
by these thoughts with memories all-powerful to lead and help
them to learn again to believe in His love, and give themselves
to Him. All their thoughts of Him in it, all their thinking of
His deeds or words of love, which its history has witnessed
and recorded, is to be emotional, as a human family's thoughts
of the affections and actions of its various relationships are
emotional always, and never by possibility purely intellectual.

Belief
"with the
heart."
9. In speaking of the emotional element of faith, illustration is better than description. The one will show more
clearly than the other what that " belief of the heart " is which
is one of the Bible's expressions of man's believing in God.
As an instructive introductory example may be taken faith in
God's Word. The authoritative analogy of family relationships bids us understand that by the similitude of a child's
belief in his father's word as to any history or expectation of
family love. Intellectual thought of the historical facts of
God's love to mankind, and of the declarations He has made
of man's condition and of His own purposes of grace, will not
come up to that model. The intellectual labour and fidelity
to truth may be great through which the mind has worked
its way to believing these against all opposing reasoning,
overcoming strongly all opposing influences. There must,
besides, be attained the child's thought of his father as the
surety for the truth of all, and the source of the value of all.
The things he believes he believes most consciously for one
reason—that they were told him by his father—his father,

who could not come short in knowledge of what is past, nor
mistake or fail in his assurance of what is to come.   The
things of a father's love which a child believes are not true
only but precious.   He rejoices to think of them.   They
bring his father nearer to his heart evermore.   So reason's
strong service of honouring study is given to God, but it is
not given alone.   Emotion accompanies it.   The high thoughts
of the most gifted believer's conscious intellectual power, the
imaginations which are apt to exalt themselves, become captive not to logical argument only; they are "captive to the
obedience of Christ"—"constrained by the love of Christ."
He thinks with the heart as well as with the understanding.
Of two children of God, the less informed may be capable
only of thinking of some few facts of redeeming love—not
able, like his brother, to generalise much knowledge into high
imaginations of God's great attributes of unchangeable love
and all-comprehending care.   The essential feature of the
thoughts of both is, that their thoughts of God's love are
thoughts of joy, and their thoughts of man's declared un-
worthiness are thoughts not of knowledge only, but of fear
and oppressive sadness.

In fullest accordance with this analogical teaching, we find Meaning of
the emotional character of the thinking of faith forced upon intellectual
us by the evident meaning of the language of faith in the Scripture.
Scriptures.   The words which we use in a purely intellectual
sense on subjects of human knowledge, we find, when employed in the Bible respecting the knowledge belonging to revealed religion, must be read so as to include emotion as well.
The *knowledge* which the Scripture characters have of religious
facts is more than knowledge.   It is exultation—the delight or
security or other prized good of the soul that comes with some
blessedness attained or assured, and so already possessed by
faith.   The man of intellect knows that there is a God.   How
did Job in early and Paul in later times express their knowledge?   "I know that my Redeemer liveth, and that He shall
stand at the latter day upon the earth; and though after my
skin worms destroy this body, yet in my flesh shall I see God:
whom I shall see for myself, and mine eyes shall behold, and

not another" (Job xix. 25-27) ; " I know whom I have believed, and am persuaded that He is able to keep that which I have committed unto Him against that day" (2 Tim. i. 12). Believers do not think of the facts and truths revealed as things which they only know. The Gospel is "good news," "glad tidings of great joy" to them. The testimonies of God are "a delight;" not known by them as things of this world's knowledge are known, but thought of with a joy which takes the thinker out of this world's life. They are his "songs"— "songs in the house of his pilgrimage"—a stranger traveller's songs of home. Again, when a good man is said to *believe* a truth in religion, the word evidently is not used of the simple credence we give to a statement upon sufficient evidence. It is the sweet persuasion of one who "rejoices to believe." If he is said to contemplate God or *meditate* on His works, his thinking—the thinking of faith—is evidently not an unmoved passionless contemplation. It is something much more akin to the luxurious musing of a warm heart upon things that lie near to it. A philosopher may think of God; he may fix his mind upon the divine character and attributes, and study them as he would any other subject of grandeur or difficulty. A religious man dwelling on His revelations of Himself does not so much think of Him as he, as it were, thinks to Him. He holds communion with Him when he thinks of Him, as with one who is necessary to his happiness. The cool speculations of heathen philosophers on the nature of imagined Godhead, compared with the warm and teeming language of Jewish or Christian believers in the revealed God, the Father of man, illustrate effectively the difference between intellectual and religious belief. The comparison shows forth, by the appropriate foil, the essentially emotional character of the thinking of true faith. What a contrast to anything we expect to read in the thoughts even of Cicero on the nature of God are the thinkings of the Scripture characters—" As the hart panteth after the brooks of water, so longeth my soul for Thee, O God:" "Whom have I in heaven but Thee? and there is none upon earth that I desire besides Thee:" "My soul thirsteth for God, for the living God: when shall I come and appear before God?" "Thy lovingkindness is better than life, therefore my lips shall praise thee." What a contrast to the emptiness of any derived satisfaction, or strength to resist evil or bear trial, manifest in the meditations of the Greek theosophists, the utter coldness, comfortlessness, hopelessness, with which they turned back from their "vain imaginations" (empty disquisitions) (Rom. i. 21) to grapple with the difficulties of life, is the rest and strength in which the prophets and apostles enwrap their souls, thinking upon the personal historical God of the Bible. "I know that my Redeemer liveth;" "Thou wilt keep him in perfect peace whose mind is stayed on thee" (Isa. xxvi. 3); "The peace of God, which passeth all understanding, shall keep your hearts and minds through Christ Jesus" (Philip. iv. 7). This is a foreign language entirely to the intellectual phraseology which speaks of "the deity," "the supreme being," "the unseen power," "the intelligence of the universe."

The essentially emotional character of the thinking of faith, which was to be looked for under the guidance of the family analogy, is thus evidently its character as seen in practice in the case which is in one sense the fundamental, introductory, but never absent, exercise of faith—faith in the words of revealed grace, the testimonies of God.

10. Particular inquiry remains to be made into what the emotions are which belong to the thinking of faith.

What are the emotions of faith?

Conventionally, Christians are apt to confine both the emotions and the thoughts of faith to that fact which is but the mighty corner-stone of the faith they are invited to — the death accomplished at Jerusalem; and, keeping by that subject of contemplation alone, speak of faith as trust in the propitiatory sacrifice of Christ. This conventional thought is due perhaps to the habit of learning religious truth in logical systems, the central propositions of which are apt to exclude the rest of their truths from usual contemplation. Its confined view, however, of John iii. 16, impoverishes the emotions of faith; if indeed logical thought be not more present in it than emotion. Our faith is in the love of God to man; of which the cross of Calvary was the completed, "finished" manifestation; but which is an unbroken history of acts, and signs, and promises of holy saving love from the entrance of destroying sin until He, who, in the fulness of times, came to give His life for man, shall come again without sin unto salvation to take His own who have believed in Him unto Himself, that where He is they may be also. The believer's thoughts of the love of God in Christ Jesus are to draw food for reasoning and emotion from all the deeds and words of God's holy love of man, and His hatred of sin, and His grace of salvation, which make the world's history—all the assurances through which the fathers looked forward and saw the day of Christ afar off, and all the accomplishments and assurances through which Christians look back and also forward, when they let their hearts fill themselves with peace and joy and holy desire in beholding ever more and more how full the fountain was, and is, and is to be, that began to flow in Eden, and was so disclosed to sight in Calvary a fountain opened for sin and for uncleanness, and will be, in the incorruptible inheritance, a river that maketh glad the city of our God. The Lord, *our Lord*, who is the same yesterday, to-day, and for ever, is in all His eternal love to man, though especially in all His earth-known coming to save us, to be " ever before us." " Looking unto Him" is to be the condition of our life, abiding in Him, and having His words abiding in us—all " His words," from the first that opened hope to Adam, to the fullest appeal to behold and believe and come to the perfected work of salvation. The emotions of faith are consequently to be all that these thoughts of faith may bring when they are singly or in combination occupying the mind. And these active emotions are to deposit, as it were, permanent habitual feelings in the soul, as they pass over it in strength again and again; so that in like manner as innumerable matters of faith's *thoughts* lie in the believer's mind, prompt to awaken to constraining force upon any suggestion, or all combined have in their quiescent condition a controlling dominion over the processes of his intellect, a permanent body of *emotions* shall correspondingly possess the soul, and keep it in a constant union of the heart as well as of the thoughts to Him in whom he believes. We cannot describe by one or by any few words that habitual state of the believer's soul.   We can only describe many active states into which it is excited to special emotions for the time towards Him who is its all in all.   But we confine the meaning of faith when we call it trust, or when we call it by any single emotional act of the soul at all.

11. It would be impossible to class the exercises of faith, which our Lord while on earth required of those who received His gifts, under any definition which would give an intelligible account of them all.   Simple taking, as a matter of course, the certainty of what He said, was all the faith that took Peter to seek the tribute-money in the first fish's mouth he caught at Capernaum, and the disciples afterwards to find the colt tied and the man carrying water in the streets of Jerusalem.   Reverential observance of whatever He might direct to be done in a difficulty, without looking for any particular kind of help, was the faith needed on the failure of wine at the Cana marriage, and suggested to the servants by His experienced mother. Thinking of Him as the sure and common Ruler of all things, was the faith He frequently rebuked His disciples for failing in—faith to walk upon the sea—to think of Him as the known Creator of food for thousands.   Assurance of the existence in Him of this authority over all things was the faith not found in Israel, but found in the centurion of Capernaum, before whose eyes Jesus appeared the Master of all the influences of life as entirely and easily as when he, the master of soldiers, was in the way of saying to any one of them, "Do this," and he did it.   Assurance of His having superhuman mercifulness of heart, as well as superhuman power, was the "great" feature in the faith of the Syro-Phœnician mother—a strong vision of His compassionateness that could not be frightened away by sight of trial or discouragement.   Such a beholding, with the ready eyes of the soul, of His characteristic goodness, as a thing above the ways of mankind as heaven is above the earth, was the general feature of the faith of those who came to be healed or saved by Him—the lepers breaking through all the restraints of religious authority to reach Him—mothers bringing their little children to Him—the blind calling after

No single emotion sufficiently descriptive.

Him in spite of all repression—friends of the incurable intruding at all hours, in all places, on all His occupations, with their peculiar distresses. An intense quietly-possessed thought of His peculiar friendship for them—a thought filling their hearts and making much of their life—was the faith that made Martha and Mary send to Him far away beyond Jordan so brief a message, even from their brother's deathbed—"Lord, behold, he whom thou lovest is sick." A thought as entirely possessed — no spasmodic imagination, but an accustomed thought of His almighty power to get help from heaven, if He should ask even a new life for their brother—was quietly spoken by them when Lazarus was dead. Through avenues of personal experience like these, diverse classes of thinkers on Jesus of Nazareth came to be able to think of Him by the description which the prophets had given of the Messiah— "the sent of God," "the one who should come," "bearing our griefs, carrying our sorrows"—the Saviour needed by mankind's life, whose coming should be "glad tidings to the poor." The bitter spiritual experience, the felt needs, of some here and there greater sinners than their brethren, received help to see also the forgiver of sins in Jesus, who was so evidently all else that the Messiah was to be ; and these came to a faith liker the chief Christian looking of faith than the others. Yet *trust* would come short of describing the state of heart of the "woman who was a sinner." Her feeling was an indescribable blessed peace —humility speechlessly thankful—a sense of being safe in Him, restored, healed, received again, God's prodigal child taken home. What was the faith of those persons inscribed in the roll of examples of faith in Hebrews xi.— the individuals we would hardly call religious—Samson and Jephthah, whose names surprise our conventional thoughts to read in the same catalogue with Abraham and Enoch ? We cannot in our thoughts of those men's history associate with their faith the richer moral emotions of Christian or of the best Jewish times. Confined within a half-barbarous state of human life in the oppressed and desperate times of the Judges, their faith seems to have been an intensely present feeling of a personal connection with Israel's Jehovah for a particular end. Jephthah was an appointed wild-handed deliverer of Israel from Ammon, himself liker an Ishmaelite than an Israelite. Samson was the trustee of abnormal strength and intrepidity, to succour the Hebrews under Philistine servitude.

12. A common element of all faith's thoughts and emotions appears, however, in these illustrations of emotional thinking. They all contemplate a person, and are attracted to Him, and are full of Him. Faith does not think of God's power or wisdom, or Christ's miraculous greatness, but of Himself. What is the faith of daily sanctification described by John ? "Who is he that overcometh the world but he that believeth that Jesus Christ is the Son of God ?" What single emotion would we name as representing that believing ? Different from trusting, or loving, or fearing, or hoping, it is a constant sight, and appreciation, and keeping hold of that great fact of our salvation, that our Redeemer, our Friend, He whom we are asked to love with heart and soul, and strength and mind, the speaker of peace to us, the desirous fellow-sufferer of our pains, who was straitened till He should be perfected in the endurance of our burden, is—JESUS THE SON OF GOD—that He is God who thus loved us. To be full of Him, absorbed in Him, taken up with living in Him, for Him, is the state of faith—looking unto Him, abiding in Him, and having His words of love and surety and guidance abiding in us, the Lord alway before us ; all the things He has done from the beginning for us, all the words He has from the beginning spoken to us, coming of themselves into our heart-thoughts, the memories of our day-dreams, the sweet thoughts of the watches of the night. Who shall define or generalise these emotions by any single term that will teach us what faith is ? If we seek for a single descriptive name for all the diverse states of mind exemplified in the history of faith, we can find none by which we may condense our knowledge in a word like trust, or expectation, or hope. We can only give a historical statement. The intellectual phenomenon of faith which observation would always find, is thinking continually of Him in whom we believe. Varying in the lines of their God-uniting thoughts, the historical "men of faith" had Him movingly, constrainingly ever before their

Common elements of faith's thoughts—Contemplation of a person.

eyes ; they endured as seeing Him. The emotional consciousness of faith exhibited in them is love, trust, holy fear, holy
desire, holy aversion and sorrow, in diverse combinations and
varying experience of feeling; no man like his brother, but
all centering their eyes on Him. We read that faith worketh
by love; it purifieth the heart, it overcometh the world ; that
it is the confidence of things hoped for, the evidence of things
not seen; that with the heart man believeth unto righteousness.
But these are exercises of faith, not faith itself; they describe
it each partially, but do not define it. What is the opposite of
an evil heart of unbelief departing from the living God? It
is a heart ever coming near to Him in its feelings, full of Him
.—a heart whose thoughts, intentional or unwatched, and its
emotions, designedly stirred, or the steady under-current of
characteristic feeling, are united to fear Him. "O God, thou
art my God, early will I seek thee ; my soul thirsteth for thee
as in a dry and thirsty land where no water is, to see thy
power and thy glory, as I have seen thee in the sanctuary."
" My soul shall be satisfied as with marrow and fatness . . .
when I remember thee upon my bed, and meditate on thee in
the night-watches " (Ps. lxiii.) This one example taken from
the mass of similar expressions of the historical experience of
faith recorded in the Psalms, shows sufficiently how ill closely-
defining terms could describe its emotional character. Descriptive language of a philosophical kind, even language
unconfined to any selection of merely descriptive words, seems
never to fit truly the free unlimited condition of faith's
thoughts and feelings; and poetical illustration, the suggestions
of metaphor, is constantly taken advantage of to help its
self-expression.

13. One human thing alone is fitted to make faith cognis-
able by the human understanding—one human thing, itself not
a possible subject of definition—the faith of all manner of human relationships, which is revealed to us as being like religious
faith. That faith of human affections is occupied evermore
with thinking of the facts of the believed-in love—in these
facts beholding evermore the beloved *person* — intentionally
musing on *him*, or with the unconscious unindividualising kind

Appreci-
able dis-
tributively
by human
relation-
ships.

of thinking attempted to be described above.   Its desirous
thoughts are chiefly spontaneous, coming in the night-watches
or day-dreams, not needing to be summoned up, coming themselves in comforting, correcting, or sustaining influence in every
hour of need.   One man cannot describe this merely earthly
belief of the heart as another will feel it.   It is indefinable.
It cannot be exhaustively described.   It can only be illustrated.   The child who can remember having no separate life
from his guiding parent—the wife who sits in the light of her
husband's countenance—the brother full of his brother—the
fearlessly fond and clinging sister—the assimilating disciple
—the soldier become veteran under a successful leader—the
friend sticking closer than a brother—the prostrate invalid
growing into life upon the physician's looks and tones—the
recovered prodigal having his comfort and courage suspended
on every trifling word or indication of restored affection,—
these, themselves experienced in that life of the soul which
is characteristically relative, a life in another lived by faith,
can understand each a part, their own rich part, of faith's
emotional thinking, but none of them can as fully understand
any of the others' experience whereby human life illustrates
the life divine.   And all these human lives of faith combined
could but show a portion, though a large one, of the positions
of faith in Jesus—the life lived in the Son of God by the sheep
that know His voice, the sick whom He healeth, the returning
ungodly for whom, when they were without strength, He came
to die, the wearied and heavy-laden drawn to His rest, the
poor in spirit rich in Him, the pure in heart seeing Him, the
hungering after righteousness fed in Him, the suffering for
His sake, the meek, the merciful, the peacemakers—who all
live their peculiar allotted lives by the faith of Him who
loved them and gave Himself for them.

14. If we seek for a general type of faith—a human experi- First use of
ence that comprehends feelings like the essential feeling of "believed
in."
religious faith, which is "peace with God"—we have appropriately enough to go back to the earliest description God's
Word gives of religious faith—that of Abraham, the "friend of
God," "the father of all them that believe."   That type is a hu-

man faith, the practice of which all may *observe*. Of Abraham the phrase is first used, he "believed in the Lord" (Gen. xv. 6). The Hebrew word translated "believed in," constructed then to express for the first time, for man's understanding, that state of the heart's life called faith, means that the patriarch was "supported," "sustained as a child is in conscious repose, felt safety, in its mother's arms." It is this peace that they who are justified by faith now have with God (Rom. v. 1).

Fundamental idea of faith—Consciousness of union. 15. Ideas akin to that original first-chosen representation of the condition of faith—thoughts of secure, happy, upholding union—are what gather about our notion of faith as we try to realise it in the states of mind of many of the recorded saints. Trust, accordingly, represents approximately many of the comforts of faith; but the feeling of union is the essential idea—union with a person, like the unions faith makes in the families of men, spoken of as making one flesh or one heart. It is union of the human being to God; varying from such as that of Samson or Jephthah, which suggests something little above mere covenant union, formal and unassimilating, up through every capable extent of affectional connection whose right progress is unto oneness of nature, a becoming "one spirit with the Lord"—one in clinging, growing into one in kind. It is this kind of union, required and promised by the Lord in the last teaching of His bodily ministry (John xiv.-xvii.), that we realise in the histories of riper faith. Its employments and affections are exactly those of faith's wholly human personal unions. We see human beings with conscious personal needs unknown to any other "resting in the Lord, waiting patiently for Him," "thirsting for Him," "desiring the light of His countenance," their "heart in perfect peace stayed on Him," "looking unto Him, their only portion on earth, all their desire in heaven," "continually with Him, held by His hand," "abiding in Him, and His words abiding in them," "living not themselves, but Christ living in them."

Reverie characteristic of faith's thinking. 16. The form of their thinking of faith is, that they live in reveries of sweet or bitter thoughts upon the things of Christ, —cherished memories of timeous comforts,—fond forelookings, —hiding at times from all eyes, because none could perfectly sympatise with it, their own peculiar gladness or gratefulness or comforted repentance—"a life" of their own "hidden with Him," of which "they *speak to themselves* in psalms and hymns and spiritual songs, singing and making melody in their hearts unto Him" (Ephes. v. 19). The musical expression of faith's thoughts, recognised in these words of Paul, is one of the expansions of Scriptural wisdom beyond mankind's systematic logical wisdom. Human nature also is, in this matter, much wiser than human reasoning. The belief of the heart, belonging to all the dearest human affections, is far oftener sung than said—sung by the heart to itself in the busy solitary times of the day, in many sweet musings and soliloquies — and in the night - watches, when awaking, it delights itself with its cherished thoughts, "filled with them as with marrow and with fatness." The songs of faith of the Hebrew Church were, by their poetical structure, a natural instrument for this recognised propensity of the human heart towards reverie in its indulgence of faith. In their repeating manner the psalmists and those whom they guided in faith seemed to dwell on the cherished thought, as if their heart were singing the glad truth again to itself, loving to taste anew the good word of faith, rolling it as a sweet morsel under its tongue; and the reverie-like chant gave congruous expression to their musing gladness. The prophets—from instruction or their own feeling, it matters not which to our present view—set their richest revealings before the onward-looking Church in this same peculiar poetry of the human heart.*

17. The thinking which makes up the heart-life of a believer Normal and occa-

* The term "faith," applied to the confidence manifested by persons antici- sional pating certain discoveries in earthly knowledge, or the coming of particular states of social or political changes, comes quite within the natural description now faith's given of religious faith. It is a faith that arises in the same way, by rational thinking. conviction being dwelt upon until it comes to possess the mind as a life-ruling thought. The confidence which sustained Columbus on his voyage of discovery, and the forecast, call it sagacity or otherwise, with which anticipators of important changes in society of a different kind have prepared for them, have both arisen from prolonged contemplation of their reasons for the anticipation, as religious faith arises from the same rational contemplation of the different kinds of grounds it has for its realising of things only equally unseen. It is in its characteristic element of spiritual and eternal union with the personal kindred object of its regard that religious faith differs from the other.

in God is this mass of emotional feelings of nearness to Him
and richness in Him, this mass of diversified unarranged
emotions, unarranged as is the happiness of a life of human
union of affection.   Such is the normal state of faith's thinking.   Other moved or moving thinking, producing occasional
effort, and temporary, though for the time ruling, interest, when
faith arises to some special working of love, or purifying of the
heart, or overcoming of the world, marks to observation the
passing of time in the believer's life; and such single thoughts,
having each an individuality of greater or less excitement, impress themselves upon overly observers as if they were all the
materials of his life of faith.   These, however, in a ripe faith
are but like casually awakened strings in a harp, occasional out-
comings of one or another part of the large full harmony that
lies therein.   All the harp's tones also wake up, like those of the
heart, to sweet living sound, though quiet and much unnoticed,
when the strong touch has made one pronounce itself aloud.

A believ-
er's know-
ledge of
his own
believing.

18. The fact that two conditions belong to religious faith—
one normal, in which a multitude of thoughts are harmoniously bringing the comforts of God to the soul ; the other
occasional, when the spirit is turned to some special emotion—
is of consequence in the question of a believer's knowledge of
the history of his own believing.   A man may be able to
assign dates to his strongly-interested, excited, intellectual
dealing with particular doctrines, particular facts of faith, or
moral efforts of faith ; but it is only such strongly individualised thinkings that he can thus set in chronological order.
Much less able, if able at all, a ripe believer may be to set
before himself what time he came habitually to have fond
musings on the things of Christ, sweet thoughts coming of
themselves at any and all times into his mind concerning the
things that have come round about his heart and possessed it
—he can only tell that the habit has come.   It is a thing of
growth almost wholly, this life-filling part of faith.   Wiseness
unto everlasting life implies not merely knowledge of the
holy Scriptures, but a past process of assimilation of that
knowledge, through familiarity of the heart and mind, intercourse of all the soul's sensibilities, with the innumerable

thoughts of our religious condition therein taught us.   That
familiar feeling, recognising, recalling, and applying of revealed
truth, comes by degrees, as different parts of revealed truth
come here a little and there a little to possess the soul after its
possessing them,—become subjective as well as objective.   New
converts, who have been turned from conscious, stubborn, or
violent departure from God to deep impressions, have chiefly
some few strong feelings as their religious experience.   They
are seldom, like older believers, "wise" in the sense of having
easy command, natural hold, of the many-formed truths of
religion, bringing out of its treasures, to guide every hour of
changing circumstances, things new and old.

19. The peculiar nature and form of the subject given to
religious faith was pointed out in Chapter II.; that it is not
all theological truth, systematically arranged in doctrines, but
the history of divine love which surrounds the existence of
man—the truth "that God so loved the world," as it is presented to us in countless forms of facts and promises and suggestive names, all giving assurance of His love, but taking all
manner of ways of manifesting it.   This matter and form of
what faith is to think upon is fitted most entirely to the character of human faith, as we have now tried to describe it from
the experience of human relationships and the language of
recorded believers in God's love—that is, a habitual emotional
thinking on the things and persons believed in.   The mass of
proof which God gives us of His love is altogether beyond our
power to exhaust by classifying into propositions.   It is indescribable.   We are to go on to know its breadth and length,
and depth and height, feeling it a thing which passeth knowledge.   It is fitted only for our rejoicing thoughts to dwell in
as in a habitation, to enjoy as a portion such as the world cannot give nor take away—to be a fulness of joy in which every
endlessly differing need and wish can find its own, and all can
be perfected in happiness, while none knows the things that
another's spirit is fulfilled with.   The believer in all which
God has told and shown us of His saving love from the beginning, realising things and beings and events unseen, lives
and moves and has his being in an atmosphere of important

The subject of faith suited to its manner of thinking.

facts, impulses, suggestions, and associations, all unconformable
to any set form of influencing him. They are living thoughts
that take plastic shape and force from occasion, and could not
be arranged in orderly propositions like the distinctly outlined
physical facts which have but one shape, and are looked at
through undisturbed intellectual sight alone, instead of perpetually disturbed emotional vision. They are thoughts
which, not fitted to be made systematic knowledge of, are
exquisitely fitted to be dwelt amongst, in musing reverie, fond
remembrance, fond forelooking, regretful love, or comforted
self-reproach ; thoughts unspoken and unspeakable mingling
with others universally understood ; thoughts that in their
combinations fill full of satisfaction, peace, and holy desire,
every capacity which the so dissimilar race of man brings to
the contemplation of God.

Spiritual result.
20. Contemplating this state of soul as the gradually-won
belief of the heart which comes with the multitude of the believer's faithful thoughts upon the things of God's love, we
come back to see how the so-called unconscious thinking, with
which we began this attempt to describe the thinking belonging
to faith, is the normal condition of a believing heart, a heart
in harmonious peace stayed on God. We are, however, brought
also to another and completing feature of the mental experience
of faith—one not in strict language part of man's practice of
faith, but in his experience inseparable from his practice of it.
Coincident with the believer's emotional contemplation of God,
a change which we call spiritual comes upon this thinking, feeling part of his being. A clean heart, a new spirit becomes
formed within him. " With open face beholding as in a glass
the glory of the Lord, he is changed into the same image from
glory to glory as by the Spirit of the Lord " (2 Cor. iii. 18).
This change of spirit—the Spirit of Christ, the mind (ways of
thinking and feeling) that was in Him, becoming that also of
His disciple as he is ever looking unto Him—is a change that
crosses the boundary-line of *man's practice* of faith. But that
line cannot be traced ; it does not divide two lives any more
than the boundary of youth and manhood does. In the thinking of faith, the good man's dutiful giving heed to the things

he has heard, his pondering them habitually, and his willing indulgence and desirous cultivation of the emotions proper to them, become crowned with a spiritual power making of these passing emotions an abiding new life of his spirit.   The words hid by him in his heart become the "leaven hid among meal" to his spiritual habits and enjoyments.   The end is to be that "the whole is leavened" in time.   The change thus coincident is co-operative.   Gifts as well as earnings of thought and feeling increase together the treasure of the honest and good man's good things.   God "shines into their hearts who have renounced the hidden things of dishonesty, to give the light of the knowledge of the glory of God in the face of Jesus Christ" (2 Cor. iv. 2, 6) ; "a new man in knowledge being thus formed after the image of Him that created him" (Col. iii. 10).   A Comforter "come unto him," "helps his infirmities," gives him desires, "shows him the things of Christ," guides him "unto all truth."   And so the reward is mixed up with the duty in part, as well as in part reserved for the end of the day of *practice ;* according to the form so distinctly given to the promise of grace, that of talents added to talents well used.   The gift corresponding to a "heart kept with all diligence" is "a heart to know the Lord" and "savour the things that be of God ;" "eyes enlightened to see wondrous things out of God's law," an "unction from the Holy One to know all things."   Spiritual discernment is the divine, the gift-part, of the humanly dutiful exercising of the senses by use to discern good and evil.   So with the *consolations* of the spirit; "In the multitude of my thoughts within me, thy comforts delight my soul."   The child of God is born again of the word (1 Pet. i. 23); which "hid in his heart," "written in his heart," "implanted" in his soul, is "the seed of God within him" (1 John iii. 9).   He receives the spirit of adoption or of sonship, whereby he "crieth to God," "Abba, Father."   The family union is attained of combined affection and nature—the reconciled soul new-made into spiritual fellow-feeling with Him who, "taking up the seed of Abraham" (Heb. ii. 16), humbled Himself to take into His redeeming nature a fellow-feeling of their human infirmities.

CHAPTER VII.

SCRIPTURAL FAITH.—VERIFICATIONS.

HEBREWS vi. 39.—*These all obtained a good report through faith.*

Verification of results.

1. THE subject of this chapter is the verification of the general conclusions as to the nature of faith come to in previous chapters. Incapable of definition, faith is represented in the Scriptures by several generalised descriptions in addition to recorded examples and analogies of familiarly-known faiths belonging to human relationships, with all which those conclusions should agree. The historical matter of faith's thoughts, and the connectional and emotional character of them, will be found amply indicated by those descriptions, examples, and analogies.

Scriptural descriptions of faith

2. The Scriptural invitation to faith, "My son, give me thine heart, and let thine eyes observe my ways" (Prov. xxiii. 26), which contains this generalised idea of faith, is exactly fulfilled by the popular descriptions of faith given in the fullest revelation, that of the New Testament—"With the heart man believeth unto righteousness" (Rom. x. 10); "Faith is the *confidence* of *things* hoped for, the *demonstration* to the soul producing *persuasion* of things unseen" (Heb. xi. 1). Faith is thus a rational contemplation of the history of God's love, producing habitual presence of it to the soul in the form of indescribable diversity of moving thoughts, working by love, purifying the heart, overcoming the world, bringing the heart of the believer to entertain the thought and acquire the persuasion of a personal connection with God, in which God's love, winning his, is to draw him closer and closer to God for

his desired life, and form anew his likings and desires and habits into likeness unto Him.

3. That the subject of faith's thoughts is a history and not a philosophy, is abundantly apparent in the Scriptural examples. It would perhaps surprise inaccurate thinkers to say that believers do not think of the attributes of God but, as the Scriptures tell us, of "His ways." The truth, however, is, that the human mind is not capable of forming definite notions of love, faithfulness, and holiness, as they are in God, infinite, eternal, and unchangeable. We only think of them as they have been experienced by man. We may put abstract statements of His attributes into our formal creeds to make a philosophy, but it is accurate and only truly descriptive to say that a child of God rejoicing to believe in those qualities of his heavenly Father, thinks of them only by thinking of one or more of the facts, the "ways" of God, by which He has shown those moral qualities to human contemplation; and what generalised thoughts or feelings of his Father's care come to possess a child of God, come by much thinking upon the particular manifestations of it. As he has occasion to think again and again and again continually of some new proof of love, a feeling more and more uninterruptedly present is acquired of the so-often seen affection; but still, whenever the heavenly child comes out of that indefinite musing, or less conscious resting in a happy feeling of his Father's love, to think of it distinctly, he comes back like an earthly child to quote to himself some particular things of that love. He returns always to think of illustrations of the attribute, not of the attribute itself. The most comprehensive exercise of trusting faith to which Scripture invites even Christians, and in which the language of creeds doubtless makes them generally think they are having faith in a body of truths, is really a faith thinking, not on any attribute, but on a fact,—"He that spared not His own Son, but delivered Him up for us all, how shall He not with Him also freely give us all things?" (Rom. viii. 32). Patriarchal faith was all of this realistic character. To Enoch God was something of an object of sense more than what we think of as a subject of faith. The large record of Abraham's training

[margin note: historical not philo- sophical thinking.]

to faith exhibits him exercised by the thought of definite facts all along.—(See Genesis xii. 1-3, 7, 10-20; xiii. 14-17; xv., xvii., xviii., xxi.) Jacob's faith, retrospective and forelooking alike, had the same realistic kind of thoughts (Gen. xxxii. 9-12; xlix.) Moses' first faith in Jehovah's grace to his brethren was faith in the God of Abraham and of Isaac and of Jacob, the God of his fathers, a faith resting on the facts of their experience of Jehovah's favour. The faith of the Israelites who came out of Egypt had to begin with the tradition of those patriarchs' experience, and to add thereto the facts of the deliverance and the miracles of the desert. Their creed, when about to terminate their pilgrimage and sit down to serve Jehovah in the Promised Land, was, we may say, the historical book of Deuteronomy. David's faith expressed in the Psalms is constantly associated with historical facts of Israel's or his own history. The faith with which the afflicted sought Jesus' heavenly kindness and help, took its courage and trust from the facts of His grace to others of which they had heard.

Its generalisations in the spirit of particular facts.

4. Generalisations of thought did arise in the experience of the Scriptural believers, but it was to thoughts still of a realistic character. Though mental constitution confined them to contemplate historical illustrations of God's love, their power to imagine and desire and expect future deeds of love was not confined to looking for only a repetition of the matter or the manner of the historical cases they thought upon, but expected in the spirit of them. The Christian text quoted above (Rom. viii. 32) bids the believer, thinking on God's gift of His Son, think freely of all subordinate things—all kinds of overflowings from so great a love; and the believers in the miracles of Jesus could generalise to an upward as well as an outward faith, and expect greater gifts from Him whose superhuman love and power had given them those from which they took courage to believe in Him. "Lord, increase our faith," was a prayer belonging to their practice of faith. The centurion of Capernaum and the Syro-Phœnician mother are remarkable examples of faith reasoning in its heart from impressive facts to greater expectations. But they were realistic expectations— thoughts of desired and needed deeds of love.

Scriptural faith shows us another generalisation serving to the easier practice of faith—the treasuring of thoughts of faith in memorial observances and names; but the thoughts are historical, not philosophical. The Sabbath, the rite of circumcision, the sacred feasts commemorative of Israel's earliest history, and those added in memorial of subsequent events such as the feast of Purim, all became to instructed faith representative facts—facts which brought with them into the mind, affecting the thinking heart, each its own history of Jehovah's love and glory, and of manifestations of His right to Israel's service and faith. The holy names, as has been already noticed (Chap. III.), were, from the time of Abraham, in faith's use concentrations of history. While some, as "Jehovah-jireh," localised materials of faith over the land—lamps of faith drawing the eye to the history of God's love of His chosen people —the great divine names progressively declared were to older Israel helping points of rest for the thoughts of faith; and the last revealed name, "Jehovah," grew during their generations to be the word of faith for all their long history of national mercies, and all the manifestations of His holiness which His saving love had made to them in ever-mingling forms of goodness and severity. To the contemporaries of our Lord the name "Jesus" grew by degrees to be the representative of a mass of facts of grace — a history of well-known manifestations of saving love, inspiring faith in Him for greater things. Believers in the Word of God now inherit all the treasures of faith-giving facts, which the thoughts of the patriarchs grouped around the first names of God—El, El-elohim, Most High God, Lord of heaven and earth, &c.; all that the Jew reading in the Book of the Law and in the Prophets associated with the word Jehovah; all that the men of the fulness of times thought of in Jesus; all that the apostolic age came in progress to be reminded of by the name of the Comforter, the Holy Ghost. Yet when we think on God and the Saviour and the sanctifying Spirit, it is the facts and promises and assurances spreading themselves over man's life, from Adam until the end of the world, that we think of; and we feed thereon our well-grounded faith in the glad tidings, matured in the fulness of times, that

"God so loved the world as to give His only-begotten Son, that whosoever believeth on Him should not perish but have everlasting life." It is by thinking of these human realities— these facts of human religion recorded by divine command— that the writer to the Hebrews (Heb. xii. 1) bids us guide the life of faith now, and get power to "lay aside all superfluous weight, and sin that so easily besets us, and run with patience the race set before us." The "cloud of witnesses," the great examples of faith enumerated in the eleventh chapter, are to be present to the believer's mind "surrounding him"—that is, are to be habitually in his thoughts, and he is to be helped by such thought of them. Helped to do what?—To exercise the like faith — to exert himself looking to the same support. "Looking unto Jesus," with which the writer completes his direction of our faith, is evidently to be a similar habitual thinking of His religious history, the facts of His faith, how He for the "unseen," "hoped-for," heart-believed, definite prospect of "joy set before Him," "endured the cross, despising the shame." The roll of names in Hebrews, chapter xi., is practically an index, slightly annotated, to the whole history of human faith. And to those familiar with the successive passages of that history, from Abel to the tried Jewish believers of latest times, and able from much thinking to call up before the mind the facts written for our learning, each name is to be the call-word, bringing to liveliness the recollection or impression of a whole class of facts of God's ways to individual men, and their faith because of them; something as the successive divine names, El, Elohim, Jehovah, God and Father of our Lord and Saviour Jesus Christ, became to patriarch, Jew, and Christian representative words, each of masses of facts greater or less according to the thinker's knowledge or his capacity for entertaining a multitude of thoughts and their relative comforts.

Standard of faith— that of a little child.

5. Besides their *descriptions* of faith concentrating in an emotional thinking on the facts and ways of God's love, a belief of the heart in things hoped for, seeing them though they be invisible, the Scriptures, in many indirect forms, and also in direct language, give us as the human type of the manner of our right feeling towards God, *the manner of a little child*; that

which was chosen to furnish a word for the name of the first recorded "faith" (Gen. xv. 6). To understand, then, how we are to think of the things of God, we may logically conclude that we should observe how a little child thinks upon the matters of his faith. The faith of little children, being the least distracted by multiplicity of thoughts among all the believings of human relationship, should be an instructive as well as relevant example of what we may practically understand by a human soul having entire belief, conviction, of things hoped for, perfect persuasion of things unseen, and of how it is the heart that such faith hangs by. It is from no persuasion of the intellect, no careful cautious proof of its being safe to confide, that a young child trusts, believes in, has ever before him, the tender, abundant, stable love of his father or his mother, so that he realises, as if he had them already in his hand, the unseen desirable things they have told him of; and he has nothing of indistinctness or indefiniteness in his forelooking to their promises. In the later bonds of friendship, and the ties which begin therewith, we are not surprised at less or more of calculating thought, the deposit of that experience of evil which the human heart cannot avoid wholly, nor perhaps ever escapes some injury from; but such a veil of caution upon the heart of a child would be to every observer as unnatural, and in need of explanation, as the absence of gaiety or of growth. Perhaps it is not going beyond the intention of the Scriptural analogy of faith, if we even think of a man's faith in the unseen things of God as designed to be like the faith which a little child has in such of these same things as he can understand. The idea of another life than this is apprehended by young children. They form notions of God, a yet invisible Being of perfect power and goodness, and of heaven as His dwelling-place and their future home. What is their manner of thinking of these unseen subjects of thought? When they hear of the death of a playmate, or when in mortal illness they are made to comprehend that they are soon to die, and leave their parents and companions, they talk of God, and Jesus, and heaven, and their already departed friends, in the very manner in which

L

grown persons talk of definitely expected persons, places, or possessions, of their worldly prospects. This is, as authoritative examples show, the very kind, and should be the degree, of faith's confidence of things hoped for, and persuasion of things not seen. If it be said that a child's faith is not the faith required of us, which must be a reasoning faith, and not a mere reflection of what we are told, is not the just and instructive answer to this, that the faith of grown persons has, when it is acquired in mature life, to be a reasoning faith, partly because they have to *reason back* over ground which they have lost; having to bring themselves to feel the reality and the importance of the things told them in God's word, by a laborious expulsion of the false impressions, and a difficult victory over the erroneous inclinations, which worldly life, acting upon a fallen nature, has produced within them, antagonistic to the things of God? They have to be "converted, and become as little children." The proper condition of faith, its only healthy state, the attainment therefore which it has to make, is that of being impressed and affected by the things of God as soon as we comprehend them, believing at once, like a child, without any "slowness of heart."

Faith of the "cloud of witnesses." 6. Just such an unhindered realising of the unseen things of God is that exemplified by the "cloud of witnesses." They are shown to us contemplating the different subjects of their faith as matter-of-course realities, they having been promised by God. Their thoughts are not speculative, but definitely expectant. They look for promised events and individuals just as children count upon the promises of their parents, however unconnected they may be with any appearances of their present world of procuring causes. Thus Noah looked forward for a hundred and twenty years to a flood destroying all life on the earth. Abraham left all, to be a pilgrim looking to the five hundred years distant inheritance; through the seed, first improbable (Gen. xviii.), next impossible (chap. xxii.) So Isaac contemplated the distinct earthly futures of his two sons; Jacob the political fortunes of the yet unborn tribes his sons were to found; and Joseph looked on through four centuries to the Exodus, and the interment of his bones in the promised land. With such simplicity of faith did Moses and Joshua and the Judges expect—what their eyes never were to see—particular events of the deliverance and subsequent progress of Israel towards the possession of Canaan. The martyrs refused deliverance from their terrible sufferings, at the price of apostasy, looking with undoubting expectation to their rising from the dead to a better life.

7. A feature of entirely childlike faith, showing the most concentrated form of realising, presents itself in some of the recorded cases ; that of contemplating not only the actual, distinct existence of the believed-in things, but the believer's own personal connection with them—a connection, persuasion, feeling, or whatever it may be named, of personal union of some one kind or another with a personally conceived God—a God of distinct historical position and affections. What more impresses itself on the imagination in realising Noah's feelings, as the hundred years passed on fruitless of any result to his warnings, than that his soul must have had a growing sense of becoming alone with God on the earth—passing from connection of being or life with all of mankind into union with God alone, his hiding-place in the coming storm, the Lord and the salvation of his obedient soul? Moses' isolation in the centre of the Egyptian court, in the solitudes of Horeb, and in the camp of the murmuring people, is similarly a dark background on which stands out his true life of conscious supporting union with Jehovah, whose servant, spoken with face to face, he was. Perhaps that union of faith is most instructively recognisable in Abraham's going forth from his country and from his father's house to his announced life of a stranger with God in the world—looking through five hundred years to the nearest rest promised for his seed in the land to which he went ; and rest in God alone for him and his descendants until then. Yet more impressive is the conscious separation from all human life and all earthly good, and union to God alone in possible life afterwards, that we must read in his going forth to the terrible three days' journey, to leave his only child, his unsuspecting son, the heir of the promises, dead on the lonely mountain even at God's command. The sense of such union of affection and support

Child-faith in a personal connection.

and spirit is the fundamental idea put into our imagination of
Enoch's life by his walking with God and disappearing from
earthly scenes, "because God took him." Have we not the
same picture of Abel thinking not of right service or reasonable sacrifice, or of judging for himself at all, but of God's
will as all he had to think about or look to? The faith of
Jephthah and Samson and Barak and Gideon, it has been
already suggested, was an impelling and upholding feeling of a
personal connection with Jehovah for a definite purpose. The
faith with which we are to think of the origin of the worlds,
the first illustration given in Hebrews xi., has for its central
thought this union of our very existence with God by the
most intimate connection of creation — the thought that our
visible being and all the worlds that surround our observant
reasoning life were called out of the unseen by His word.
This same element of union, theoretically the centre thought
of Christian faith, whose symbols are the union of the newborn
babe hungering for its pure milk, the union of branch with tree
grown or engrafted—this union by relationship, adoption, and
new creation, whose closeness of connection is likened to that
of the divine Father and Son—we find the centre thought of
Paul's faith, in which he says, "For me to live is Christ;" "I
live, yet not I, but Christ liveth in me "—" Christ formed within you," "dwelling in your hearts by faith."

Emotion in Scriptural faith.

8. The emotional element of faith, inferred from Scripture
language and the analogy of human life, is very distinctly seen in
the Scriptural examples—the believing with the heart. What
place are we to expect to find emotion holding relative to reasoning in Scriptural faith, considering the analogy of human
affections given to guide us in understanding what faith is?
We have considered one aspect, the simplicity, of the primordial
least fallen faith of human relationships—that of little children:
how their faith follows immediately upon the little reasoning
that is needed to set the authority of their believed-in facts before them. A higher instrumentality, however, than reason, produces much of that faith. Certainly children do not rely upon the
constant care of their parents, because they reason with themselves that it is safe to confide. But take, as more relevant to

reasoning faith, cases of affection in mature life—life burdened with disturbing experience, bringing on slowness of heart to believe. It is not a laboured proof that our friend is true which at any trying time makes us turn to him in faith for relief. A wife does not day by day formally think over the moral securities she has for her husband's affection. The faith has another hold besides intellectual argument. In many cases reason has in previous experience, with differing celerity of thought, and therefore of consciousness, gone through its diverse tasks of considering the permanency or the guarantees of the faithfulness of the trusted ones, but the amount of evidence sought has been exceedingly various; and after an experience which the heart more than the mind has felt sufficient, the heart takes to itself this work of inference, and waits not for the steps reason would have to take; and it overrules the temporary difficulties which bare reasoning stumbles at, by some indescribable means—perhaps by the unconscious rapid use of former experiences, or abiding feelings which they have left behind them, but evidently sometimes, as in the case of children, by something which is not the fruit of experience.

9. Just such a process of the heart's quick feeling and acting, not upheld by immediate reason, and refusing to be hindered by it, is what we read of in Scriptural examples. An early instance is Abraham's intercession for Sodom (Gen. xviii. 17-33). The temerity of that prayer makes the flesh thrill as we read on its encroaching and encroaching petitions. A strong heart, holding fast its sureness of Jehovah's exceeding great merciful love to man, must have repeatedly put down the fear which reason cannot but have forced up in the man's heart, speaking as Abraham spake on that day to God. We can see this thrice at least in the language of verses 30, 31, and 32. What but a *belief of the heart* in Jehovah's faithful promise, rising above all the disabilities of reasoning—hoping more than against hope—against seeming possibility—led the patriarch afterwards out those three long days of tried faith to burn in sacrifice to Jehovah the childless son by whom He had promised him to be the father of many nations? Through what fearful conflict of reasoning must his heart-faith in Jeho-

Examples of belief with the heart.

vah's perfection of holiness and love and wisdom have trodden its way, as with garments rolled in blood, to be able to believe that he could have heard aright the command to offer to Him a human sacrifice—that He, the God of goodness, would have commanded him to kill his own son as a service to Him! When the father could rise up from his vision to do it, and that not in an instant of terrible ecstasy, but having to contemplate it during the journey of three days, with his son by his side, questioning him in his ignorance, " Where is the lamb for the burnt-offering ? " what clinging to the Invisible, whom he had once seen face to face, must have sustained his pierced and bleeding but not blinded heart in that dark treading of the wine-press alone! Job's exclamation of faith in the sure faithfulness of God, who knew his heart, " Though He slay me, I will trust in Him," was a protest of the heart against all the human reasonings of his friends upon what man for his deservings should expect from God. Reasoning on the case before him should have deterred Moses from more than one of his intercessions in the wilderness for the backsliding people ; which yet he made with a strength of heart-trust, a boldness like that of a child or servant who cannot offend, which was well-pleasing to Jehovah. The language of faith to be read in the Psalms so generally is the language of reasoning, but of reasonings which are the heart's own combinations. " Thy love is better than life, therefore shall my lips praise thee." " Thy loving-kindness is before mine eyes, and I have walked in thy truth." " Thou art *my* God," is the expression of one who has come nearer to God than bare argument could come. " When my father and my mother forsake me, then the Lord will take me up," is an assured faith anticipating the grace described in Isaiah's promise, " Can a mother forget her sucking child . . . she may forget, yet will I not forget thee," but one as clearly beyond the merely rational inferences which best human affection can exercise. The 91st Psalm gives a picture of faith in God's providence, which goes forth beyond all the bounds which the expectations of mere intellect would see—with a freedom of expectation, an uncontrolled consigning of the form of desired good to God's wise love which belongs only to the heart's unconditioning confidence in the love and loving choice of those whose favour, and not their gifts, is its life. The longest of the Psalms is a large diversified informal communing, fitting either a wise or a wayfaring man, of the experience of a life of faith—the heart living with God in a union of dependence, confidence, desire, sufficiency, oneness of spirit, likest of all things to the Christian formula of faith, "Abide in me, and let my words abide in you."

It is in the case of God's nearest manifestation of love, which came close to mankind's sight and touch in a human life like the love of body and soul and spirit of one of their own kind, that we should most expect to see instances of this belief of the heart absorbing and subordinating the slower insight of man's intellect; and the expectation will not be disappointed. Such was generally the faith of those who sought Jesus' miracles. It was a faith which intruded beyond the warrant of precedents, and persevered in beseeching Him through the discouragement of great difficulties and against the opposition of those most likely to make the suppliants fear refusal. Two examples, however, are eminently illustrative : those of the Syrophœnician woman and the sisters of Lazarus. For some reason unexplained, but resulting in priceless encouragement to all after-times, it was His purpose to try the faith of the heathen mother by all the discouragements which reason or sympathy could well bring upon her ; but the trial served well to illustrate for our help how the belief of the heart is to hope against hope, and say, "Though He slay me, I will trust in Him," clinging to His loving-kindness against all mere reasonable representations of want of warrant to trust, or even appearance of designed refusal. Matthew gives the story most fully (chap. xv. 21-28). Her maternal affection, tried by her daughter's agonies under demoniacal possession, having to turn from all hope of relief by ordinary human means as vain, had been drawn or driven to think strongly upon accounts, that had travelled across the borders of Galilee into Tyre, of a Jew who was doing miracles of kindest healing to all in Judæa and Samaria and Galilee. She knew how every Jew held her race, and all but the worshippers of Jehovah at Jerusalem, in despite or

worse aversion, and would refuse to show kindness to any such
as she was; but she believed, or it was borne in upon her heart,
that He who could do what she had heard of, could she but
come to His presence, would be greater in His compassion than
those thoughts of man, however inveterate or reasonable.   She
had, with the quick learning of the needy hearing of a deliverer,
heard of the divine character or mission of " the Son of David,"
the title by which some receivers of His greatest miracles had
called upon Him, and she came to Him appealing to Him by the
name of promise, " Have mercy upon me, O Lord, thou Son
of David; my daughter is grievously vexed with a devil."
Perhaps the very fact of His entering or so nearly entering the
heathen land, though so privately as it was, gave her courage
of heart (perhaps it was so meant) to rise up when she heard of
it and go to Him.   If it did, her heart must have been thrown
back into the chill pain that comes with disappointment when
it aggravates the desolation of helpless suffering, relief from
which was looked for.   The Being whom she heard of as sympathy itself—He who was spoken of everywhere as the healer
of all, the comforter who never refused comfort—answered *her*
not a word, but seems to have turned and walked away from
her.   His strange disregard of her anguished cry, a disregard
so pointed and so different from all that He had ever shown to
others, would have killed all merely reasoning hope.   Hers
must have been a " hope against hope;" she clung to her prayer
and to Him.   Her evident condition of misery affected the
disciples, who on other occasions repeatedly manifested no
overflowing sympathy for distress; or they may have wished to
get rid of her importunity; and even against His manifest
turning away His ear from her petition they came to plead for
her.   " They came to Him and besought Him, saying, Send
her away, for she crieth after us."   When they received the
answer for her, more forbidding than that strange disregard, " I
am not sent but to the lost sheep of Israel," it silenced them,
if it was in compassion that they spoke, but her hope would not
be put to death.   She must have seen their blank look of surprise—theirs who knew Him, and could judge what approach
could be made to Him.   Her heart held fast by what she had

heard of His sympathy, and it arose to beseech Him only the more vehemently. She had probably been, after her first paralysing shock, halting behind, only crying forth her heavy-laden prayer. She came up again after them to His presence, and prostrated herself before Him, saying, "Lord, help me." Sore beyond mere reason's power to bear up under was the answer that she was to get when He at last spoke directly to herself, but spoke in words so terribly different in spirit from all she had ever heard of the healer and consoler. "He answered her and said, It is not meet to take the children's bread and to cast it to dogs." What words could like these crush a soul that could only reason with itself? And it was not the answer of reason that she gave, but a true device of the heart, at once going round about all the difficulties of reason with some happy taking hold of a word let fall by the besought and trusted though refusing One. "Truth, Lord," she said, "for it is the crumbs the dogs eat, which fall from the master's table." He tried her no farther. He stopped the revealing discipline of heart which brought her, the first fruits of the Gentile world, to look so closely on Him, and know what faith she could have in Him, and He said to her, "O woman, great is thy faith; be it unto thee even as thou wilt." The belief of the heart which appeared in the sisters of Lazarus was of a different type. It was not a newborn inspiration, rising in an hour when sore need and unlooked-for opportunity met, and making fast quick use of tidings of Jesus' widely exercised power and compassion to encourage the helpless heart to come to Him for help. Theirs was a faith which had settled itself down in their hearts during many months of a strange happiness they had passed through in intercourse with His more than earthly wisdom and attractiveness. It was a faith that did not speak much except within, but it sat much at His feet to listen to Him, or took itself up with ministering to Him in silent service and honouring, and did not express in words their necessities or their strong desires to Him, even in the time of utmost need, feeling that He would know and would do all that love should. When death was approaching their brother, they sought the help of their friend by this message only, "Lord, behold, he whom thou lovest is sick." No word of complaint or request they sent from Bethany thirty miles beyond Jordan, where He was sojourning, sure that that message would bring Him who loved Lazarus. This faith in His readiness of affection was tried by seeming neglect. "Jesus abode three days in the place where He was," and death, and even the grave, held their brother before his friend arose to go to Bethany. Yet behold how the silent heart of each held fast its faith in Him, and questioned not why He had not come to save, but, even with the forbidding hand of death holding back all reason's power to hope, still spoke to itself of His love and His power. "Lord, if thou hadst been here my brother had not died," was the thought that still filled their hearts. It was all that Martha said, when, hearing that He was come, she went out to meet Him, leaving her younger grief-oppressed sister with their kind neighbours in the house; and when they came to bid Mary go out to Him, she spoke to Him but the same words, "Lord, if thou hadst been here my brother had not died." How true heart-words were those words of undefining petition, unprescribing trust—trust even when He *did* slay instead of healing! Other words were to follow, how high above all the courage of reasoning, yet a pure reasoning; only one of the heart cleaving to God as a little child's heart, not of the mind building for itself hopes whose growth men would recognise. Lazarus was in the grave four days. Martha herself had realised and spoken of the dissolution then certainly reducing his body to corruption, *yet* she added the words—indefinite and meaningless to rational thought alone, but how full of meaning as the words of her clinging to Jesus for help, she knew not of what kind, a faith startlingly marvellous when interpreted by the result—"But even now I know that whatsoever thou shalt ask of God, God will give it thee." He answered the unexpressed but understood appeal of the heart's faith—which was one surely called forth by His own Spirit savingly communing with her spirit, and helping her infirmity so to believe in His divine power and grace—with the promise, "Thy brother shall rise again." Her faith was but partly de-

finite, partly grasped with conscious firmness ; and true to all
human nature's experience of infirmity in the emotions of its
faith, she began immediately to shrink from laying hold of the
definite blessing, and to put it far off to the time of all the
bereaved's blessedness. "I know that he shall rise again at
the resurrection, at the last day." But her soul, though she
knew it not, was ready to receive all; and He that was mighty
to save strengthened her with the reproach of love wherewith
God and man, God's child, alike strengthen failing faith. "Said
I not unto thee, that if thou wouldst believe thou shouldst see
the glory of God ?" "I am the resurrection and the life: he
that believeth in me, though he be dead, shall live ; and he
that liveth and believeth in me shall never die. Believest thou
this ? And she said, Yea, Lord, I believe that thou art the
Christ, the Son of God, which should come into the world."

10. The verification of the conclusions come to in Chapters Completed
II., V., and VI., by comparison with recorded examples, which faith.
has now been hastily gone over in the histories of patriarchal
and Hebrew faith, and faith in the visible Saviour, should be
practicable in the case of Christian faith, the completed religious faith which contemplates Christ no longer seen. The
faith accordingly which we can see in the disciples after He
had "gone away," and the faith which they direct in all who
believe through their word, is one, the elements of which are
those above described—a thinking of facts belonging to the
personal history of God manifest in flesh; realising "things"
now that they are no longer seen, things of performance or
promise or manifestation of character ; and thinking on them
with a reasoning which is not of the intellect alone, but of the
heart. His own direction to man's faith was, "Abide in me,
and I in you." Who was the "I" and the "me"? Necessarily
that very Jesus whom the writers of the Gospels knew by face
and voice and manner of affection and behaviour to them—the
Jesus we know "by their words," that personal uniquely individual Redeemer, the Son of God become for our sakes the Son
of man—the human-hearted Messiah who grew up from a
human infancy in our sight in favour with God and with man.
It can be no indefinite Godhead set before our conception by

reasoning on doctrinal attributes, but the Jesus of history, the Jesus of fulfilled prophecy, of minute biography, and of a definitely promised future. "To have Him ever before us," to "endure as seeing Him, now He is invisible," is to have in habitual, most facile, or rather haunting remembrance, a history—a mass of illustrations of personal qualities and relative affections; words of grace and truth; miraculous helps of all temporal needs, typical of awaiting spiritual and eternal salvations—a mass of divine facts become human, which the heart fuses into a beloved portrait, which it can fill up with affecting details on the call of any individual need or desire of faith faster than the unmoved intellect. What is it to have "Christ dwelling in our hearts by faith," "formed in us," "in us, the hope of glory," when the Spirit has glorified Him by taking of His and showing unto us? What Christ can be in us but the historical Jesus of Nazareth, whom alone we have been taught—God manifest in flesh, distinctly realised from the words of those who companied with Him; realised, and, though yet unseen by us, ready to be recognised; an individual being surrounded with distinct facts of hope, which are to be inherited *jointly with Him*, in "*union*" with *Him*, in a *place prepared for us by Him*, in His and our Father's house, a divine and human heaven, clearly described in outline to us in Heb. xii.? What is it in the mean time to "believe on Him, and not let our heart be troubled"?—the direction He gave at the end of His familiarly-known human life (John xiv. 1). He explained immediately that to know Him was to know the invisible Father, and that they should have known Him in the long time He had been with them. To "believe in" Him thus now must be to think of Him in terms of the Gospel narratives of His sayings and deeds; to think with heart-assuring thoughts of His definite help, of no general but particular perfectly instructed sympathy in any class of troubles from without, and in any fears from within, arising from sinless weaknesses—the help and sympathy brought recognisably to faith's sight by facts of His sufferings, tribulations, and weaknesses of the same kind. Paul's new life was lived by this historically-instructed faith (Gal. ii. 20), a faith holding fast a per-

sonal union with Christ the Son of God, who loved him and
gave Himself for him. The historical love of Christ constrained him to live unto Him (2 Cor. v. 15)—Him realised in
a particular manner, Him "who died for us and rose again."
Peter exhibits to us faith advancing on the path of holiness to
heaven in constant sight of the historical Jesus—Jesus of
a past and of a future alike definite. "Whom having not seen
ye love; in whom, though now ye see Him not, yet believing,
ye rejoice with joy unspeakable and full of glory, receiving
the end of your faith, the salvation of your souls" (1 Pet. i. 8-9).
"Through the knowledge of Him who hath called us to glory
and virtue . . . are given unto us exceeding great and precious
promises, that by these ye might be partakers of the divine
nature, having escaped the corruption that is in the world
through lust" (2 Pet. i. 4). John's thoughts were heart-
rejoicing thoughts of closest relationship, that of "sons" to
God, the future gloriousness of which was not yet conceivable
by him, but was all embraced in promised closeness of place
and nature to the personal Jesus, whose beloved disciple he
had been. "We shall be like Him, for we shall see Him as
He is; and every man that hath this hope in him purifieth
himself, even as He is pure" (1 John iii. 2-3).

11. A verifying illustration by Scriptural language, doctrinal
or practical, of more minute parts of the process of faith, has
been interspersed in the foregoing chapters. Let the following
short consecutive comparison be added. *Verification of the process of believing.*

12. The first step of faith in the things of God—viz., arrested
attention leading to remembrance, consideration, and intellectual conviction—was the reason of Jehovah's "getting Himself
honour upon Pharaoh," and of the systematic providence by
which He afterwards made "the nations know themselves to
be but men," and acknowledge that there is a God that
"judgeth on the earth." Israel's shortcoming in this readiness
of perception or remembrance was reproached as *unbelief*
throughout their early history; *e.g.*, Deut. i. 32, Ps. lxxviii.
22, 32, and Ps. cvi. 24. In the New Testament it is the
explanation of Paul's words (1 Cor. xiv. 22), "Tongues are
for a sign, not to them which believe, but to them which *Arrested attention.*

believe not;" and of the wayside hearers' failing to attain
the faith that cometh by hearing (Mat. xiii. 19). In our
Lord's language "little faith" meant want of observation
(Mat. xvi. 9), and want of consideration (Mat. viii. 26).

Thinking on facts.

13. That the intellectual process of the believer's acquiring
faith is his own thinking upon facts of God's love, universal,
national, or personal, appears universally in the Psalms, the
fullest Scriptural collection of examples of the practice of
faith, and in Paul's chosen illustrations of faith in Heb. xi.
The "faith of God's elect" (Titus i. 1), the "faith delivered
to the saints" (Jude 3-7), the faith preached by Stephen to
the Jewish court (Acts vii.), and by Paul to the synagogues
and his Greek audiences, was essentially bodies of definite
facts.

Impression, appreciation, recognition.

14. The proper result of contemplating the things of God—
viz., impression, appreciation of their character and importance,
and recognition of their affinity to man's conscious condition
—is the meaning of faith widely in the Scriptures, Gen. xlv.
26; Isa. liii. 1-3; 2 Kings xvii. 14; Jonah iii. 5; Luke v.
19; John ii. 11, iii. 18, iv. 50, v. 46, vii. 48, viii. 24, 32,
xi. 45; 2 Tim. ii. 13. Unseeing eyes, unhearing ears, hearts
that could not be impressed, was the prophesied unbelief of
the Jews (Mat. xiii. 14), and that condemned in heathens
(Rom. i. 20). The unbelief of Aaron and Moses at the rock
(Num. xx. 12) was failure to appreciate the honour due to
Jehovah in their action. The unbelief of the Lord's brethren
(John vii. 5) and of the Pharisees (v. 38-47) was not recognising His divine character; the cause in the Pharisees being
that their minds did not value His Father's praise, but were
engrossed by desire for honour from man. Nicodemus's failure
in faith was failure to recognise Jesus' description of the
motions of the Spirit, which He called earthly things, rudimentary matters of spiritual perception. Extensively in John's
writings faith includes recognition of the congruity of the
things revealed with man's conscious condition. The Psalms
largely illustrate the same condition of faith. They are rich
in the language of affinity, attraction, appropriation. "My
God"—"my portion"—"my soul thirsteth for Thee"—"in

the multitude of my thoughts within me Thy comforts delight my soul." The necessity of subjective preparation to recognise divine truth is systematically taught in the New Testament— by our Lord, John iii. 19, 20 ;—by Paul, requiring believers to be "rooted and grounded in love" in order to study success- fully God's love, the subject of faith (Eph. iii. 17), and associ- ating real "unfeigned faith" with a "pure heart and a good conscience" (1 Tim. i. 5) ; and assigning as the reason of the Jews' failure to "profit by hearing the word of God," that they were not "mixed with those that hear it," *i.e.*, not in spiritual affinity with the whole body of the children of God, an exact description of the Jews' proud, conceited separatism, their national sin and stumbling-block (Heb. iv. 2) ;—by James (ii. 22), describing Abraham's faith as being perfected, exer- cised, disciplined to perfectness, by his faithfulness, "his works." Compare 2 Thess. ii. 10 and Rom. i. 17-21 for spiritual affinity associated with belief and unbelief.

15. The intercourse of the heart implied in this spiritual attraction to the matters of faith's intellectual contemplation —the possession of the thinker's heart by these, filling it with consciousness that comes in emotional reveries, accesses of in- tense thought, musings not always conscious, so making a hid- den life within the life which is visible to others, a life only sometimes impressing its existence upon observers—appears very much in the Psalms ; *e.g.*, Ps. xxiii., xxiv., xxx., xlii., li., xxxiv. 8, lxxiii. 23-28, cxii. 1, 4, 7. Isaiah describes richly this life of the heart in God in his twenty-sixth chapter. In apostolic descriptions believing "fills the believer with peace and joy" (Rom. xv. 13). It is a reasoning of the heart (Rom. x. 10), an admiring contemplation (2 Thess. i. 10), making riches of inward enjoyment (2 Cor. iv. 6-15, James ii. 5), in which the heart "sings to itself of its happiness, and makes melody to the Lord" (Eph. v. 19). *[Thinking with the heart.]*

16. The idea inseparable from faith's being a thinking of the heart upon the things of God—that it is characteristically not an act, but a state of the believer's spirit—is included in faith's expressions in a great mass of cases throughout the Psalms, and in the subjective notices of it in the New Testa- *[Faith not an act, but a state of spirit;]*

ment; *e.g.*, 1 John iii. 24; 2 Cor. v. 5-8. The key-note of Christian exhortation to faith is, "Abide in Me, and I in you:" "if a man abide not in Me, he is cast forth as a branch, and is withered" (John xv. 4-6). It is called the "work" of God (John vi. 29), the business God gives to man's life, man's occupation in serving Him, the habit of all religious life—"we walk by faith, not by sight" (2 Cor. v. 7). It is an essentially self-developing thing, habitual thoughts going out into virtue, and that into inquiry, &c. (2 Pet. i. 5-9). It is a "patient work" (Jas. i. 3), a process of overcoming "the world" (2 John v. 4), an acquisition of which good men are "full," as were Stephen and Barnabas; and men fail in from having "no root in themselves" (Matt. xiii. 21); a thing in which they must be "settled," "established," not "going back" (Heb. x. 38, 39). The faith of the Thessalonians and the Romans, which became famed abroad among the churches, must have been a condition abiding enough to be well recognised.

dealing with definite thoughts and indefinite trust.

17. That the condition of believing — the "thinking" of faith—deals with all manner of definite remembrances and anticipations, and also with an indefinite mass of thoughts producing a state of peace properly called "trust" in God (Isa. xvi. 3), is abundantly verified in Scripture. Hebrews xi. is a catalogue of cases of faith having specific objects. This was the faith generally required by Jesus from the receivers of His miraculous healings. Christian faith has to contemplate a definite prospect of resurrection, and heavenly life, and sanctifying help from God fitted to individual needs. Indefinite trust, for felt or foreseen occasions of need, placed in a definitely realised Person, the Lord Jehovah their strength and song, and ever becoming their salvation, was the common complexion of the Old Testament saints' language of faith; Ps. xxvii. 13, xxxvii. 5, xl. 4, lxxi. 5, cxli. 8; Isa. xii. 2; Dan. vi. 23; Hab. iii. 17-19. It was such faith as Jesus, in John xiv. 1, makes faith in Him now to be—which is to be trust in a definite forgiveness (Gal. iii. 22), and trust for all special supplications (John xiv. 13), but also for all watchful care (John xiv. 18; 2 Tim. i. 12; 1 Pet. iv. 19), beyond what the truster can ask or is able to think of definitely (Eph. iii. 20).

18. Diversity in attainment, capacity, and matter of most Diversity
in matter
and manner
of thought. frequent contemplation, which should appear in the thinking of faith since it comprehends special trusts, and an indefinite state of peace and joy in God, nurtured by endlessly different exercises, is amply recognised in Scripture language ; *e. g.,* Paul's picture of the human and divine education of faith (Eph. iii. 16-19), his "helping" of the Corinthians' faith (2 Cor. i. 24, x. 15), his language about the "weak in faith" (Rom. xiv. 1) contrasted with those of comprehensive faith (Rom. xiv. 22 and 1 Tim. iv. 3), about the "strong in faith," the "steadfast," the "established" in faith, the "proportion of faith" possessed by prophesiers or teachers (Rom. xii. 6). Diversity of ruling thought is the connecting link of Heb. xi., and of many trusts, all called by the one name of faith, which our Lord required or recognised in the objects of His miracles. The spiritual "gift" of faith is classed among gifts whose prominent characteristic is diversity (1 Cor. xii. 9).

19. The divine operation in the production of faith is doc- Divine
operation. trinally taught in, *e.g.,* 2 Thess. i. 11 and ii. 17, *contra* ii. 11 ; in the rich description in Eph. i. 17, ii. 10 ; a help corresponding to man's progress of acquired capacity—" from faith to faith" (Rom. i. 17). It is necessarily to be inferred from the universal connection of faith with the "Word of God," its " coming by" hearing the Word of God (Rom. x. 17), the "word dwelling richly" in the believer (Col. iii. 16), "incorruptible seed" of which he is "born again" (1 Pet. i. 23), "working effectually in them that believe" (1 Thess. ii. 13); from the purpose of "the law" (Gal. iii. 23), and from our Lord's requirements as to His own "words" (John xv. 7, xiv. 26, xvii. 8, &c.) The Psalms largely illustrate this feature of the practice of faith, the experience of divine co-operation. The common subject of the longest of them is the believer's habit of seeking faith by the Word of God, and God teaching it to man's spirit.

20. The beginning and the end of the education of faith, Conscious
connection. what may be in general terms called a consciousness of connection with God—a connection of our being and our life of soul with God, apprehended through all kinds of welcome and

M

unwelcome consciousness—is an idea declared in much of the most authoritative—*i.e.*, the directly divine—language of the Scriptures respecting faith, and is the element which gives a uniting meaning, a common character, to all cases of faith, whether destructive or productive of peace, as the believing of devils (James ii. 19), the terrors of guilty men (Rev. vi. 16), and the comfort of habitual trust (Ps. lxxiii. 23). The conscious connection is illustrated in all diversities up to spiritual union. In unwelcome faith, the feeling of connection with the dreaded object was exemplified by Pharaoh and the hostile nations of Canaan. A connection of direct help, or infused power for a special purpose, is the faith we must recognise Samson and Jephthah to have been conscious of. The power of working miracles (Matt. xvii. 20, xxi. 21) comprehended a similar manner of faith, sometimes but not always associated with a higher spiritual condition of heart (1 Cor. xiii. 2). Associated with a higher moral subjective, faith exhibits the consciousness of a union of sympathy in such cases as Mark v. 36, Matt. ix. 21. The fact of such a connection of sympathetic dependence on the one side and support on the other is the truth taught by the metaphors of the vine and its branches, the olive and its ingrafted bough, the body fitly framed making increase together, the living stones of the building of which Christ is the chief corner-stone. The consciousness of such a union is the lesson contained in the metaphors of human relationship, original and adopted, and especially in the metaphor of the sucking child (1 Pet. ii. 2). The believer's consciousness of such a sympathetic union with the head and the body of Christ is necessary to make intelligible our Lord's principal discourse on His people's connection with Him (John xiv.), which, however, it fills with rich and appreciated meaning. It is the interpreting idea required by John's first epistle; by all the didactic or illustrative language respecting Christ in the believer with which Paul's writings abound—*e.g.*, 2 Cor. xiii. 5 and Col. ii. 6-10 ; and by all the language of reciprocity which distinguishes the Scriptures' manner of speaking of the believer's connection with God. The fact that the word for " faith " has also the import of " faithfulness," is illustrative of

the manner of all the affections of the divine life; which are
essentially affections not bestowed or received as between beings
distinctly separated and independent, but interchanged, and
needed to be so on both sides, as the enjoyment and support
of a natural union which cannot be broken or intermitted but
with suffering. A union that must be conscious pervades
Col. i. and ii. It is spoken of expressively in Paul's experience (Gal. ii. 20): "I live; yet not I, but Christ liveth in
me: and the life that I now live in the flesh I live" (not in
the flesh anxiously given up to, having my conversation in, the
things of the flesh, but) "in the faith of the Son of God, who
loved me, and gave Himself for me" (consciously enjoying,
given up to, the pleasure and security of His love and saving
help).—Compare 1 Pet. i. 8, 2 Cor. v. 5-8, Phil. i. 6, Ps. lxiii.,
Jude 19-25. Less definitely reasoning, but strongly sympathetic, consciousness of the need and sufficiency of union to
Jesus was the faith of two widely different cases among His
personal followers (Mat. ix. 21, Luke vii. 38). James (i. 6)
seems to make the union of conscious dependence essential to
the prayer of faith. Paul (2 Cor. x. 5) sets it forth as the true
condition of a hearer. In Heb. iv. 2 he makes conscious union
with the body of believers—being of one heart and sympathy
with them—essential to profiting by the word of faith.—Compare Eph. iv. 11-13. The reader of the Psalms will recognise
this consciousness of connective sympathy, appropriate dependence, reciprocal possession, relational oneness, spiritual
assimilation, richly characterising their subjective language.

The fact which is contained in this consciousness, that religious faith contemplates one object continually—a person
whom it thinks of directly in connection with all the facts of
religious fear and love and salvation—a person who has been
in this manner the object of all religious faith from the beginning of revelation—will be considered in the next chapter.

CHAPTER VIII.

THE OBJECT OF FAITH.

JOHN viii. 58.—Before Abraham was, I am.

LUKE xxiv. 27.—Beginning at Moses and the prophets, He expounded unto them the things concerning Himself.

ACTS i. 11.—This same Jesus shall so come in like manner as ye have seen Him go into heaven.

HEB. xiii. 8.—Jesus Christ the same yesterday, to-day, and for ever.

The same person the Object of the faiths of all times.

1. THE subject of faith is, " God so loved the world." The fact given to be thought of as proving and showing forth that great love is, that " He gave His only-begotten Son, that whosoever believeth in Him should not perish, but have everlasting life" (John iii. 16). That fact, looked forward to, beheld, and looked back upon, has been the matter of faith's thoughts from the beginning of God's love being revealed ; and so it comes to pass, that to all positions from which mankind have looked unto God's love, the object that has been always before them has been, is, and will be, He whom we now think of as Jesus. When the patriarchs thought of the great promises, they " saw His day and were glad" (John viii. 56), and "esteemed the reproach of Christ greater riches than all the treasures of Egypt" (Heb. xi. 26). When the men of " the fulness of times" looked upon the work of redeeming love, they beheld "Him that was to come"—Christ the power of God and the wisdom of God unto salvation, and who was " to come again," " this same Jesus," to " receive them unto Himself." When Christians look back or forward upon the ways of God with man, thinking upon the work of mercy and salvation from the promise of the seed of the woman to the preparing of the house of many mansions,

it is the same being of love who went about doing good among the generation of the fulness of times that they see from the beginning to the endless end, showing and promising redeeming love to Adam's race. The " same yesterday, to-day, and for ever" (Heb. xiii. 8), it was He, " the only-begotten Son, who is in the bosom of the Father," that " declared " the Father to every period of fallen man's hearing the glad tidings as well as to the Jews of Pilate's time.

2. Not the mere declarer or perfected manifestation of the love of God to man His coming from Adam's days to that last " day of the Lord," when He shall come without sin unto salvation, *is itself the love of God*. The fact of Christ is the fact of which all other facts of God's so loving the world are parts, expositions, or consequences ; and so religious faith, the faith of salvation contemplating these, becomes, like all faith known in the authoritative analogy of family life, faith in a person—faith in the Son of God, the Saviour of the world. Christ the Love of God.

3. The opening description of the Object of Christian faith in the Epistle to the Hebrews, "His Son, whom He hath appointed heir of all things, by whom also He made the worlds " (Heb. i. 2), prepares and suggests the thought of this connection of Jesus of Nazareth, the personal Christ, with the whole history of mankind's earth ; leading us to think of that history as embraced by, embosomed in, this great being, the " Son," the visible part of whose earthly connection with it was His coming to " purge our sins " (ver. 3). The writer in that passage gives us to recognise as the central historical thought of his faith, that the person known as Jesus of Nazareth, the " Son in whom God spake " to mankind in the last days who had spoken by prophets in earlier times, is the same being who was the manifestation of God at the creation of visible things and will be at the consummation of that temporary condition, and is the upholder of that condition while it endures. The " heir of all things," by whom God " created the worlds," " who upholdeth all things by the word of His power," is He "in whom God spake to man," " who being the brightness of His glory, and the express image of His person, when He had purged our sins, sat down on the right hand of the Historical conspectus in Heb. i.

Majesty on high" (Heb. i. 3). It is of immeasurable comfort to faith to be able to gather up all its thoughts of God's will and ways with mankind into this one assuring sight, Christ Jesus; and behold the history of God's love made one in Him —the same love yesterday, to-day, and for ever—the things of it that took place in heaven and the things on earth and the things in the new heaven and the new earth, all one love assured and administered by one unchanging Saviour. The title of Pantocreator given to Christ in the worship of the Byzantine Church is a happier recognition of this truth than modern creeds contain.

Human history embraced in the history of "the Son."

4. When we carry with us the fact that wherever, in the full revelation of truth which New Testament Scripture contains, the love of the heavenly Father to the race He made in His own image is offered, expounded, or enforced, it is in terms of "His Son," we see a peculiar importance in the history of human kind being thus all embosomed in a personal history of "God's well-beloved Son" as itself part of that history. It is a historical contemplation, given to our faith, of the fact declared in words in 1 John iii. 2, which gives a force of assurance beyond the force of words to that commissioned declaration: "Beloved, now are we the sons of God; and it doth not yet appear what we shall be: but we know that, when He shall appear, we shall be like Him; for we shall see Him as He is." Man's present life is a part of the life of the Eternal Son, the well-beloved Son of God. "My Father, and your Father;" "because I live, ye shall live also" (John xx. 17, xiv. 19), are words natural to it, belonging to our true condition, our condition now, and from the beginning, and for evermore. Our Saviour, the image of His glory, in whose image we were made, inseparably associated in our thoughts with the creation of our world, and of ourselves a part of that world, we are to associate in inseparable personality with all the history of providence. And we are to think of the human future by one essential character, that of its being His anticipated possession—thinking of Him as the heir of all things, most prominently of all human things—His everlasting life identified with our kind new-created in His image—we, the many brethren, sons of God, of whom He is the first-born—He the heir of all things, of which we are to

be joint-heirs with Him in God's newly blessed life—and that
life "the restitution of all things" from an imposed "vanity"
(Rom. viii. 20), a bondage of corruption under which creation
groans and travails in pain until deliverance come to it when the
adoption comes to the sons of God.   The keeper of spiritual
Israel, all human faithful life, stands at the beginning of time
—the human world's portion of duration—"the Lamb slain
from the foundation of the world;" at the end of time, the
consummation of all things, He stands the same "Lamb which
had been slain," the Object of heaven's adoration of redeeming
love.

5. Did faith need only, or did it chiefly profit by, theological *Proof of*
proof, that it is the Saviour of the Gospels that we read of in *identity.*
all previous times of revelation, under the diverse names of
"the Angel of the Lord," "Jehovah," "the Angel of the covenant," and who was adored with such riches of affectional
attributes by the patriarchs and the faithful of Israel, a sufficient proof is, the statement that "no man hath seen God at
any time; the only-begotten Son, who is" (ὁ ὤν, always is) "in
the bosom of the Father, He hath declared Him" (John i. 18);
and when "the mystery of godliness"—the formerly hidden
object and *source* of all religious life—was a mystery no more,
but had been "manifest in the flesh, justified in the Spirit, seen
of angels, preached unto the Gentiles, believed on in the world,
and received up into glory" (1 Tim. iii. 16), He claimed the
same names and showed the same attributes by which the
near object of the patriarchs' and Israel's faith had made Himself known—viz., "I AM" (John viii. 58, Rev. i. 17).   The
appropriate comfort of faith, however, in the identity thus
declared, is to be able to *recognise* the Saviour of the fulness
of times from the beginning, along all the line of historical
manifestations of God to holy men of old.   The means of such
an identification, by declaratory names, moral peculiarities,
and phrases and incidents explained only by the appearing of
Jesus, it is now proposed to point out generally.   They seem
ample enough for critical evidence, exceeding by much the
amount of proof which is held as conclusive in other historical
researches.

6. At the very beginning of God's work of love, the creation of a race He was also to redeem from misery to a new eternal life, the identification begins also. A comparison of the history and attributes of Wisdom in the 8th chapter of the Book of Proverbs with the language of the New Testament, and especially of the 1st chapter of John's Gospel, respecting Him who was called the "Wisdom of God," shows us, by manifestations of identity which would be enough and to spare of evidence in any historical question of identity, the future Saviour of the world, the impersonation of God's love to man, looking forward from the bosom of the Father to that manifestation of love; waiting to accomplish the work which He finished in the fulness of times. "The Lord possessed me in the beginning of His way, before His works of old" (Prov. viii. 22). "In the beginning was the Word, and the Word was with God" (John i. 1). "When He prepared the heavens, I was there: when He set a compass upon the face of the depth: when He established the clouds above: when He gave to the sea His commandment: when He appointed the foundations of the earth: then was I by Him, as one brought up with Him: and I was daily His delight, rejoicing always before Him; rejoicing in the habitable part of His earth; and my delights were with the sons of men. Now therefore hearken unto me" (Prov. viii. 27, &c.) "Whom He hath appointed heir of all things, by whom also He made the worlds; who being the brightness of His glory, and the express image of His person" (Heb. i. 2, 3). "All things were made by Him; and without Him was not any thing made that was made. In Him was life; and the life was the light of men" (John i. 3). "The only-begotten Son, which is in the bosom of the Father" (John i. 18). "This is my beloved Son; hear ye Him" (Matt. xvii. 5). The remarkable phase of Jewish theology at the beginning of the Christian era noticed above (Chap. III. p. 49)—viz., the identifying of the Word of the Lord with Jehovah in the Old Testament—is a fact which it is relevant to refer to here, as indicating how the first Christians, the personal scholars of John, would understand his language as carrying back the personal history of Jesus to the beginning of human time.

7. In the history of human salvation, inaugurated as de-

scribed in Prov. viii., we should expect to *recognise* Him who Human was the power of God and the wisdom of God, in the records ances. of His very present helps to the objects of His love. Do we find anticipations of Jesus of Nazareth in Divine Love's early communion with man, when it came, as Jesus of Nazareth afterwards came, to bless, or promise, or save? We do. We see foretastes given, earnests recorded, even of that characteristic assurance of saving love which the manifestation of Jesus was to mankind—the assumption of the fellow-feeling condition, God the Saviour coming to man in the very form and lineaments of his own kind. On three occasions, which we must look at as forepointing epochs in the history of God's selecting love of that race which was to bring the knowledge of His grace to all the peoples of the earth—1st, when He came to tell Abraham of the immediate fulfilment of that promise of seed, the consummation of which was to be the accomplished salvation of men; 2d, when He came to Jacob, the immediate father of the chosen family, to give him the name of divine honour, Israel, God's name for His own people; and 3d, when the fulness of times was come for the holy nation entering upon the conquest of the promised land, and He appeared before Jericho to Joshua, saying, "As the Captain of the Lord's host am I come"—He came as He came in the great fulness of times, in the *form* of man. And with the same *human sympathies* He came; the hearer of prayer to Abraham's marvellous intercession; humbling Himself to the weak estate of "His servant Jacob's" human nature so as even to suffer the patriarch to wrestle as a man with Him and prevail; taking, to uphold Joshua's faith, the burden of Israel's conflicts upon Himself, as now, the "Captain of our salvation," He takes ours.

8. The identity of "The Word," the declarer of God to Identifying men (John i. 18) in the fulness of times, with the old "mes-titles. senger of Jehovah," "the angel of His presence," the declarer of His love to representative men in the preparatory times, should be no surprise to us, but a thing we should miss if it were not taught, since we read of both bearing the name and surrounded with the attributes of God, and working alike as

the whole purpose of their manifestation among men, one peculiar work, that of man's Saviour. The identity *is* taught however. He whom Abraham received at the door of his tent in the plains of Mamre is called Jehovah throughout the narrative; and the "man" who wrestled with Jacob, Hosea tells us (xii. 3-5), was "the Angel," "God," "the Lord God of hosts," "Jehovah." He was "the Angel" whose blessing Jacob invoked upon the sons of Joseph, who had "redeemed the patriarch himself from all evil" (Gen. xlviii. 16). When the time came for Israel's deliverance from Egypt, the first words. that Moses heard (Exod. iii.) from "the Angel" (ver. 2), "Jehovah" (ver. 4), out of the midst of the fire, was a declaration of the identity of Israel's Saviour with the Saviour and friend of Abraham and Jacob : "I am the God of Abraham, the God of Isaac, and the God of Jacob." And the next words spoken by the God of Abraham to the prophet, the incommunicable name I AM, carry on the declared identity to the divine presence known to man in Judæa and Galilee, and to Him who shall sit on the throne in "the new heavens and the new earth." That name by which the peculiar people were in all their wanderings and settlements to think of their deliverer and trust in Him, the name of eternal inherent existence, "I AM," was never repeated to human ears again after that first declaration of it until Jesus of Nazareth repeated it as His own attribute on earth—"Before Abraham was, I am" (John viii. 58); and Jesus, exalted to the glory which His own are to behold and rejoice in for ever, declared Himself, "I am the Alpha and the Omega, the beginning and the ending, saith the Lord, which is, and which was, and which is to come, the Almighty" (Rev. i. 8). How more clearly could declaratory evidence tell us that it is one being who is to be the beginning and the end, the first and the last object, of our faith's realising thoughts when thinking historically of God's saving love ? How more distinctly could we have set before us "Jesus Christ the same yesterday, to-day, and for ever," as the central fact of revelation, the fact ever present, the tree of righteousness planted in the earth, whose sheltering branches and healing leaves all other facts of God's love are ? It is enough of critical proof to identify the Jesus of the Gospels with the object of the patriarchs' faith, the "I AM" of Horeb and the "Jehovah" of Israel. And the Jehovah of Israel had no changed manifestation from His revelation to Moses until the fulness of times. Isaiah (lxiii. 9) epitomises the history of Israel as being all a fulfilment of Jehovah's promise to Moses (Exod. xxxiii. 14)—"My presence shall go with thee, and I will give thee rest;" and in identifying Israel's Saviour from Egypt with their Saviour from all succeeding troubles, he impressively sets before us the same manner of salvation, all-comprehensive and all-sympathising, which belongs to Jesus of Nazareth alone : "In all their affliction He was afflicted, and the angel of His presence saved them : in His love and in His pity He redeemed them ; and He bare them, and carried them all the days of old."

9. The moral identification of the Jehovah of the patriarchs and Israel with mankind's Jesus, which Isaiah illustrates in the passage now quoted—the recognisable likeness, the sameness of expression and ways, in those old drawings-nigh of God to man, with the words and ways of Him who spake as never man spake—is what faith will most rejoice to find in the early testimonies, and most will get edification from. An attentive perusal of the narratives of man's early communion with the object of his faith—"the Angel of the Lord," "the Angel of His presence," the Saviour of Israel's temporal salvations, the King of Israel's so redeemed national life, who is identified by the incommunicable name with "Jesus," the Saviour of His people's sins, the "Messenger of the covenant," the "Angel" of the Apocalypse—will show as distinct identity in moral characteristics, presenting that unique union seen in Jesus of divine grace and human sympathies. The accounts given of those early communions of God with man look like as if He, whose marvellous love was to be manifested in the fulness of times in taking the very condition of man upon Himself, had from the beginning, in desirous anticipation, frequently realised His coming nearness of approach to them ; foretasting it in spirit, watching over and yearning after His own with that " desirous desire " which afterwards longed for His best earthly communion with

Moral identification.

them (Luke xxii. 15); and as if He had again and again broken through the invisibility which concealed Him from those who never were from His sight, to give *them* also an indulging fore-taste of that perfectly near love and sympathy in which He sought them to have faith and comfort. Faith increases its comfort immeasurably in " Jesus, who saved His people from their sins," when in the light of so sure recognition it can think of Him as no messenger of the fulness of times only, sent then into the world by the Father to seek and save them that were lost; but can behold Him with them from the beginning of the world, Himself the Father of Old Testament assurances, or one with the Father in a union which may foil our intellect to explain, but which comforts our hearts to think of—it puts away so happily all thoughts, as if we had a heavenly Father a being of wrath chiefly, and a separate Saviour, who was to us only a shield from His deserved vengeance. It is a sadly hurtful effect that is produced by our thinking of the saving love of God in a chronological light, as if once it existed not, and be-came ours when it was dearly purchased by the Friend of man. The manifestation or unveiling—*i.e.*, revealing—to human sight of the Father's love was a thing of chronological progress, for man's power to realise so great and undeserved affection was so; but there never was one love of the Father and another love of the Son. It was one love that watched over the chosen race from the beginning. The Son was the Father's love : " He that hath seen me hath seen the Father." It was one love—the same yesterday, to-day, and for ever—which had its delights with the sons of men from the foundation of the world; and during their waiting generations yearned to show itself to them ; and did again and again unveil its presence to give a glimpse of sight to their faith of what were the riches of the promises it bade them believe in, which eye had not seen, nor ear heard, nor had it entered into " the heart of man to conceive."

Early facts understood only by Christian light.
10. The human appearances made to Abraham and Jacob and Joshua, and perhaps to Adam and to Enoch, are anoma-lous in Old Testament representations of God's intercourse with mankind; but they become consistent, and fall into most natural place, when looked back upon over the narratives of

the Gospels, when the mystery hidden from ages and generations was manifested in the flesh. In like manner, the Gospel pictures light up into their true expression the remarkable moral features of patriarchal and Jewish communion with Jehovah. The human sympathies manifested by the "Angel of the Lord" are similarly anomalous when read of side by side with the contemporary human notions of the Most High expressed, for example, in Solomon's language respecting the great temple Jehovah had allowed him to build to His honour: "But will God in very deed dwell with man upon the earth?" They are set in recognisable position, and take their place with manifest fitness, in the love which is the same yesterday, to-day, and for ever, when the life of Jesus of Nazareth sheds its revealing light back upon them. Faith, believing on rational grounds in an identity fixed by such an interlacing of divine names and attributes as makes the individuality of Jesus and the Angel of God's presence, Jehovah, one, rejoices with heart-seeing belief and edifying satisfaction to recognise the same Jesus, from the earliest narratives of God *with* man, the first as well as the last Saviour of Adam's race in all their afflictions, the giver of all their blessings.

11. Was it the same "Wisdom of God" (1 Cor. i. 24), Christ Jesus, the heir of all things, who in the fulness of times endured the cross, despising the shame, for the joy of man's salvation set before Him? was it He who in the beginning took the same name and the same joy for His inheritance, and before the race was created rejoiced in the places where they were to dwell? (Prov. viii.) The cry of wisdom "in the top of the high places, by the way in the places of the paths: O ye simple, understand wisdom; and, ye fools, be of an understanding heart. Hear; for I will speak of excellent things," is the cry of Jehovah by His prophets to faithless Israel—the very cry of Jesus of Nazareth to the sons of men. The "joy in the habitable part of the earth, the delight with the sons of men," is properly to be placed, surely, as an early chapter of the same "life, the light of men" (John i. 4), which was manifest in flesh in the days of Pontius Pilate, and now intercedes for the sons of men in heaven—a forelooking love, as then and now—an active

The "cry" of Wisdom and of Jesus.

love, concentrating itself on mankind so as to suggest the very words of the New Testament's description of the love of Jesus Christ: "He loved us, and gave Himself for us;"—"O Jerusalem, Jerusalem, thou that killest the prophets, and stonest them that are sent unto thee, how often would I have gathered thy children together, as a hen gathereth her chickens under her wings!"—"If thou hadst known, at least in this thy day, the things that concern thy peace!"—"I have a baptism to be baptised with; and how am I straitened till it be accomplished!"

Foretastes of the Flesh and its sympathies.

12. Scripture does not *describe* other human appearances than those above spoken of vouchsafed in the early times by the Friend of man; but faith, having familiarly before its eyes the *man* who appeared at Mamre, Penuel, and Jericho—the man who ate bread with Abraham in the door of his tent, who reproved Sarah forbearingly with so human-like appreciation of her state of mind, who took Abraham into His confidence as to His designs on Sodom with a seeming friendly afterthought so like our own, saying to Himself, while Abraham walked with Him part of the way from his tent, "Shall I hide from Abraham the thing which I do?" and then suffered, with endlessly-expanding fellow-feeling, the old man's persistent intercession for the cities of the plain—will be prone to associate some such visible phase of love with the earlier narratives of Him whose voice was so well known to the first pair in the garden, and with whom Enoch walked, and was taken to heaven by Him without tasting death.

Eden and Cana.

13. Do we recognise the same hand which in Cana of Galilee turned water into wine—the first, and the type of all the divine deeds of His human life—preparing, long before, the garden eastward in Eden for man's dwelling-place, when "out of the ground Jehovah God made to grow every tree that is pleasant to the sight and good for food, the tree of life also in the midst of the garden" (Gen. ii. 9); preparing, too, the first trial of faith, "the tree of the knowledge of good and evil"? Was it the very "seed of the woman," the pitying, desirous Propitiation Himself, that hasted in the first day of fear to bring to the fallen pair the glad tidings, "The seed of the woman shall bruise the serpent's head"? as it certainly was after-

wards Abraham's promised seed Himself, the blessing of all nations, that in human form gave the waiting and repeatedly wearying patriarch the distant promise of that seed, and the promise of its immediate earnest, Isaac, " born to one as good as dead" (Heb. xi. 12). In both narratives it is by the name Jehovah that the divine visitor is called—the I AM of Moses' subsequent revelation, and of Jesus' full declaration of Himself.

14. Perhaps it is instructive that in Gen. vi. and vii., in the description of the conflict of feeling taking place in the divine mind over the wickedness of Noah's generation, upon which the Flood was sent, the names God and Jehovah are both used—the name of Godhead, and the name, appropriated to God's redeeming coming nigh again to mankind, by which He made Himself known to typical Israel ; and while it is of God (Elohim) that we read the inexorable judgment (vi. 12, 13), it is under the name of Jehovah (the future I AM and Jesus) that the narrative places the so richly emotional elements exhibited in it—grief to the heart at man's sins, but forbearance for yet a hundred and twenty years ; repentance that He had made man, and a resolution to banish the unholiness by destruction of the race ; but love still, and a new trial of the race—" Noah found grace in the eyes of the Lord." It is the very mixture of feelings which Judæa and Galilee often heard in the fulness of times in the lamentations over Jerusalem, and the denunciations of Chorazin and Bethsaida. Under the same name of Jehovah we read of the merciful confounding of language at Babel, which restrained the quick spread of new corruption. Faith, dwelling on the compassionateness of the severity, will spontaneously associate it with the similarly unique confusion of senses at the hill of Nazareth and the garden of Gethsemane, as the work of the same long-suffering Spirit who "restraineth the remainder of man's anger."

15. The history of Jehovah's communion with the father of the faithful is fitly rich in food for faith's assuring thoughts recognising the oldness of that love which we get peace from having ever before us. How often did He, who in the days

Distinctive mercies of Jehovah—those of Jesus.

The Flood and the towns of Galilee.

Babel, and Nazareth, and Gethsemane.

The Friend of man with Abraham.

of His flesh prayed for Peter's after-days of frailty and trial that his faith might not fail, come to Abraham's help—a man of not unlike strength and weakness—in sustaining manifestations ; repeating and reassuring the great but far-off promise, in the single-hearted belief of which the patriarch had left his native land for ever for his strange, blind, sojourning life ! How like the same Jesus overpassing the bounds set to His mission—"the lost sheep of the house of Israel"—to heal the centurion's servant and the Sidonian mother's child, is Abraham's Angel of the Lord going after Hagar into the wilderness to recall her to duty, to uphold her with promises almost a shadow of the promise made to Abraham's self ;—and Abraham's Jehovah even appearing in visions, not of severity but of kindness, to the idolatrous Egyptian and Philistine kings for Abraham's sake, as afterwards to Laban on Jacob's account ! The 18th chapter of Genesis is full of the Christian's Lord. How human-like, meek, and lowly are the incidents ! First, the suffering without any confounding discovering of His real character, the freedom of Abraham's unrecognising hospitality. Then the manner of announcing Abraham's long and of late wearily wished-for child of promise, and the sympathising observation of Sarah's emotions on overhearing the intimation, and the forbearance with her wrong but confused denial of having laughed. Then the soliloquy in the very language of uniting human friendship, "And the Lord said, Shall I hide from Abraham the thing that I do ; seeing that Abraham shall surely become a great and mighty nation, and all nations of the earth shall be blessed in him ? For I know him, that he will command his children and his household after him, and they shall keep the way of the Lord, and do justice and judgment ; that the Lord may bring upon Abraham that which He hath spoken of him." Who can fail to see in that day's manifestations—that day's, in which Jehovah came as a man to the tent-door of his friend—the yearning after man to love and be loved by, to trust and be trusted, which appears afterwards in Him who, not for a day, but for thirty years, humbled Himself to be found in fashion as a man, and then so needed human sympathy, and sought it oftener than He found it—

that yearning which yet looks desirously for human love and
reliance as the travail of His soul, the purchase of His pain?
But that narrative's treasure of the thoughts needed by faith
in the Saviour is most impressively rich at the close, where
there stands before us so surely our Intercessor at God's right
hand, showing us, in His grace to Abraham, by what unlimited
measure we may think of the intercession He is prepared, by
His knowledge of what is in man, to make for His own—and
how without measure may be the unfainting prayer which He
will hear from His own as well as make for them. The
appalling persistence of Abraham's intercession for the cities
of the plain almost takes away the breath to read, put as it
is in a stronger light by the patriarch's own feeling of his pre-
sumption; but what shall we say of Him who, the Eternal
God, stood before Abraham as a man to hear it, and rebuked
it not, but yielded and yielded and yielded seven times, till
Abraham ceased to intercede, not He to hear? One other such
hearing of entreaty is recorded. It is that which Jesus heard,
and the Syrophœnician woman, standing before Him, found
courage and faith to make. The hearer and the very present
helper of Abraham and of that suppliant was One—He who
saw good to encourage unfainting prayer even by the strange
parable of the unjust judge, but who is a nearer helper still,
who "heareth the desire of the humble, and prepareth their
heart, and causeth His ear to hear" (Ps. x. 17). Yet how
much is His love made mighty to save in our eyes by this
sight of its having been always as near to man—as perfect in
sympathies, and as strongly yearning after man's love and
salvation in the plains of Mamre, as, thousands of years
afterwards, in the very neighbourhood of the cross! Mamre's
modern name, El Khalil, The Friend, is a delicious memorial
of that old grace.

16. A few years later we behold, in that far-back time of Abraham
revealed love, no little of the required and invited practice of Christian
the very faith which Christian times were to have in the fully- faith—in
manifested Saviour. That ripened faith received its best God's Love,
recorded illustration in the educating human experience that
took place when "God did tempt Abraham." The self-deny-

N

ing love of God for man, which the fulness of times has to think
of—that it could go on even to the giving up of an only-begotten
son—Abraham was called to measure and learn to think upon
with the ever-present thinking of faith, by passing through the
same heart's experience himself. The surrender in faith, un-
helped by any sight, of our all of this world's possessions for
Christ's sake which is directed in His words by the severe trial,
" He that loveth son or daughter more than me is not worthy
of me," Abraham, and no believer of the fulness of times, was
the great Scriptural example of, when " he that had received
the promises offered up his only-begotten son, of whom it was
said, In Isaac shall thy seed be called."   And where shall faith
in Jesus' own promise of His comfort in " a little while," when
the forewarned tribulation for His sake is accepted in meekness,
find so assuring facts of that promise to dwell upon as concluded
the story of that sore tempting—the hasting call of the relieving comforter when Abraham was about to break his heart in
obedient faith and slay his promised son—the hasting cry of
the unseen watching Saviour, "Abraham, Abraham! lay not
thine hand upon the lad, nor do thou any thing unto him : for
now I know that thou fearest God, seeing thou hast not
withheld thy son, thine only son, from me" ? (Gen. xxii.)

and His
Providence.
17. Faith in the eternal love of Christ Jesus, that it will
overflow with all sufficiency of temporal mercies, has to take
as the measure of its peaceful dependence His words, " Take
no thought for your life," " your heavenly Father knoweth
what ye have need of ;" and His disciples were once appealed
to by Him after a trial of that faith, " Lacked ye anything ?"
That education to all-confiding faith, the Christian faith in
Providence, was but a repetition of a human experience of the
self-same care which lights up to our instructed eyes the long-
back yesterday of Abraham's days with the light of the same
Saviour's countenance. Abraham's whole wanderings in the
land he never saw till he came to it in faith's blindest following of the divine impulse, and in which he was never to possess more than room to bury his dead, were a life lived by
faith in all the richness of very present love in which they
that trust in Jesus' promise have peace ; and his sojournings

in Egypt and Gerar, stained by unbelief strangely reproved, were the very failures which Christians were to be ashamed of in their faith. Graphic touches of a faith, the very likeness of that of the Galilean youths who left their boats and their father's house to go wherever Jesus bade them, are presented to us in Eliezer's journey to Padan Aram (Gen. xxiv.) The bright trustfulness of his prayer, "knowing in whom he believed.' brings up before our eyes a strong-in-faith suppliant of the fulness of times, and the self-same very present hearer and answerer of prayer, as little visible, but as little leaving His trusting servants comfortless.

18. With what invisible figure is it that we are to fill up the narrative of Jacob's exile—coming to him in the vision of Bethel, frustrating ten times Laban's oppressive bargains, enriching the worldling for Jacob's sake, restraining his avaricious designs when pursuing Jacob on his escape, turning Esau's vindictive heart back again to his timid brother? Who was "the God that fed him all his life long, the Angel which redeemed him from all evil"? (Gen. xlviii. 15, 16.) That "Angel" wrestling as a man with Jacob at the brook, and letting Himself be overcome by the believing clinging patriarch, is an anomalous sight in Old Testament representations of God. But the whole history of that exile is like a passage from the fulness of times regarding Him who knew the willing spirit and the weak flesh of His best disciples, who " suffered how long" their slowness of heart to believe, and the worse contradiction of perverse sinners, and who " being found in fashion as a man, humbled Himself, and took the form of a servant." *He that humbled Himself.*

19. Do we think of the prayer, " Lord, I believe ; help Thou mine unbelief," as not only the very accent of needy man's most fully instructed seeking unto God, but as expository of the very genius of Christian grace—that sympathising tender help which knows our need before we ask, and works in us to will and to do? and do we think of that grace as a thing of the latter days, when the Spirit, causing men to walk in God's ways, was to be poured out? Moses sorely needed such grace when he stood before the burning bush to receive the commission which the Saviour of Israel had chosen him for ; and he *"Help thou mine unbelief."*

received the very help which we recognise as the befitting help Jesus would have given in the latter days, who had a fellow-feeling of our infirmities—help not in the almighty inspiration of God's command, but in the form of his own brother's companionship sharing the necessary enterprise and difficulties of the service. It was just as Jesus afterwards sent forth His disciples to their first mission of preaching and doing miracles, not singly, but two and two together. The same manner of Saviour helping to believe in Himself stood in a later generation by Gideon, and tenderly met all his desires of assurance. That yielding, without reproof or reproving instruction to the young man's timid and ashamed request for a repetition of the test of the fleece, has much of the softened colouring that warms faith's picture of Thomas's Lord, who did not break the bruised reed nor quench the smoking flax (Jud. vi. 39).—Compare His help of Paul and of Elijah (Acts xviii. 9, 10 ; 1 Kings xix. 13-18).

The Saviour proclaiming Himself on Sinai.

20. Thus richly in the visible works of the invisible Jehovah of the patriarchs can we see the lineaments of the human-hearted Saviour of the Gospels — Jesus, Immanuel, God with us—as if the eye of faith needed but to be accustomed to look into the imagined obscurity of the times of lesser revelation to see Him whom we should see there, since His love is the same yesterday, to-day, and for ever—who is the creator, the providence, and the heir of all human things. The long patriarchal and Jewish ages which brought on the times of full manifestation were not obscure. They are called "times of ignorance at which God winked." Their darkness was a darkness in the eyes of men, not upon the countenance of God. Some, as Abraham and Moses, saw even then the light that lightened the fulness of times. And bright heavenly lights broke at times through the comparative darkness. Such was the revelation that passed little noticed over the minds of Israel—a brightness afar off, above their earthward eyes— which was given to Moses to put new strength of faith into his soul when, depressed and despairing for Israel, he went up into the mountain to receive the second time a writing of Jehovah's commandments. " The Lord descended in the cloud, and stood

with him there, and proclaimed the name of the Lord. And
the Lord passed by before him, and proclaimed, The Lord, The
Lord God, merciful and gracious, long-suffering, and abundant
in goodness and truth, keeping mercy for thousands, forgiving
iniquity and transgression and sin, and that will by no means
clear the guilty " (Exod. xxxiv. 5-7).

21. Unappreciated by the demoralised people as that revela- His peculiar grace
tion was, we, with the light of Jesus' life, can see even then the in the lives
of Moses,
living working of its grace, afterwards the very grace of God Samuel,
manifest in the flesh, evermore enduring, pitying, loving, help- &c.
ing, seeking to save. The holy but unfearing daily intercourse of
Moses with Jehovah in the tabernacle of the wilderness is like
the near communion, almost that of equals, to which John and
Peter and the family of Bethany were admitted.   It is in the
language of human happiness in man, not of one far off from
man, that Jehovah speaks of His servant Caleb, and Job, and
David the man after His own heart.   The history of the
wilderness was a history of richer human-like forbearance
with sinful man, though not with sin, than even Moses' faith
was prepared for, even as Jesus' love of Lazarus astonished
the Jews.   The sorely-needed salvations given to the times of
the judges were the peculiar help which Jesus gave promise
of as His giving of rest—the help which the wearied and
heavy-laden needed, and were drawn and driven by their
afflictions to seek and trust to get—a help which showed
how near them in all their afflictions He was, and how surely
Himself afflicted in them.   How like the considerateness of
Jesus' compassion, making the stripes of correction as gentle
and persuasive as might be, was the sending of the child
Samuel to tell Eli, the weak but blameworthy old man, His
words of reproof and threatening ! So considerate of the best
way to save, like the fellow-feeling thoughtfulness which the
court of the temple (John viii. 7-11), the well of Sychar (iv.
16), the upper room (xiii. 22-27) in Jerusalem, beheld, was the
reproof of David by the mouth of Nathan, and afterwards the
choice of punishment given to him, and the help to choose
correction by the Lord's hand, and not by the hand of man.
There is something greatly suggestive of Jesus' manner with

little children in the narrative of Jehovah's voice in the chamber of the tabernacle waking little Samuel night after night, until the child got the explanation of the call from his kind old friend telling him, with awestruck reverence, that God had spoken to him, and bidding him, when called again, say, "Speak, Lord ; for Thy servant heareth" (1 Sam. iii.)

. When the chosen people became a nation, and Jehovah's dealings with them became general, we cannot gather so frequently this food of the peculiar manner of faith in which we think of Jesus of Nazareth ; which is a faith that thinks much upon incidents of His near communion with individuals. In that period He necessarily came to be more as one behind a veil, though near and watchful and helpful as abundantly.

Footprints of Jesus sowing words of faith, 22. Another class of anticipatory manifestations of the Saviour of the latter days then began to be laid up in the instructive writings of the times, to be choice food of faith as to the long-back earliness of His love, when His disciples should come upon them in after-times in their searching of the Scriptures that testify of Him. Numerous revelations, unveilings of Himself, are scattered over the Psalms and the prophets—expressions descriptive of the earthly condition, or some incident of it, in which He was to appear, or of His own peculiar moral character, or of the spiritual life which He was to bring to man's earthly habits—expressions which were *not prophecies,* and are not claimed as prophecies in the New Testament, but which to the eye of faith, now instructed by the Gospels and by the spirit of Christian religiousness, appear as *early footprints* of our own Saviour, Jesus of Nazareth. They show Him, as it were, walking concealed by the side of man in those early generations, and, in His desire towards them, all but betraying His presence ever and again ; they show Him as if He were dropping tokens by the way, thinking of how they would be found by His own afterwards, and they would more abundantly believe in His love and rejoice in it, seeing by these how it was of old from everlasting. Examples of these sown words, living seeds of future fruit, language lying for generations in ambush, to lay hold on faith when the full time should come, and draw its glad eyes back to see how long that love in which it rejoiced had looked forward to be fully known, are: "My God, my God, why hast Thou forsaken me? . . . All they that see me laugh me to scorn: they shoot out the lip, they shake the head, saying, He trusted on the Lord that He would deliver him: let Him deliver him, seeing He delighted in him" (Ps. xxii.) "They weighed for my price thirty pieces of silver. And the Lord said unto me, Cast it unto the potter. And I took the thirty pieces of silver, and cast them to the potter in the house of the Lord" (Zech. xi. 12, 13). "And one shall say, What are these wounds in thine hands? Then he shall answer, Those with which I was wounded in the house of my friends. Awake, O sword, against my Shepherd, and against the man that is my fellow, saith the Lord of hosts: smite the Shepherd, and the sheep shall be scattered" (Zech. xiii. 6, 7). "Who is this that cometh from Edom, with dyed garments from Bozrah? this that is glorious in His apparel, travelling in the greatness of His strength? I that speak in righteousness, mighty to save. Wherefore art Thou red in Thine apparel, and Thy garments like him that treadeth the winefat? I have trodden the winepress alone; and of the people there was none with me. . . . And I looked, and there was none to help; and I wondered that there was none to uphold: therefore mine own arm brought salvation unto me" (Isa. lxiii. 1-5). "Then I said, I have laboured in vain, I have spent my strength for nought, and in vain. . . . And He said, It is a light thing that Thou shouldest be my servant to raise up the tribes of Jacob, and to restore the preserved of Israel; I will also give Thee for a light to the Gentiles, that Thou mayest be my salvation unto the end of the earth" (Isa. xlix. 4, 6). These are examples of descriptions lying here and there in the Old Testament fitting the redeeming life lived by Jesus, which are not given in their places as prophecies of the Christ, nor are claimed as prophecies in the argument of the evangelists and apostles, but are peculiar features of the life of saving love that was to be lived upon earth; and in them faith, taught by the Gospels, recognises Him who is the theme of the evangelists, and sees Him, as it were, standing by the side of the prophets, and, while He helped them to look forward to the fulness of times, letting fall in His inspiration of their speech expressions which would have to wait full recognition until the mystery of godliness was manifest in the flesh,—but would then betray His own forelooking love.

23. Did not the first disciples love to recall such expressions to their minds, and rejoice in any new one that occurred, as some peculiar event of their Lord's life, or some remarkable phase of conduct, brought up suddenly its description in old revelation? A confessed example is in John ii. 17. Seeing their Master's strange access of holy indignation, and His as strange authority in expelling the traders from His Father's house, they remembered that it was written, "The zeal of Thine house hath eaten me up" (Ps. lxix. 9). So did the evangelists themselves "remember," and see far back the footprints of the Saviour coming through the long ages to the history they were to write. Matthew (ii. 15) sees Jesus in Hosea's words of Israel (xi. 1), "I called my son out of Egypt;" and in Jeremiah's picture of the captivity (Matt. ii. 18, Jer. xxxi. 15), "Rachel weeping for her children." John beholds incidents of His crucifixion painted long before in the Psalms (xix. 24, xxii. 18), "They part my garments among them, and cast lots upon my vesture;" (xix. 36, xxxiv. 20), "He keepeth all his bones: not one of them is broken." Paul, feeling the greatness of Jesus, and the direful ignorance which crucified the Lord of glory, recognises the grandeur of the Christian times foreshown in Isaiah's unconscious words of Jehovah's grace to penitents of his own time (1 Cor. ii. 9, Isa. lxiv. 4): "Since the beginning of the world men have not heard, nor perceived by the ear, neither hath the eye seen, O God, besides Thee, what He hath prepared for him that waiteth for Him." Other recognitions of Jesus in Ps. viii. 5 and xl. 7 appear in Heb. ii. 9 and x. 7. Did our Lord design to bid faith open the eyes of its mind, and see Him the same yesterday, to-day, and for ever, when (John i. 51) He sent Nathaniel's thoughts of Him back to Jehovah's communion with Jacob at Bethel (Gen. xxviii. 12), and afterwards (Matt. xxiv. 30) quoted without remark, in speaking of His day of judgment on Jerusalem and the world, Daniel's vision of the Son of man? (Dan. vii. 13.)

(margin: recognised by the New Testament writers.)

24. Akin in the kind of anticipation of the Messiah's times Anachron-
isms of
history,
are the strange geographical combinations familiar in the
inspirations of the Psalms and the prophets, but totally beyond any thought which history could have suggested to the
writers. The kings of Tarshish and the isles bringing presents,
the kings of Sheba and Seba offering gifts (Ps. lxxii. 10),
describes a meeting of Eastern and Western civilisations not
both in existence in the Psalmist's times. Princes coming out
of Egypt, Ethiopia stretching out her hands to God (Ps. lxviii.
31), Rahab and Babylon, Philistia and Tyre, the birthplaces
along with Zion of the people of God (Ps. lxxxvii.), was a
geographical combination utterly above all Jewish religious
sentiment; but brightly descriptive of the style of the world's
tribute to Christianity, the only thing which its powers have
with one practical, though unknowing, agreement served.
They were anticipations that could not be human. They were
forelookings of His who was to make them history; and faith
is to recognise Him desiring with desire, and make the psalmists
and the prophets speak strange words of, the redemption of
the children of men, and is to feel more, because of the sight,
how from everlasting His saving love to man has been.

25. Beyond these anticipations of history, a moral picture and of
religious
sentiment.
appears in those old writings, also recognisable only when He
appeared in whom all the religious life of Jewish ordinances
and instruction was fulfilled. The joyous childlike whole-
hearted faith of the Psalms did not fit into the times of the
kingdom of David, and never appeared in suchlike verbal
description again but in the Gospels. Christian readers of the
Psalms, and the prophetic utterances which record the religious
thoughts granted to Israel's teachers during their needed times
of severe discipline, are constrained to see His glorious greatness often breaking forth in them; as if, in the spirit of His
human manifestations to Abraham, He yearned to show Himself to those whom He so loved and waited to redeem, and in
consequence often gave them thoughts stretching boundlessly
beyond their present circumstances—thoughts of great joy to
them which, though not yet clear, would be in them living seeds
of pondering anticipation and growing desires, drawing their

souls forth after Him. The minor prophets, the commissioned comforters of Israel and Judah when the captivities were at hand, had allotted to them a specially rich portion of such spiritual thoughts—thoughts unfitting, as their descriptions of Israel's restoration were, to any future that Israel ever came to, but bright reflections, to be recognised by Christian times, of the fulness of grace which was to become historical fact to them. They were glimpses of a historical salvation over centuries of which we of the latter days have the joy of looking back to see, in those old unveilings, the Saviour desiring the coming time; and lighting up His way of salvation in the growing desires of His faithful servants and in their anticipating faith.

Designed fruit of words thus sown.

26. What end is served by all those pregnant words, those expressions and descriptive features of earthly future concerning Christ, lying for centuries in waiting, to be understood only when He became known in the flesh, some of them perhaps not until, or nearly until, His second coming without sin unto salvation? No prophecies to indicate His approach, nor claimed when He came as verifications of His person; they were but marks of His presence with the minds of the speakers, unrecognised by them. Parents often gratify their affection for their children, and knit their own hearts more to them, by placing, unnoticed by them, tokens of their own watchful affection about their daily path, that *they* may find them unawares, and feed their faith in that careful love thereby. If this was the designed effect of these tokens of our Saviour's presence laid in wait to surprise believers' hearts in following ages into joyful faith in the oldness of that solicitous love which we are apt to think of as but a modern thing, it is no design unworthy of His grace. It is a great gift given to our faith, seeking amplest room wherein to joy in Him, when we have to think of the love, not of one who came in the latter days of the world to work a short awful work of salvation; but of one whose love had suffered long, as human sinfulness had been long, and loved through all the contradiction of sinful men, not for thirty, but for four thousand years; and still has so to love, and does love—always wounded in the house of His friends,

always leading His loved ones like the good shepherd, always looking in vain for His people to help, treading the wine-press alone, and His own arm bringing salvation.

27. We think of the great preparatory dispensation of Moses, Israel's whole religious history—the Law—as having been a schoolmaster to bring the chosen people to Christ; a long training under close commandments as to cleanness and uncleanness to habituate them to thoughts of holy obedience to a pure God, and under the burdensome laws of sacrifice bringing them to thoughts of the necessity of atonement; and a long providential government of goodness and severity keeping them or bringing them back to the thoughts which were to work in their souls habitual feelings of a pure and holy God loving them so as to redeem them by the sacrifice of Himself. But we are apt to think as if a marked chronological line of division separated that preparatory dispensation from Christ Himself; and that though we are clearly taught that it was "the Spirit of Christ" that was in the prophets (1 Pet. i. 11), and "the reproach of Christ" that Moses chose in Egypt (Heb. xi. 26). What a relief to our faith thoughts—what a comfort, bringing into our view of the grace of God that simplicity which belongs to all other thoughts of our God's ways when we understand any of them well—it is to look on that long training as being wrought out by the loving Saviour Himself; and to know that He Himself was the Angel of God's presence who saved His people of old, that it was He who was afflicted in all their afflictions, who in His love and His pity redeemed them, and bare them, and carried them all the days of old! What a relief from thinking of the Messiah as one who was waiting, all the long period of man's existence and his needs, apart in heaven until the time for His coming in the flesh should arrive; and of mankind as having been prepared for His appearing by some far more distant supervision than that which Jesus of Nazareth exercised over the fulness of times! It was not another supervision, but His own; He it was, not in heaven, but as now both in heaven and on earth, watching over the race whom He loves, with only a hidden presence, as parents watch with overflowing and sometimes self-betraying

[margin note:] Christ present in all "The Law "—Himself the "Schoolmaster."

love, behind some concealing thing, over the efforts of their little ones left purposely alone to try their powers and guide themselves by rules. He himself was the schoolmaster, bringing them, by the constant checks, corrections, humiliations, and pointings of the law, to seek and find, and believe in His own unknown love, His personal value, and His grace to them. The whole history is full of the Christ of the fulness of times—His own often-perplexed heart turning about to every hand in holy anger and yearning love ; pronouncing sentence of destroying punishment ; turned from it willingly by the intercession of Abraham, or Moses, or David, or Hezekiah, to sparing mercy ; hasting with fulness of blessings, like the prodigal's father in His own parable, to meet and encourage every return. In the Old Testament histories we are wont to look for types, resemblances of His work of saving and blessing which the fulness of times was to begin. Those old events were not types of His work ; they were His own earlier works of salvation, and types only as the miracles of the three years were types of eternal healing and forgiveness and purifying—assurances, properly speaking foretastes in relative or the same manifestations of grace.

Old histories not types, but parts of the love of Christ.

28. The historical identification illustrated in the preceding pages is in excellent agreement with the description which the Bible gives of what is the study of faith ; that it is to " comprehend what is the breadth, and length, and depth, and height, and to know the love of Christ, which passeth knowledge, that we may be filled with all the fulness of God " (Eph. iii. 18, 19). We recognise this one love filling all extensions of man's condition, this one loving being the object of faith in all times. It is a view of man's faith in the love of God being really one faith in all periods which is satisfying both to the understanding and to the heart to attain. It is a sight of faith which unites most clearly the characteristics of faith advanced in previous chapters ; manifesting that it is an emotional thinking, a contemplation by the heart of the love of God ; not reasoning on it as an attribute, but looking on it in a person—that person the engrossing object of adoring human love, and grateful and desirous possession ; one whom we can

Recognition of Christ the study of faith.

form an imagination of to ourselves as a visible being apparent
to our senses, and whom we think of by a history. We have
now to see how in Christ, the object of faith, there is set before
us the essential form of affection which our faith is to contemplate in the love of God—viz., the family affection, the union
to God both by relationship and nature which Scripture language requires and invites us to think of as man's connection
with God.

29. That this peculiar manner of love—family love—is the *The Gospel*
nature of God's love of man, was indicated and assured by the *revelation,*
that of
habitual adoption, in His revelations all through the prepara- *Sonship;*
tory dispensations, of names implying family ties ; and by the
faith in such family love which He enabled His servants to have
towards Him. When His love and our invited faith became
fully unveiled in the fulness of times, this was the distinctive
form in which it was to be seen by us. Our Redeemer, the
first-born of us His many brethren to immortal life, who
revealed God to us as being His God and our God, His Father
and our Father, is called the Eternal Son of God. In this
language all the perfected instruction given to man in the
New Testament of what he is to believe in is expressed. The
Old Testament prophetic names are superseded—the Messiah,
the Prince, the Messenger, the Branch of righteousness, the
Counsellor, Immanuel, &c. The Christ, the full revelation, is
God's own Son. " This is the record, that God hath given to
us eternal life, and this life is in His Son " (1 John v. 11).
How is faith to use this so marked form in which the " glad
tidings " are given to us ? In two ways, giving us separately
assurance of God's love. That " record" is the declaration of
a connection guaranteed by such a title as that of sons. It
is also the revelation of such a relationship as being an essential fact of our nature, as created originally, and by salvation
" quickened " from a state of death.

30. First, What is given us logically to gather of assurance *declared in*
of peace with God and grace from Him by everything being *Christ*
Jesus;
offered and guaranteed to us in terms of His Son. The thought
of Jesus Christ as God, and yet as the Son of God, must be
always beyond our power to make a distinct thought logically

intelligible; and it is not philosophical to seek after more distinctness of theological idea upon the subject than Scripture language presents to common readers, which, by clear declaration and habitual assumption, sets Christ Jesus before us as God Himself, and as clearly requires us to think of Him as the only-begotten well-beloved Son of God, the brother suffering for man, and heir of all things with man. John's 14th chapter, which is a treasure of faith if we think of the Father and the Son as one, is unintelligible if we logically separate the individualities. While, however, difficulty never yet surmounted overpowers the attempt to place these two teachings of Scripture in logical connection, if we think of that divine sonship as implying separation of individualities and possible difference of feelings, such as we would associate with a human sonship having a similar work of propitiating suffering—and we thereby run great risk of importing into our religious thoughts logical elements which the heart, seeking salvation, is disturbed and distracted by— we may take richest logical food of faith, though not of philosophy, from the thought of sonship which envelops all the perfected revelation of God's love to man. Though we cannot lay open to mental comprehension the operation of the relationship in which Christ is spoken of as the Son of the Father in so many different lights, every connection with us in which He is so spoken of sets before us, in a new and completing light, God's love to us as the same love that a father has for an only son, while it adds also an assurance wanting in the experience of the strongest human parental love, in the fact that the guaranteeing love is one that is inseparable from the idea of self-love ;—" I and the Father are one." God's love to man is as great and as assured as that of a father of prodigal children who would give up a son in whom he was ever well pleased to save the undeserving children from death. God's love to man is as near and as perfect in fellow-feeling as if a brother would give himself to death to save prodigal brothers and sisters, and be straitened till, by the sacrifice of himself, he could accomplish their recovery. Our right feeling of the consequence of sin, is as if

a father could not pass it by in a weak and tempted child
unless his only other son, who knew no sin, took upon him
all its shame and all its punishment, so that he would atone
for it even with his life. The assurance we have of the sufficient bountifulness of God's love is what unworthy children
might have in a father's love who had delivered up his well-
beloved son for them, that after that he would freely give
them all things. Our hope of the eternal inheritance is made
as sure, notwithstanding our feeling of undeserving, as if the
enemies of a great benefactor were made by him joint-heirs
with his own only son. Our blessedness of the everlasting
inheritance is full as that of the only child of a perfect father;
appropriate and perfect in kind as the blessedness of likeness to such a father combined with the blessedness of his
affection. Our saving, blessing union with God is to be as
close and sure as His who is God himself;—"That they all
may be one; as Thou, Father, art in me, and I in Thee, that
they also may be one in us" (John xvii. 21). Our new and
everlasting life is to be as sure as His own. It is that of
the "branch grafted into the vine." These assurances are
unavoidably, some of them expressly, contained in the *declaration* of man's sonship in Christ.

31. A second form of assurance is to be found by faith in *revealed in Him as* the *revelation* of man's sonship to God which the sonship of *man's* Christ made to the world. We throw away much consolation *nature, original* offered to us in those key-words of full revelation, "life in *and re-stored.* His Son," if we think of the new life thus revealed as altogether and in all respects new. Are we to think of the rela-
tional oneness of man with God, the union of affection and
nature, as coming with Christ Jesus, or rather as restored by
Him from long obscuration in consequence of the darkness of
man's understanding, and restored to conscious possession from
long suppression of all feeling of it by the power of sin? The
coming of Christ was no first uniting of the human nature to
God; it was the perfect discovery of a unity that is original
—a sonship which was part of our created nature, though
needing to be "redeemed" (Rom. viii. 23) and "quickened"
(1 Cor. xv. 45). Adam was the son of God (Luke iii. 38).

The mistranslation of Heb. ii. 16—"He took not on Him the nature of angels ; but He took on Him the seed of Abraham," instead of, "He taketh not up," or helpeth, "angels ; but He taketh up the seed of Abraham"—must naturally misguide the thoughts in this matter; but it is not the *nature* of man that He is said to have taken upon Him, but the *form* and *likeness*—"the form of a servant," "the likeness of sinful flesh," "the fashion of a man." It is not said that He who created us in His own nature needed to take that nature upon Himself. We had fallen in character—we were no more "worthy to be *called* sons" of God ; but He had not changed His nature when man dishonoured it. He had not arisen far away from our first nature, repudiating it in its disgrace. Hiding Himself, withdrawing from our unworthy eyes, was not any putting away of the likeness that we had defiled. In that nature He waited, unseen by man, but not afar off, until the fulness of times, when He could be unveiled in it, to win back the fallen, deceived, apostate ones to seek to be created anew, restored to that lost estate. And the time which the I AM chose to call Himself the Son of God was when He was manifest as also the Son of man—when again the two parts of man's first condition were for a season brought together before the eyes of the world. But in all periods of God's saving communion with man we may see the relational oneness of nature between God and man, in those historical traces we have reviewed of the presence of our own human Saviour to the lives of believers in the old dispensations. It is an unchanging God and Father that we see, and an unchanging manner of fatherly love that the faith of all times is desired to think of. The human appearances vouchsafed to Abraham and Jacob and Joshua, and the human sympathies that fill up so much the pictures of God's drawings-nigh to man from the beginning, were no accidents of the manifestations. They belonged to the very being of the manifester. It was Himself He was showing, in body or in spirit, to their love and their faith. "Adam was the son of God" was no metaphor expressing that Adam had proceeded immediately from the hand of God; it told Adam's nature. Is it Luke's own expression, or that of some early genealogist setting down the tradition of the race? It took up, in the day of completed unveiling of the love which had long been darkened—but only darkened to man's power of believing, because of sin's disablement—what was the essential fact of man's first nature, that he was made in the image of God. That revealing was part of the work of love of the second Adam, who took not the nature, already His own, but the condition of the first. He did not originate at that time the divine nature in man, but He unveiled its existence and provided for its quickening. "No man hath seen God at any time; the only-begotten Son, who is in the bosom of the Father" (ὁ ὢν who was evermore in the bosom of the Father when man went out, Cain-like, from His presence), "He hath declared Him" (John i. 18). "No man knoweth the Father but the Son, and he to whom the Son will reveal Him" (Matt. xi. 27). He is the "way" in which God is manifest to His children desiring their return; He is the "truth" of our assured condition, the reality, the actual manifestation of our blessedness, our status as children; He is the "life" assured to us as His own is sure. "His life is the light of men." "Because He lives they shall live also" who believe in Him.

32. The overwhelming importance attached in apostolic teaching to "faith in Christ, the Son of the living God," becomes appreciable by us when we carry with us how in every subject of faith's thinking of God's love, both historical records and doctrinal revelations of it, He who was Jesus of Nazareth is always the central object of every sight presented to our contemplation, and that He is presented in the completed revelation of God's love with the essential condition of Sonship, personal, and including all believers in Him. Having that "same Jesus" continually set before us—the manifestation of God's love from the beginning—the "eternal life" given to us (1 John v. 20), it is surely but truly represented as the greatest sin and the greatest folly in any one of mankind not to be possessed by that habitual emotional thinking of Him, which is the natural state of man's heart towards any constraining object of his trusting love. Justly is he "condemned already"

Importance attached to faith "in Christ."

O

who believeth not in (is not built up in all peace and child-like sense of blessed safeness, the meaning of "believing in" when first used in Gen. xv. 6) "the only-begotten Son of God" (John iii. 18); who appreciates not, has no "witness in himself" to the value of, the eternal life given in that living form and assuring name. "He maketh God a liar who does not believe," is not impressed to perpetual thought by, "the record God hath given of His Son" (1 John v. 10). Necessarily the sin of the world is branded as this one thing comprehending all, "They believed not on me" (John xvi. 9). On the other hand, the study appropriate to saving faith is most logically marked as "to comprehend what is the breadth and length, and depth and height, to know the love of Christ, which passeth knowledge;" and so is the appropriate help of the Spirit, which is "to take of the things of Christ and show them unto us." Fitly the moving feeling in our life is to be "the love of Christ;" thinking on which is to "constrain us" to the perpetual judgment of ourselves and choice of life which turns to Him, to live not to ourselves, but "unto Him who died and rose again for us" (2 Cor. v. 14). If it was He always from the beginning who by His acts of love saved all good men from the world, the temptation or tyrant of our fallen state, it is but the human side of the same truth, the necessary practice of faith, that is expressed in the question, "Who is he that overcometh the world but he that believeth that Jesus Christ is the Son of God?" (1 John v. 5)—who, by having the precious contemplation habitually in his heart of the love and assured sonship to God declared in him, conquers worldly lusts. He who has been the "all" of love and help and watchful salvation "in all" diversities of man's needs, could not be thought of by us as historical truth requires if our "speaking to ourselves" of religious things took not the accent of Paul's words, "I know nothing among you but Jesus Christ and Him crucified." One thought, centralising in itself all the perfected glad tidings—the collective thought produced by all the facts of God's love must possess us—"Christ formed in our hearts by faith." For faith's thoughts, whether they be of gratefulness or trust, motive or desire or gladness—whatever makes or moves life,—if they be historically intelligent thoughts will be thoughts containing Him ; and their progressive result will be that " Christ will be formed in us " (Gal. iv. 19)—a sight which gives us "the hope of glory " (Col. i. 27). And, preciously conformed to the contemplation of the personal Saviour by our faith, the promised teaching of the Holy Spirit is partly to be Jesus' own "words "—no words of a messenger inviting faith in another, but His own words of love offering Himself, "the love of God," to be confided in by man—those *own words* of Jesus which human nature has found itself more under the power of than of any other words.

33. If any obscurity seems to hang over the language of Scripture as to the Object of Faith, when we read of a personal Christ formed in our hearts—no doctrines about Him, but Himself in some sense—it will be cleared away by again turning to the illustration given by human affection's thinking. The commonest experience of pure human affection, the life it lives, is to have the object of its love in such a manner present always to its conscious or unconscious thoughts, that it would say it has him dwelling in its heart, as Paul wrote of his beloved converts, "Ye are in our hearts to live and die with you" (2 Cor. vii. 3). As more full and intensified, in a degree which we cannot make use of comparison to understand, we may think of the presence of Christ in the believer's heart, because with the believer's own emotional thinking of Him is combined the Spirit's effectual glorifying of Christ in his eyes by taking of the things of Christ and showing them to the thinker's heart. But the result of all this " fellow-working " is to form not any abstract thought of Jesus' love or faithfulness or condescension or saving grace, but a lively sight of Himself, in which the facts of the world-long history of His manifested love are habitually going to and fro before the believer's eyes —each one expounding in their " free course " its peculiar lesson of the grace he is to rejoice to think upon. Constitutionally, human love does not think of the qualities of its object, but of that object himself—his own self, as his words and deeds and looks set him before its musing eyes.

34. What, then, must human love's faith in Christ think

[marginal note: Christ formed in the believer.]

upon ? Conformably to human nature's own manner, and the Spirit and the Word's chosen way of showing Christ to the soul, faith's choicest musings will be at all times of that human life of the Object of faith, which we think most easily of under the name of Jesus—that " life" which has been indeed " the light of men"—those narratives by His disciples which, and not the doctrinal instructions, however precious, of the apostles, Christians have always called " the Gospel," the good news, the " glad tidings "—those very exhibitions of God's love of man, those historical pictures of how " God loved the world," which are not assurances, but very sights, of God's human heart, His tender mercy and loving-kindness for His needy sons and daughters—not similitudes, but portions, foretastes of the nearness of His everlasting love. That living picture will be the choice thought of faith—not the subject but the object of its studious contemplation and its habitual musing — Jesus of the evangelists' stories — Jesus of the miracles, doing those almighty works of tenderness, helpfulness, healing, and blessing—Jesus of the boundless sympathies with human affections and joys as He went about doing good—Jesus whom little children knew, and distracted parents, and desolate sufferers, and outcast sinners — Jesus, who had a baptism to be baptised with, and was " how straitened" till it should be accomplished. Only a filling out of the picture are His " words," such as never man spake ; His own words, inseparable from His human sympathies which gave them comprehensiveness to His brethren's hearts, or from His almighty deeds of actual or typical salvation which filled them with assurance. It is said that the world would not contain the books that might have been written of that human life, the length and breadth, the depth and height of the labours and endurances, cares and sorrows, and intercessions and joys of His love of man ; and in the narrative of it single words are continually occurring that sum up crowded days of miracle—His " healing multitudes," " as many as had diseases," " all manner of diseases and infirmities and plagues"—many sources opening of trouble to keep full for ever the cup He had to drink, which made Him a man of sorrows and acquainted with grief. But what reader of those things which are written has, in the longest life's musing on the few selected pictures, formed within his own breast all the fulness of the picture of God's love of man which is to be gathered therefrom, line upon line, into his thought of Christ Jesus, the realisation of our sonship and eternal life? And faith will deprive itself of much of its needed comfort of thought concerning Christ and the sonship He restored, if it look not back through all humankind's time upon the "same Jesus," and behold Him dwelling from the beginning in the habitable parts of the earth—again and again opening the veil of the invisible to look with human face upon man, or felt, but not seen, guiding the songs of the psalmists and the prayers of the saints, and giving the prophets to taste of the riches of their own visions, opening their spiritual eyes to see what manner of Comforter sought mankind's faith, and was waiting to take their low estate ; or if it carry not its realising musings, unbroken by any historical gulf, past the period of earthly life's time unto the—"days" no more—the life of heavenly promise, and look upon "this same Jesus" in the house of many mansions with them whom He "willed to be with Him to behold His glory," and look upon them likewise in the "union" which He desired, the union of all with Him.

35. Indeed, the eyes of faith will only see with true vision, *The day of* and gather the designed comfort of its "looking unto Jesus," *Christ.* when, in its thoughts of the history of His love, it melts all religious chronology into one life-full watching desiring day, the endless day of Jesus' human-hearted love—the day of the Travail of His Soul, which may have had in one sense a noon of light, when "the mystery of godliness was manifest in the flesh, justified in the Spirit, seen of angels, preached unto the Gentiles, received up into glory," but had no morning except that in which the stars sang together and the sons of God shouted for joy, and will have no night at all :—

HIS DAY *of holy saving love,* in which "the joy" was set before Him ;—joy yet to come unmingled, but not till faith ceases to be faith, and His "work" is "finished," and the "rest" is "entered into."

HIS DAY *of merciful visitation,* the same yesterday, to-day, and for ever, that beheld Him on earth receiving graciously the strangely-persistent prayer of Abraham, and the kindred supplication of the Tyrian mother two thousand years after, and in heaven beholds Himself interceding for men with the same unfainting prayer ;—

HIS DAY *of unchangeable judgment,* in which, with the same sorrowful holy anger, He destroyed the cities of the plain, and condemned the heathendom of Tyre and Sidon and the unrepenting Chorazin and Bethsaida, and will judge the world because it " believeth not on" Him ;—

HIS DAY *of long-suffering patience,* in which He spared, and taught, and waited for the generations of the old world, and chastened the new at Babel, and made Himself known in waiting forbearance in Egypt and Canaan, and among the peoples of the Isles and of the River, and winked at their times of ignorance, and instructed them in ways known and ways unknown to human history, sending prophets to Egypt and Assyria as well as to Israel, and "wisdom" among the children of the East, and bare with them, and had long patience, until the night came of their time in which they would not be wise ;—

HIS DAY *of fellow-feeling of man's infirmities* filled to the Saviour of men all along its ever-present, ever-passing course with the endlessly-changing diversities of His human-hearted sorrows and joys—the first rejoicing in the habitable parts of the earth—Eden in its gladness and Eden in its darkening—the new life of outcast Adam, and of the repentant hoping woman looking for the promised " seed "—the wanderings of pitied, protected Cain—the godly, deathless life of Enoch —Noah's hundred years—the sojourning of Abraham, His " friend," with whom He ate bread, His chosen who lived by faith of Him looking afar off upon His day, and making himself glad in it—gentle Isaac's meditations—worldly and world-tried Jacob's exile and bereavements—Joseph's afflictions, and his forgivingness and saving love, so like a foreshadow of the love of the Son of man—the cry that came up from Egypt—Moses in the court of Pharaoh, in Horeb, in Sinai, in the wilderness,

and on Pisgah—the passover in Egypt, the tabernacle of witness, the lamb slain morning and evening so long—Gilgal, and
Shiloh, and Mizpeh, and Nob, and Gibeon, and Jerusalem, and
Babylon, and all that they beheld—the times of Israel's afflic-
tive judgments and delivering saviour-judges or kings—Eli
and Samuel's lives, like types of the weakness and strength of
men's service of Him—Saul's mingled faith and mingled fortunes—David's as great though different diversity of soul's
experience, of fleshly sin and spiritual desires, bright faith and
dark fears, hardness and bitter repentance—the weak and faithless luxurious kings and nobles, and the fearless prophets
whom He sent unto His people then, "rising up early and
sending, but they would not hear"—Hezekiah, and Asa, and
Josiah, sights of joy amidst their darkened times—and beyond
the chosen race, the lives of Abraham's Pharaoh, and Abimelech,
of the king of Salem, the man of Uz, and the Mesopotamian
prophet faithless to light and given up to his idol and destroyed
in his sin—His grace to Benhadad and Hazael, and the king
of Nineveh, and Nebuchadnezzar, and Cyrus His "servant"—
the obscurer lives also which men saw not, but He looked
upon who seeth in secret and rewardeth openly, the domestic
lives of faith, those gentler softer lights of redeemed human
life, like Ruth, or Hannah, or like the women of Bethany, and
of the sepulchre, and of Berea, and Thyatira;—

His DAY that brought to Him, in the fulness of its time, *the
wondrous manifestation in human flesh*—the man's life of sorrows acquainted with grief—the contradiction of sinners—the
love of a human mother—the longing after the comfort of
human friends—the baptism of death for man, gaining and
quickening *him* back to sonship—"the joy" also that broke
over those years, lights of the eternal day, in the fields beheld
white to the harvest, and the foretastes of their fruitfulness
which solaced His wearied spirit in the love of John, the
faith of Peter, the coming of the "publicans and sinners" to
Him, to follow Him and sin no more—the human home of Nazareth and Capernaum—the days by the Lake of Galilee, and at
Bethany, and at Sychar, and in the temple of His Father—His
intercession for Peter—His opening of heaven to Stephen's

sight—His " cheering " of Paul—His vision to John in Patmos
—the ages also of His Spirit's helping of His servants' infirmities, and guiding them unto all truth, while, like the springing-
corn, the truth that is to save "springeth and groweth up,"
"man knoweth not how"—the foolishness of preaching, in
which the doings of that endless day of His love become the
power of God and the wisdom of God unto salvation—and
the second coming, without sin, to take His many brethren to
His Father's house, where He hath prepared a place for them,
that where He is there they may be also.

The Rest— 36. Such is faith to see the day of the Son of man, exercis-
and the
day of   ing itself and rising up in power to see it thus; looking as if it
man's
Lord.   could look with His all-blending eyes, while He looks on the
whole life of the race whom He so loved—beholding all earth's
history one day of His love, unbroken by the terms of human
time—one day that embosoms in His never-slumbering care
the countless lives, measured by so-called years, of fallen and
repentant and believing, or impenitent God-grieving men—a
day of care and sorrow still to His love as well as of satisfying
sight of the travail of His soul; but in which that shall decrease,
but this shall increase until it is finished.   That day faith is to
behold ending to Him and to man, not in night, but in " rest "
and the joy of man's Lord—not the " rest " which man's body
needs, the rest of night and sleep, nor the absorption of lost life
unconsciously sinking into the being of another, the sad dream
of heathen philosophy which knows nothing of salvation, and
seeks but the end of suffering—but the rest which man's spirit,
his human heart, recognises and seeks as its own rest even
now, and which recruits even his fleshly body more than food
and sleep can do—the rest of love and union with the loved.
That rest and union the Saviour and the Friend of man also
beholds and desires as yet, because it is yet unperfected—
when they whom He loved and who love Him shall enter
into a union called oneness, that will not absorb but mul-
tiply the consciousness of redeemed eternal life — and into
a "rest" in which that new life shall go forth in joyous
liberty and everlasting power, in all the ways of kindred
love's communion and admiration that are the life of man's

heart which God our Saviour made in His own likeness. It shall be that life of union and of rest the endless good of which He sets before us now in a wealth of suggestive relationships, in which distinctness of feature is sacrificed to cumulative assurance—the union-life of sons in their recovered Father— the assimilating life of brethren with their Brother, who gave them new life, when they shall see Him as He is—the life, gathered again into one in Him and in one another to be separate no more, of the spirits of the just made perfect, by whose even earthly union the world is to believe that He has come.

CHAPTER IX.

THE DIVERSITY OF FAITH.

MARK ix. 40.—He that is not against us is on our part.

1 COR. xii. 6.—There are diversities of operations, but it is the same God which worketh all in all.

2 COR. iii. 18.—We, beholding as in a glass the glory of the Lord, are changed into the same image.

Diversity in emotional thinking, normal. 1. THE habitual thoughts of a variety of persons upon one and the same long history of love, the central object of which, though one person, is presented in many strongly-impressive aspects, will not exhibit uniform phenomena. The emotional contemplation, which is the thinking of faith, will be marked by characteristic diversity, both because of the diversity of permanent or occasional mental conditions of the thinkers, and because of the immense range of matters of thought, among which their faith finds appropriate attraction. Every person's individual state of feelings, however arising, from the providential mould in which the habits of thought have grown up, or from natural temperament, the soul's gift received from the body's peculiarities, must always direct the thoughts to some classes of subjects more than to others. With the same knowledge, the habitual thinking of believers in God's love will be diverse. The children of God will differ in propensities of thought and in their impressions of particular things of their family relationship, as do the children of an earthly father. This diversity is recognised in, or at any rate accords with, Scriptural language respecting spiritual conditions—the "house of *many* mansions, and *places* prepared" therein—"diverse stones built into one temple"—"some *least* some *greatest* in the kingdom "—" *last* who shall be *first*, and *first* who shall be *last* "—" *babes* in Christ needing to be fed with milk, and *men* in understanding able for strong meat." In accordance with such language, the illustrative and instructive characters and lives written in the Scriptures exhibit the renewal of nature which goes on under the operation of faith—not as of one uniform habit, but presenting many activities of spiritual life and directions of spiritual growth.

2. The fact that the renewal of men's nature, through faith's beholding of Christ Jesus, is to be in His image, by no means disagrees with differences in men's contemplation of Him ; for in Him the human character was many-sided, as it does not appear in individuals of mere mankind. The natural temperaments, which are distributed much more than combined in our individual characters, united in Him ; even as, in His circumstances, the diversified conditions of His own met together in a way that made the Jews think all the prophecies of the Messiah could not refer to one person—power and privation, social happiness and social trial, popularity and persecution, consciousness of holiness and intensest association with sin in relationship, temptation, oppression, and blame. The Saviour of the world, who, when lifted up, was to draw all men unto Him, was Himself perfect man—*the complete man*, in whom the feelings met of all human needs, human sufferings, and human joys. Believers in Him, "having Him ever before them," "looking unto Jesus" from all the different sides on which their lines of circumstances and suggested thoughts lie, are to be, by beholding Him, renewed in His likeness. But while the standard of their ultimate attainment is " the measure of the stature of the fulness of Christ," their present conscious copying is directed to special points—those which are most obvious or attractive to them. All men are drawn up to Him, but along their different lines of thought to the different phases of His nature which their own conscious nature makes them think most upon and feel most in Him.

Imitation of Christ not uniform but diverse.

3. By diversity of faith is here meant, not diversity of accepted creed or difference of opinion as to the truths which the understanding has become possessed of, but difference of habit

Meaning of diversity of faith.

of thinking about them—a diversity which appears, as to the portions of truth most thought upon and habitually seen by individuals, the facts, or classes of facts, in the knowledge of God's love, which come most readily into different minds. All believers are, in the progress of faith's thoughts of Jesus, converging to "unity of faith and of knowledge of the Son of God" (Eph. iv. 13). It is of their present state of progress, continuing to the end of this bodily and earthly life, and of the different states which at any time the converging minds and hearts will show as yet that the term *diversity* is used. And considering the sources of that diversity, no thoughtful Christian should be surprised at great want of uniformity of feeling and expression of the truth as it is in Jesus among His disciples, but should suspect the reality of a faith which confines itself to any very close uniformity of language. It has been aptly said that "in the same meadow the ox sees the herbage, the dog the hare, and the stork the lizard."

Causes of differing propensity of thought.
4. What things of man's own nature and condition are there of obvious power to give a direction to individual thought upon any emotional subject—things because of which we should be prepared to see different individuals make different selections of things of Christ to think most upon, be attracted most by, make most use of in self-discipline? The temperaments are recognised parts of human character, and their peculiar manifestation is exactly a diversity of propensity in the thoughts; the choleric, the phlegmatic, the sanguine, and the melancholic, each having its own range of subjects in which it finds itself absorbed—the things it "has ever before" it. Sex, age, and race are also recognised sources of difference in the habits and propensities of thought and feeling, determining the character or feature of character in a friend with which any thus differing individual can be *en rapport*, the manner of person he or she is likely to cleave to as an object of faith, or be taken up with. In the most uniform and natural condition of the members of a family, a sister's lines of thought differ from her brother's, a child's from his parents'; and their needs of sympathy—the objects their souls draw to in faith—also differ. Worldly condition, which

modifies original character, does so by inducing habitual thoughts. The ruts of work and difficulty, the sets of associations in which an individual's thoughts are so far confined, will certainly produce in him habits of looking most at particular things, and feeling most some particular truths. Special studies whet the perceptions in their own class of thoughts, not without the risk of a loss of appreciative power on subjects essentially different. Physical and metaphysical studies need, for instance, to correct each other's effects in order to keep a hard student in either fit for healthy general thinking. Race has likewise an influence that is well known. Celts and Saxons look at different features of the same matter. The French and German minds are notably different from each other, as to the excitements they are susceptible of, and the mental exercises attractive to them. It is plain how these diversifying influences, residing in the propensities of temperament, the needs of sex or age, the inherited proclivities and capacities of race, and the second nature of associations produced by employment, &c., will tend to determine the moral qualities which can be the subject of trust, or which will exercise an attractive influence over individuals. The effect will be the same in religious as in other subjects of emotional thinking. The thinking which different believers in Jesus, looking to Him as their salvation and their desire, will indulge themselves in, will be of differing things of Christ, although their formal creed may be the same. Their confession may be the same, but their practical creed, the matter of their habitual, constraining, attractive, besetting thoughts, will differ — yet an equally entire cleaving to Jesus may characterise all those who so differ in the proportions of their care for the components of a formal creed.

5. This normal diversity of the thinking of faith is put beyond the sphere of controversy by what we know of those who had been the personal attendants of the Lord. They manifestly differed in their propensities of thought, their ways of feeling things, their quickness to recognise, and their tenacity in holding fast particular truths. They understood not one another wholly, and had disagreements as to the truth in

Difference appearing among the Lord's personal disciples.

its application to life; but they all understood Him, and felt that they were understood by Him (as Peter in John xxi. 17) with a completeness which filled each individual's needs, though the thoughts of one would have left empty some part or over-filled others of any brother disciple's consciousness. It would be most instructively and satisfactorily illustrative of the diversity of faith which we are to expect to meet, if we were to compare the differences which appeared among those believers who looked most nearly upon the Object of faith. What lines of thought concerning their Lord and their God was John prone to go into? What different lines were most natural to Peter and to James? Of the many-sided perfectness of their Lord's character each saw and felt and thought of one side chiefly. No one's sympathies had grasp enough to take such strong hold of all—each corresponding to but a part, reflecting that part, having that part his object of habitual contemplation, the part of his Lord's perfect complete humanity and divine grace with which his own peculiar nature or condition felt in closest relative connection. John's thought of Jesus' love, and of our love of Him, and its product, a spiritual life of love, fuses present and eternal life into one contemplated state of being " in Him " who was in the beginning with God, and was God, and came unto His own, and in Him was life, and His life was the light of men. Peter—it may be because of more of some kinds of experience of the necessity of self-discipline—sees impressively the process of salvation through Christ, and the eternal prospect rousing to present endeavour after holiness. Paul and James differ much. The goal shines before Paul's high susceptibility, and his soul is under the necessity of pressing onward, forgetting all *attainment* as now *behind*, laying aside every weight, and running the race yet before him. James, while having before his mind the sure help and prize, looks more on the human side of the struggle, and sees man's difficulties and his propensity to self-deceit, which may make the prospect he sets before himself a delusion, his character being incompatible with it; and accordingly James's felt necessity is, to press upon the imagined believer that he must constantly test his expectations by his life. In the picture of the Christian's life—Faith working by love, purifying the heart, overcoming the world—Paul's eyes were chiefly attracted by the faith, John's by the love, and James's by the obedience. Other characteristic diversities in the mental turn of the three most famous apostles, Peter, Paul, and John, naturally drew them to different things of Christ, which appear prominently in their writings. Peter, distinguished by the special qualities which direct and confine the motions of an active man—courageous and confident, so as even to walk forth on the sea, but holding much by the tangible—had his thoughts of Christ, though he was the first to behold in Him the expected Messiah, so closely united with the law of Moses, which He came to fulfil, that he could not for long think of the Saviour separately from its ordinances, nor of Christians as not obedient to them. Paul, profound, and thoughtful of the principles of things, going below all forms and institutions for the roots of faith and conduct, was able, though he had been educated a straitest Pharisee, to behold in Christ not a portion of the law, its corner-stone, but the meaning of the law, to whom it was only a forelooking, the king of an Israel of God wide as humanity. The formal and positive sink in his eyes accordingly out of sight, as the consummation of the spiritual appears ; that which is old passes away when that which is perfect is come. And so Paul and Peter came to variance as to the faith and conduct of believers in Jesus, until Peter's slower reasoning, aided by a divine vision, came to see clearly also. John, essentially different from both—contemplative, affectionate, having his life in near love of his Master, rejoicing in personal liking and faith and service— occupies his Gospel with the personal glory and goodness of the Lord, and fills his forelooking not with the fight of faith here, which fills Paul's thoughtful stewardship, but with the holy, eternal, spiritual life of love, which is gathering together now by all the divine means of positive and moral, formal and spiritual kinds that here are mingling or succeeding each other in the Church of salvation.

It has been remarked upon already how the four evangelists set the subject of their Gospels before us in characteristically

different lights — Matthew thinking more than any of the
others of the Messiah of Jewish prophecy, the fulfilment of
the law; Mark beholding the work of the Redeemer as He
travailed in it in the greatness of His strength, mighty to save;
Luke gathering before his eyes constantly how true and near
to human nature and human estate He was who came the
friend of man; and John gazing upon the eternity of His
divine love of man, whom He calls "His own."

We cannot set before ourselves so well the other first disciples who have not shown to us in written manifestation
their ways of thought. Would the same things of Christ
habitually rise up before them all? Would not the Israelite
indeed, in whom was no guile, draw to his musings a different
set of facts concerning his Master from those Thomas would
turn to, who was ready to question, and needed much proof?
Jesus' one betrayal of omniscience first attracted the one; the
other's faith, having failed after much knowledge, was compelled
all at once to enthusiasm by his Master's calm, compassionate
making allowance for all his doubts, and loading him with evidence. The two events would often arise on the two disciples'
thoughts, separate bonds of each soul to his Lord. The sons of
Zebedee in their early discipleship differed widely in their
habitual thoughts from the spirit they were of long after. The
conduct of Nicodemus at the dangerous close of their Master's
earthly career would make us respect the sustaining power of
his faith as much as we could respect Peter's. Their previous
manner towards Him showed a great diversity in their constraining thoughts of Him. Peter, confident without consideration, refusing even his Lord's bidding to think of dangers he
needed to think of, and failing as eminently as he professed,
must have had a different thoughtfulness from the ruler whose
discipleship never comes into the foreground until the time
when all the eleven had been panic-stricken, but to whom
Jesus had spoken of the profounder things of His work some
considerable time before He had revealed them to Peter or his
brother attendants on their Lord. The thought with which
Mary of Bethany looked back upon Jesus, and the things of
Christ to which the eyes of her faith would be wont to turn,

most readily, would be a different selection from those which would arise before the mind of the "woman which was a sinner." The one must always have looked to Jesus, and could not help it, through His remembered visits of so sympathetic human friendship, and the great fact of His bringing her brother back from the dead, which linked that human love to Godhead's, and pledged the omnipotence of God to human sympathy, in her thoughts of His saving grace. The other could as little help thinking most of Jesus the forgiver, the consoler, who had given her remorseful heart peace without a word of upbraiding, and taken fear for ever from her by so accepting her humble caressing of His feet. Jairus, Zaccheus, and the Syrophœnician mother, had begun their affectionate thinking of Jesus from different forms of emotion as starting-points ; and without doubt the strong original emotion continued to assert itself prominently amidst all habitual thoughts of grateful, humble, worshipping feeling which filled their life afterwards. His perfect entering into the sore afflictions of family affection—His power to rebuke worldly lusts away from the heart—His power to see and draw out from its most secret place faith in His grace under every form of repressing difficulty,—these different parts of His all-comprehending perfections would give special colouring to the differing thoughts of Him which those three would find natural to them. Had they all become preachers of Christ, they would have preached different truths powerfully. Had each of them compiled a creed, the fruit not of intellectual controversy, but a representation of his or her conscious thoughts, they would have been three different though not discordant creeds.

6. These examples of recorded faith exhibit sources of diversity in the thinking of faith, arising in both elements of that thinking—diversity in the matters of thought offered to faith, and diversity in the thinker's peculiar preparation to deal with them. Both these diversities are of great practical consequence.

Diversity in the presentation and in the appreciation of truth.

The maxim, sound in religious as in other knowledge, that "truth is one and indivisible," does not exclude diversity in men's habitual thoughts of Christ so long as their knowledge of Him is fragmentary, and that diversely. Each must think most of what he knows most. Nor is uniformity of faith a consequence necessarily following upon faith's being the gift of God, and the "things of Christ" being shown to us by His Holy Spirit. The "spirit of system," which hinders as well as helps induction in science, seeks much after uniformity; but uniformity is not God's system in His other works, and in the work of grace we are told of something of the same manner —that the Spirit's work, giving birth to the thoughts and feelings of the new life, is like the motion of the wind, unconfined and unpredicable, discovered only from its varied effects. Did He show John and Peter and Paul and James the self-same features of their Lord's character, with the same force, or did He guide them unto all truth so as to lead them to a uniform impression of the features of the earthly life which was to be His service? Shall other men be expected, under the same Spirit's teaching, to see the things of Christ, His redeeming affection and its ways, and man's reasonable ways of service because thereof, one uniform sight in every man's eyes; with no different suggestions made to any soul of special indebtedness or peculiarity of affection due by it, with no different lines of abounding duty opening up before any one? To expect such sameness of result would be a mere assumption of what must be meant by the Spirit guiding believers unto all truth. No human teacher could make different persons by his lessons form in their own minds the very same picture of however simple a case of human amiabilities and moral excellence. Is there anything but the spirit of system, forming an a priori assumption that the perfectness of divine teaching must produce uniform results, to make us think that intelligent learners under the Spirit of God will not, like those learning under human teaching, appropriate the same set of lessons of God's love with a difference? It would surprise us beyond measure, in the case of any other book telling many impressive things, to hear that all readers retained the same impressions of the same parts of the book. The consequence seems unavoidable, that the so rich diversity of Jesus' manifestations in Bethany, in His teachings, in the Transfiguration, with little children, in the Temptation, in Gethsemane, under the eyes of the Scribes and Pharisees, before Pilate, in the so different miracles, in the parables, &c. &c., must have left in beholders different deposits of chief thought; and will always have their portions of mankind, sometimes capable of being united in concurring societies, who will in their religious thoughts see one phase or one or two phases of the Saviour's character more than they see anything else.

7. It is in exact accordance with different parts of religious truth being readiest to affect different persons, that the Epistles, reflecting so far individual human souls and individual views of the truth as it is in Jesus, do not draw the feelings of all ages and conditions to their frequent perusal as the Gospels do, which exhibit no one chief cast of human excellence, nor chiefly any human view of truth logically arranged, but simply set forth all the sides of the love that is to be savingly attractive to man, as it was according to natural opportunity manifested in facts and assurances in the life of Jesus. Of the same significance is the fact that the Book of Psalms has always been so necessary a part of the Scriptures to every class alike. The reflection of no individual soul, nor of any one chief condition of life, but recording the emotions experienced by persons of diverse positions and under great variety of God's discipline, both in personal history and in national fortunes at many periods—part describing minutely the emotions and religious self-discipline of David's life, which stands alone among recorded human lives for its diversity of worldly fortune and moral experience—the Psalter has proved an inexhaustible store of spiritual nourishment for the so different cravings, needs, propensities, and peculiar states of heart which occur in the dissimilar multitude that has to be turned from every kind of dead and evil works, every manner of weakness and corruptness, every form of trouble, unto Him who was lifted up that He might draw all men unto Him. The whole sacred Scriptures are distinguished from all purely human religious books by the same diversified exhibition of the truth fitted to lay hold on different habits of thought and varied moral needs ; though the narratives of God

[margin note: Presentation of truth in the sacred books.]

manifest in the flesh, and the book exhibiting the emotions of a great diversity of human religious conditions, are the most universally ready for this "catching of men" (Mark i. 17). The most systematic writings of the apostles are not systematic after the manner of theological treatises, but discursive, casting out lines of thought on all sides of a main argument. They have also a peculiarity of immense disseminating influence in those terse expressions with which they abound, which to a logical mind often sum up and condense a lengthened argument, but which possess so much of the convincingness of axioms as to be enough of reasoning on their different subjects for those not accustomed to argument. And these reasonings and maxims of the devotional Scriptures are besides set in the midst of constant practical application to religious conduct, the effective exposition of doctrines to all habits of mind and states of heart. Their theology is in fact not theology, but the application of theology to human life in great diversity as it presented itself on the occasions which called forth the Epistles. The mass of the sacred books contains little of even that degree of doctrinal teaching, but exhibits the ways of God, His designs and will, in the very way fitted for universal instruction; i.e., widely diversified illustrations of divine grace, and examples of human feelings and conduct under its influence, narratives of God's dealings with man, lives of God's servants which readers can apply to their own conscious wants as they do the narratives of the Gospels.

Diversity of thinking propensity.

8. The supposition that in religious things, differently from all other subjects of human study, the Spirit guiding unto all truth must produce uniform thoughts of the truth, thus ignores the fact, the source of any amount of diversity in man's necessarily fragmentary knowledge, that the truth is multiform. It has to ignore also the fact characteristic of human condition, that diversities in perceiving, being struck with, caught by, constrained by, different things in emotional subjects, arise from bodily temperament, period of life, race, sex, and place in human relationships; all which confine or induce particular moral and emotional activities more than others. Of these we can most easily illustrate the effects of temperament.

The temperaments.

Persons of choleric temperament, warm, uncompromising, and zealous, will find themselves thinking often upon Jesus' indignant hours, and His stern reproofs of all hypocrisy and guile. His expressions, " whited sepulchres," " that fox," " blind leaders of the blind," " evil and adulterous generation," have often seemed meet language for Christians in the eyes of strong masculine natures zealous for the purity of the Church. Gentler natures will find enough to fill heart and mind with in the meek and lowly language and doings of the Lord at other times.—" He that is not against us is on our part," " Spare it this year also, till I dig about it and dung it," " He beheld the city and wept over it." Their desire to put off the necessity of strife for the cause of religion, or to avoid proceeding to measures of severity for the faith in the family or the church, will be confident of appreciation and much sympathy at His hands who did and said these things. The early part of His ministry, when He is seen so long letting His works and His character work their way to influence in the public mind without self-assertion on His part, will give faith of being right to many whom more excitable neighbours may think unzealous or cold—many who seek by their conduct, personal and towards religious things, to let the cause of Christ in their life be advanced, as by " an epistle known and read of men," more than heard by men, feeling that in that department they can work and have patient faith, while they would not see their way to usefulness in polemical service. Calm faith (the experience of their phlegmatic temperament, while they wait the promised result, working for it in their peculiar way) was in His perfectness as well as the powerful aggressiveness in which choleric natures think they are like Him.

Those burdened with what theoretically may seem not very compatible with strong faith, but what was, notwithstanding, much seen in Jesus—viz., melancholy depression because of the difficulty of influencing men to their peace—and those who, like Paul, are oppressed by the consciousness of inherent evil, the law of sin in their members, the body of death, the divided inner man doing what they would not, will look unto Jesus as their peculiar Saviour, Comforter, fellow-feeling Helper, and think

often, with solaced faith, upon how He mourned over His fruitless desires, and pains taken with an unbelieving generation, and
with slow-hearted disciples; how yet He pitied the disciples,
whose spirit was willing but their flesh was weak; how kindly
and not oppressively He reproved the "little faith" of His
disappointing followers; how He prayed for Peter, when Satan
desired to have him that he might sift him as wheat, that the
disciple's faith should not fail; how He warned him of the tribulations of His service which awaited him; and how He himself
shrank from suffering in Gethsemane. A great guide of faith
to such persons will be the experienced apostle's words, " Consider Him who endured such contradiction against Himself,
lest ye weary or faint in your minds." And sanguine spirits,
equally with stern, mild, calm, or disheartened, will have part
and lot in Jesus the Son of Man, who was perfect in our exercise of endurance, that He might succour us when we are
tried. Peter never fearing, as well as Paul often fearing, could
lay hold on things of the very human nature of Christ himself,
to keep him sure that he was known by Him. The disciples
marvelled at their Master's alacrity going up to Jerusalem
when He had told them He was to suffer death there; and as
they followed Him, they were afraid. The recollection of that
journey was to them all—and to Peter very much, we may
believe—a thought giving them strength and courage in their
faith of His sympathy when the days came that they had to
meet bonds and imprisonment and death for Him. His words
belonging to that, the sanguine part of His character, were to
be glad tidings to them, and to every buoyant-hearted striver
with worldly difficulty and trial in His service—" In the
world ye shall have tribulation; but be of good cheer, I have
overcome the world."

Bearers of these so diverse temperaments could not turn
then or now to each other for the comfort and support of being
thoroughly understood; but how fully, without doubting or
trouble at all, could and can any one turn to Him who
" knoweth what is in man," and recognises as His own—kin
to His own perfect humanity, at first formed after it, drawn to
it now, and to be corrected and sanctified by it unto perfec-

tion—every diverse-featured looking of love to Him and His
honour. Consciousness of upright desire will be as confident
of recognition from Him as contrition will be of acceptance.
Fervent zeal and timid fears, the naturally exacting and the
naturally willing to make allowance, diverging though their
human paths of religious action would be, will have remembrances of Him by which their spiritual thoughts converge
and approach towards a coming oneness.

9. If we think of any man's faith, not as the propositions of
a creed, but as his heart's favourite thoughts, the emotional
thoughts of the facts of God's love, which are, because of
determining peculiarities as well as selecting education, wont
to come into his mind at any and every time—diversity of faith
is not a thing to alarm, but one to be looked for as the normal condition of the "body of Christ," a sign of separate individual life in a body of men and women, in whose hearts Christ
dwells by faith, while the whole body is making increase and
perfecting itself in love. Such diversity of consciousness is a
consequence of the fact, that all are looking unto Jesus from
the midst of things of their own spirits which others know
not, and that all believers, while the time for faith lasts, are
in progress, and at different stages, none having attained to
completeness of thoughts, all going on to know the Lord. The
step from such a habit of thinking of and being affected dominantly by one or more selected truths of divine grace and
relative human sanctification, is manifestly a short one to a
propensity, should circumstances induce the construction of an
intellectual creed, to form one logically depending from those
particular truths as centre truths. Creeds, attempting uniformity of so much of the faith of believers, are theological, not
religious, things. To some extent they are chronological
things, the records of ecclesiastical diversity at particular
times; but records also of the progress of faith, whether, like
Paul's, a progress in understanding revealed truth, or, like the
early Hebrew creed—expanding in Moses' time from the prophet's first announcement of Jehovah as the God of Abraham
to the many thoughts of the Book of Deuteronomy—a progress
because of increased revelation. But creeds, could they be ex-

(margin note: Normal diversity of faith affecting creeds.)

haustive of formal religious knowledge, can never by possibility be exhaustive of religious truth. Not the few objective thoughts of the creed, but the multitude of the thoughts within the heart, make a man's faith as far as it is saving faith. Uniformity in these spontaneous thoughts would, like uniformity of result in any education of human thought, be possible only by the process found associated with that uniformity, the repression, starving, or eradication of the free emotions and spiritual activities of the human being. While, therefore, diversity even of creed is defensible as being an unavoidable consequence of forcing into forms of feelingless logic material which essentially comprehends feeling, diversity of actual faith is in every truly-believing Church immeasurably greater than all diversity of creeds in the family of Churches. This fact makes creeds subordinate things in the household of faith. The faith of Christendom is more comprehensive than all its creeds. And if diversity of turn of thought, or start of thought, or capability of appreciating new truth, makes men still sometimes diverge in outward fellowship, saying, "I am of Paul, and I of Apollos," it is as in the days of those professions not probably, because they are not of Christ, but because they differ only as the apostles differed from, and were not understood by, one another; while all knew the Lord, and felt that He who knew all things knew that they loved Him.

Lines of thought— "I am of Paul," "I of Cephas."   10. There is a recognisable sense in which wise and well-instructed Christians may, with full faithfulness to their Lord, be expected to follow different human leaders, as if they said, "I am of Paul," "I of Cephas,"—a sense in which, when they say, "I am of Christ," it is thinking of different things of His glad tidings. A contemplative mind, turning engrossingly to what shall be hereafter, will be attracted by enjoyed sympathy to John's Epistles; and will find correction there too of the tendency of that state of soul to lose itself in gazing up into heaven, by being brought down with the apostle so frequently at once to see what the earthly life must be to which such heavenward forelooking belongs. The practical soul which feels the life that now is so much that its readiest outlook is for its covert evils, will come as to a master spirit of its own kind to James; but come only to have its habit of confined vision corrected by his close intense connecting of the practical outer life of this world with the thought and sight and feeling of the everlasting presence of God his Saviour in all his labours and exercises of faith and patience. Among our Lord's most direct revelations of the forms and extent of His grace, of which His followers are to think—viz., His miracles—will not every separate miracle draw to Him a separate state of mind, or diverse allied states, as the story is pondered, vivid with its picture of a particular need of our condition met or sought out by His saving help, and of the receiver's faith in His peculiar help drawn out by Him in ways fitting so many different conditions of understanding and confidence? Even this most closely personal following of the Lord in the thinking of faith must be thus by differing lines of thought. The diversity of matter of thought offered to the mind by the different books which were undoubtedly included in "the Scriptures" which Jesus bade the Jews search for their witness to Him, obliges us to think of a blessed wideness in the subjects of thought which it is God's purpose to make paths by which men shall come to Him who is "the Way, and the Truth, and the Life." It seems, perhaps, from afar off, that the mundane wisdom of the Book of Proverbs leads to the truth as it is in Jesus. That reading, however, has been in its turn the first convincing proof of a revelation to minds wise in human knowledge or observant keenly of human ways. The gloomy views of life written in Ecclesiastes, so far below Paul's bright visions, yet struggling into some light, have been congenial introductory thoughts of faith to others.

11. To what conclusions do these considerations lead us? *The unity of the faith—what is it?* Is diversity in the subject or manner of religious thinking to be held up as the right rule of faith which man should follow after? Certainly not. It is not a rule at all—not a guide to be followed—but a condition of man's earthly state, to be expected, and not to be misinterpreted mutually by those who are different in their habitual thoughts. If it is a truth of man's nature that subjective condition will influence faith in objective truth, there is a companion truth, the revealed truth

of man's necessary religion, that his self-education, by the means of grace and the help of the Spirit of God, is to bring his subjective condition into harmony with the objective truth which God sets before him. Temperament and circumstances will tend always to direct the unwatched thoughts. Faith's first business is intentional watchful thinking, not upon subjectively attractive points of revealed truth, but upon all truth. And the end of faith's purposed reasoning, considering, thinking " on these things " of Christ, is to bring every " high thought and imagination into captivity to the obedience of Christ " (2 Cor. x. 5). The design of all the ministry of the Word is that all may come to " the unity of the faith and of the knowledge of the Son of God "—to one knowledge, or in some sense uniform way of thinking of the Son of God; having before them, as the measure of their aim, to become a " perfect man," to attain the " stature of the fulness of Christ;" that they be " no more children, tossed to and fro and carried about with every wind of teaching, but speaking the truth in love, may grow up into Him in all things, which is the Head, Christ; from whom the whole body fitly joined together and compacted by that which every joint supplieth, according to the effectual working in the measure of every part, maketh increase of the body unto the edifying of itself in love " (Eph. iv. 13-16). The apostle's figure points to a diversity which will accompany the perfectness of the members of Christ, as elsewhere he speaks of one star differing from another star in glory. It is the beautiful diversity of harmony which is so attractive in all the other works of Him who works man's sanctification. Man's way, however, of working towards that diversity which is to belong to his perfect state, is not by thinking of and following after diversity of ways now, but by " thinking the same things "— " being of one mind." The diversity is that of members made one through the head—growing up into one body. This is our rule for the practice of faith.

To be attained by study of the historical Christ.

12. To approach to the harmony of diversity set before us in the body of Christ, we have chiefly to work towards uniformity. All are to have one object of faith, Christ Jesus. The process of our following after unity of faith is not by

repression, eradication, starving of our diverse natural affections or propensities of thought, but by unity of study of the
Son of God, which is the meaning of unity of knowledge of
Him—by bringing those diverse living capabilities or propensities of our spirit into captivity to obey Him. In contemplating Him—having Him ever before the mind—the things
of His nature and love taken and shown to the soul—every
diversity of impulsive whole-heartedness, steady caution,
holy zeal, holy sorrow, unfearing courage, or depression under
burdens of trial, will find, besides its needed sympathy, its
needed guidance and sanctifying correction. In Him dwelt
all the fulness of innocent manhood as well as of Godhead—
all perfectness of the diverse human temperaments, which mankind possess not in such harmony, as well as all fulness of that
divine grace which every varying needer of His sympathy could
cleave to. And in contemplating Him perfect in man's nature,
and perfected in experience of man's conditions, each will find
the correspondence with and understanding of his case which
he needs; as Peter did in his time of seeming greatest removal
from likeness to his faithful Master, and, in the depth of self-
reproach for his own untrustworthiness, was able to say to
Him, " Lord, thou knowest all things: thou knowest thatI love
thee."

13. This correction of subjective differences bringing diver- Correction
sity into harmony we find illustrated in the same cases of our of propensities.
Lord's personal disciples, which gave so full exemplification of
diversity of natural propensity.

John, for whatever reason he was the disciple whom Jesus John.
loved, was, as all his writing shows, distinguished among the
attendants of the Lord by his love of Him personally. He has
been called the φιλοιησους, as Peter was the φιλοχριστος, seeing
the *person* as the other saw the *mission* of his Lord dominantly.
The corrective influence which that constant contemplation
had on his natural ways of thinking was very apparent. John
was not in those first years the gentle disciple we call him now
—his and his brother's spirit was vehement. They were Sons
of Thunder. They asked for the highest places in the kingdom
of their Master, ready to drink of His cup, and to be baptised.

with even His baptism of suffering. They rebuked one who
cast out devils in their Lord's name, because he was not one
of their company. They sought to call down fire, " as Elijah
did," to destroy a Samaritan village, merely for inhospitality
shown to Him. How corrected and harmonised with the spirit of Jesus became those strong human propensities of soul
in John by the time he wrote his Gospel and Epistles! There
his strong love looks with increased absorption of thoughts
upon the person of the only-begotten well-beloved Son of God;
but he has come to speak of himself and his fellow-believers in
Jesus, to whom he writes, as little children now, and not ambitious, strong, striving men. Amidst the propagation of philosophical theories explaining away the historical character of
the Christ, he is the strong uncompromising asserter that it
was a true person, a real individual, the Son of God, and God
Himself, who came in the flesh. But the early rebuker of a
different manner of following Christ from his own is now no
polemic nor controversialist, even against heresy. He but sets
forth in its own strength the proved truth of Jesus' declaration
of Himself and the divinely moral teaching of His faith, and
lets these condemn the heresy; as His Master had let His works
show Him to men, and demanded their faith upon that ground
alone. He who before the Samaritan village knew not what
spirit he was of, in Patmos knew his own spirit, " the Spirit
He hath given us " (1 John iii. 24); and the vindictive avenger
came to think and write habitually of self-sacrifice for the
brethren, and said, " He that hateth his brother is a murderer,"
" he that loveth dwelleth in God," " if any man love not his
brother whom he hath seen, how can he love God whom he
hath not seen?" " we know that we have passed from death to
life because we love the brethren."

Peter.   John's dissimilar fellow-disciple and afterwards companion-
apostle, Peter, associated with him in that so common attraction of differing temperaments which seems to indicate that
diversity is a law of human progress to perfection through
mutually-sought complement, is another example of natural
temperament adopted into the new life through a correcting
process effected by the contemplation of the things of Christ.

Peter's ultimate moral character was announced by Jesus when his brother Andrew brought him into His presence, and He said, "Thou shalt be called the Rock" (John i. 42). Peter's natural propensities and capabilities were akin in some particulars to that coming steadfastness in the faith. He was rough and stubborn; but he was not stable as yet. By union with the living Rock, the Rock of Salvation to him, the union of constant contemplation producing its promised change into the same likeness, he became firm and immovable unto the end—the "power" which he "received from on high" perfecting in good his own constitutional tendencies, which had before shown the natural risk of unsanctified affections to take a turn to evil. Peter, rudely presumptuous, rebuking his Master for speaking of His humiliation, stubbornly self-confident in the upper room, violently courageous in the garden, totally overthrown in the judgment-hall, to the loss of all courage, fidelity, and self-respect, was the selfsame Peter who afterwards, with modesty and firmness equalling one another, held fast his faithfulness against the browbeating of the Sanhedrim, and under Herod's imprisonment of him with the prospect of death hanging over him after the slaughter of James. It was the same rock of offence to his Master, who afterwards became the rock of stability to the early church, "strengthening the brethren" (Luke xxii. 32). There is all Peter's early faithfulness, but none of his forwardness, in his and John's answer to the high priest, "Whether it be right in the sight of God to hearken unto you more than unto God, judge ye; for we cannot but speak the things which we have seen and heard." The former earthly-mindedness of both, and their views of discipleship, were in like manner gone when they went out from the presence of the council after they had been beaten and forbidden to preach Jesus Christ. "They rejoiced that they were counted worthy to suffer shame for His sake." The hastiness which was the sometimes faulty character of Peter's early declarations of his belief in Jesus and his fidelity to Him—which produced these confessions conspicuous for their early manifestation of faith in the dignity of Jesus and appreciation of His needed work, "Thou art the

Christ of God;" "To whom shall we go? thou hast the words
of eternal life"—but which produced also the rash self-ignorant
walking on the water, and the profession of fidelity unaccepted
by the Lord on the night of the betrayal—that hastiness to
profess and to act counting no cost, estimating no difficulty in
himself, became in his training not hastiness of promise but
preparedness for confession and promptness in obedience. The
two periods of Peter's moral life were made parts of one whole
by the faithfulness which was the rock of his nature. Peter
never did anything like merely professing; in his rashest time
his ebullitions were true manifestations of the inner man.
His humble, grieving, almost remonstrating words at that mid
point of his life, when the discipleship was ending and the
apostleship was to begin, "Lord, thou knowest all things, thou
knowest that I love thee," asserted a consciousness of integrity
which belonged to him before as well as after. The peculiarity
of Peter's line of Christian thought, in which he is compared
with John and called the φιλοχριστος, while John was the
φιλοιησους, distinguished the apostle as markedly as the disciple. The Messiahship of Jesus was Peter's distinguishing
early confession. It was he who recognised the meetness of
the association of Jesus with Moses and Elias in the Transfiguration, and he who answered in these words expressing the
only hope and refuge of man, "To whom shall we go? thou
hast the words of eternal life" (John vi. 68). It is the same
human spirit who, of all the teachers of the church, sets before
the earthly life of disciples so brightly, as its hope, stimulus,
and upholding, the work of Christ—His atonement, His
example of enduring suffering on earth, and the "exceeding
great and precious promises, the inheritance incorruptible, and
undefiled, and unending," which His prepared heaven holds
forth. Christ's work, Christ's example, and Christ's heaven,
are in Peter's teaching not distant things in human contemplation or influential expectancy, but made to bear on the lives
of His servants. Travelling Zionwards by these thoughts,
Peter's disciples converge to the same state of spirits of just
men made perfect as John's, and minds congenial taking his
guidance, are approaching by another line of thought — the

thought of Jesus himself, His personal worthiness of love whom they are to be "like, seeing Him as He is" (1 John iii. 2). Both look and endeavour onwards to "an abundant entrance into the everlasting kingdom of our Lord and Saviour Jesus Christ" (2 Pet. i. 11).

14. The progress of an individual's faith to fuller and fuller *Progress in* thoughts of Christ and His salvation, implying different faiths *perceptic.* at different times, all of which were right, but changing in order to perfection, is more clearly seen in Paul's religious history. *Paul.* Saul's religiousness did not begin on the road to Damascus. He was a man whose sincere regard to revealed truth before made his susceptible spirit nerve itself to a course of action for the sake of the truth as he saw it, in which the sense of duty alone could have sustained him, for it must have required him to suppress painfully the human sympathies with which his nature was very largely gifted. His perceptions of the truth were defective, not his practical emotional thinking of it, having it "ever before him," constraining his life. He only did not then see Jesus Christ as the end of the law. His conversion was not from a man without God in his thoughts; that is, without faith. It was from shortcoming sight and thought of the truth revealed under the law to so far complete sight of it, and to immediate acceptance of it by his spirit, already a believing one. So Ananias described his change as a progress of faith: "The God of our fathers hath chosen thee, that thou shouldest know His will, and see the just One, and shouldest hear the voice of His mouth. For thou shalt be His witness unto all men of what thou hast seen and heard" (Acts xxii. 14, 15). Why Paul, to whose great intellect all Gentile Christians look up, should have been blind to what they see taught in all the Law and all the Prophets, is a question of only comparative difficulty, an illustration of the origin of the normal diversity of faith. Saul's blindness was shared by the Jews generally, whose nation is blind to this day, "not able to see to the end of the law" (2 Cor. iii. 13); and especially was it the blindness of Saul's religious sect, the Pharisees, who could not see in Jesus of Nazareth the expected Messiah, because they had come to habitual think-

ing that they saw in the prophecies another manner of position and person in the Messiah than the mean human position
Jesus assumed and the divine nature which He asserted; and
unlearning is always more difficult in religious truth than
learning. Saul's faith had also, after his vision at Damascus,
still to make great progress in recognising the whole truth of
the Messiah's salvation taught in the books so familiar to him,
the Law and the Prophets. As he needed a special revelation
to see Jesus as the Christ, he and all the apostles needed
afterwards help of the same kind to see the truth, declared by
Jesus to Nicodemus, that " God so loved the world that *whosoever* believeth in Jesus shall have everlasting life." At least
six years beheld him preaching Christ from no more far-seeing
point of view than the Jewish Christians were long confined
to. During part of that period he appears as the companion of
Barnabas, and always named second to him. Contemporaneous with his beginning to bear the name of Paul, though in no
indicated connection therewith, his thoughts appear free to
contemplate the will of God as being the salvation of all
nations, and not of the Jews only. That freedom of faith
marked another diversity among the very leaders of faith; for
Paul's confident vision of the end of Jewish ceremony was not
shared in by the others so soon. His case is peculiarly instructive in the present consideration. Had Paul written a
creed at those three different periods of his life, they would
have been three different creeds; but they would have illustrated a feature of what is here meant by diversity of faith.
They would not have contradicted one another; only each
later creed would have been fuller than that going before it.
They would have been, as diverse human creeds, the spontaneous expressions of believers, are, and as the creeds of churches
should be if they were full confessions of faith, records of a
" following on to know the Lord." In all his after-progress Paul
never departed from the simplicity of teaching Christ and Him
crucified, the hope and life of God's prodigal children arising
to go to their father; but he was for ever learning spiritually,
adding to his influential thoughts, ever correcting the old
exclusive religious pride of the " young man Saul," and be-

coming one in sympathies and self-abegnation with the body
of Christ, Jew and Greek, barbarian, Scythian, bond and free.

15. Paul's faith, like John's and like Peter's, had a line of
thought of its own, in which, like theirs, it went on to know
the Lord, not changing views of salvation so much as enlarg-
ing them. John's love of Jesus himself gathered about it
personal things of Christ, one after another accumulating the
fulness of Christ from "the Word" of "the beginning" to the
Lamb by the throne. Peter's sight of the work of "the Christ,
the Son of the living God," drew more into one line of vision
terminating in Him, the pilgrimage of working, suffering,
tempted life, and the inheritance incorruptible and undefiled
and that fadeth not away, in which the object of his faith's
vision was always Jesus who had gone to prepare it. Paul's
recorded faith started from before the fulness of time. It
came forth richly furnished with the so full but yet unfinished
revelation of the truth of God's love; and it was in connection
with the forecasts of Jewish ordinances, and with the necessities which Jewish law compelled his soul to feel, that he
learned the things of Christ to the fulness of that great feeling
of them, which came to him after his eyes were memorably
opened to see the end of the law. The law was to Paul a
schoolmaster to bring him to Christ, in the full recognition of
dependence, need, union, sympathy, spiritual connection, he
was by it prepared for. The faith of the Jew was not thrown
away by him. The veil on his Jewish-taught heart was rent,
and Christ, the fulfilling of the Law, was beheld close to his
sight. There was no conversion from Judaism to Christianity
in the sense of converson from one religion (connection with
God) to another. The faith of the Jew and the faith of the
Christian were one, as spiritual and eternal life will be found
to be one unbroken thing. The old revealed truth, pondered
upon and become familiarly his own, fed the new thoughts.
His faith converged with John's and Peter's to the same
Object of Faith, at whose name every knee shall bow. But
it was the same faith in which Abraham, far back in the history of faith, travelled along his solitary way, seeing afar off;
and Moses and David, and the cloud of witnesses whom history

Paul's advance through Hebrew into Christian faith.

Q

remembers travelling and looking Zionwards, widely apart from each other, on the many narrow paths of the world's life.

Use of the means of grace.

16. These three described examples illustrate the use of the means of grace to the diversified nature of fallen man. The "perfecting of the saints," the conforming of broken temperaments, the harmonising filling up of their diversities into likeness to Christ Jesus, is the work of the Gospel, of its study as of its ministry.

It would have been instructive in this matter if we could have had such records of the faith attained to by the female compeers of those disciples, and by persons in diverse social circumstances, as they saw or thought more and more of Jesus of Nazareth. The means of grace assimilate all original differences as life goes on ; and the likening work is helped by the coming on of the state of old age, the sameness of whose few feelings upon all points is so great a contrast to the early antagonism or contrasts arising from sex, education, and position in life's relationships or occupations. But in the time of the freshness and strength and fulness of emotional capability, diversity arising from these present estates of the living soul is not all disease needing cure, but is partly a fulness of life, a richness in the heart's fruits of faith glorifying God, which seems the true service of earthly human life; and which, ripened and completed into harmony, may, much rather than may not, be thought of as giving a diversified beauty and joy to the everlasting inheritance of "the heir of all things," whose lifting up is to "draw all men to Him."

Historical divergence of creeds —how caused.

17. From these illustrations of diversity in the great examples of faith, we may read with understanding what consequence is attached to the occasions of diversity adduced in the beginning of this chapter, and see thereby a more comfortable explanation than a charge of heresy is, of the historical differences of creed. In considering what things must be accepted as probable sources of diversity of faith and of creed next—should a creed become a necessity—we find *political*, like social peculiarities, leaving their impress on the habits of religious thought, and that even in the case of the logical creeds which are the result of constrained thinking,

and often of conforming compromise. Of course, then, the propensities of thought which, even when forced into confining order, show such prominence of different features at different periods of the world as the creeds of Christendom do, must, in free, self-indulging, ruminating thought, be far more abundant in living individual peculiarities. The effect of *race* upon propensities of thought, appearing in the *religious sentiment* which, when compelled to logical expression, is apt to make differences of creed, is inexplicable, but quite recognised. Teutonic and Celtic Catholicism differ in the proportion in which religious sentiment dwells upon the Virgin Mary as one of its objects. Her altars, which are for the most part prominent objects in the churches of France and Belgium, are not so in those of Germany. Though interchange of religious reading has had no little influence in removing peculiarities of religious writing, and so far, consequently, of thinking, critics still think they have some definite meaning when they speak of a German, or a French, or an English, or even, diverse from English, a Scotch, way of looking at a religious subject. Who would expect the old Greek mind delighting in subtle disquisitions, and the Roman mind bent habitually upon practical organisation, to have set the multitude of revealed things of religion before a body of hearers, such as the Church, in the same shape of human system? Two churches, departing from and denouncing each other, were the early consequence of East and West coming together to discuss philosophical systems of religious truth. Dean Stanley traces the indomitable affectionate Benjamite in Saul of Tarsus as well as in Saul the king. He has pointed out the general characters of the descendants of Esau and Jacob, appearing throughout history divergent as those of their progenitors were. The Jew has been cautious, persevering, stooping to escape difficulties rather than rising to grapple with them; chastened and deterred only by centuries of discipline from time-serving adoption of idolatry. The Idumean has been impetuous, grand, generous, greedy, unstable— Herod hearing John gladly, and then beheading him for a rash promise; Herod Agrippa, almost a Christian, but laughing at the idea of his being caught. The race was characterised by

Josephus as a turbulent unruly race, rejoicing in changes, roused to arms by the slightest motion of flattery, rushing to battle as if they were going to a feast. What is the religious end of the two as yet? The Jew is immovable in his Judaism—blind, and unable to think a generous thought of any other people. The children of Edom have gone astray into the wild fanaticism of Mohammedan sectaries, and that creed's lavish sensuality, fatalism, and imposition of religious forms by the sword.

A source of diversity of way of looking at subjects of thought, curious in kind, but exceedingly important because of its extent, lies in the imperfection of language as an exponent of thought. The principle is well known, that language is, to some extent, the leader of thought, the exigency of expression often bringing to hand words which, by association, will change the line of thought from what it was exactly meant to be. This influence, most perceptible in hasty expression under excitement, is so far dominant in the case of all thought that has to be expressed. Those intimate with the spoken language of the Scottish Highlands say it almost excludes logical address, and subjects all religious teaching to the risk attaching to the perpetual use of metaphor. Chevalier Bunsen, a clear writer in several languages, quotes, with some amusement, the result, in his own case, of writing in German or French or English, that to his intimate friends he seemed to differ in habit of mind with the tongue he used. His German relatives would have mistaken him for a Frenchman when they read his French writing; and he promised them to be an Englishman when they should read his 'Egypt' in the English language. Language, unavoidably an imperfect instrument, becomes, within the confinement of any nationality, chiefly fitted for expressing the ways of thinking which are seen to become peculiar to a nation, the result of all its associations of history, employment, climate, geographical feature, &c., and thought cannot keep but partially out of the established rut.

Originally and properly the result of impression and thought, language thus becomes in its turn the origin of both. This is one of the sources of the religious influence exercised by the sacred writings. The language of the Bible could have arisen in no country but the so exceptional one of Palestine. No nation but the Hebrew one could have had the associations of mountainous and level scenery, maritime and pastoral habits, nomad life, and African, Asiatic, and European civilisation. No other language, accordingly, is so wealthy in metaphorical expressions of all origins. Hence the appreciation and effect of the historical and devotional language of the Bible are so wide—all peoples finding in it things familiar to them which influentially guide their farther thinking. The opposite condition of languages like the modern European tongues instanced by Bunsen, if it had such effect upon his expressing himself, who, a master of thought and of fitting expressions, was entirely familiar with the different languages which he used, must be expected not only to confine expression, but to drag the thoughts into a certain line in some lesser or greater degree, just as an imperfect tool becomes the workman's master always to an appreciable extent. It is much as bodily temperament, peculiarity of brain, or other bodily organ, or healthiness or unhealthiness in the organs connected with thought or emotion, confines, suggests, or leads to these. For the leading effect of Aryan and Semitic languages towards polytheism and monotheism, see Max Müller's 'Chips from a German Workshop,' vol. i. p. 358.

18. The eleventh chapter of the Epistle to the Hebrews, enumerating under the same authoritative term of "faith" such dissimilarities as belong to the instances there quoted, exhibits strikingly what diversity we are to look for of this possession under differing circumstances of outward life. What human writer would, without such authority, have classed Gideon and Barak and Jephthah along with Abraham, Moses, and David, as examples of faith? Yet the wild character which belonged to two at least of these four eminent men among Israel's deliverers differed from the ripe righteousness of Abraham and Moses and David no more remarkably than the wild distracted state of the tribes, overborne and oppressed by the Eastern Midianites and the Western Philistines, differed from the domestic peace of Abraham's general state, or the life Moses

Recognised diversity of faith in the cloud of witnesses.

passed, consciously as it were, under the shadow of Jehovah's wings, daily taken into His presence in the tabernacle, or the days in which David, " dwelling safely in the midst of Jerusalem," was the sweet psalmist of Israel. And one quality of faith belonged doubtless to the history of the Father of the Faithful, to Moses the man of God, to David His anointed, and to those who, to human sight, are only national heroes, wild patriots, leaders of the forlorn hopes of the people in their several times. It is that quality we have already been led to infer as the fundamental consciousness of faith, its universal feature, its essential part but with undefinable additions—the feeling of union with their Jehovah, having Him " ever before" them, "in all their thoughts." Before those four worldly heroes, Jehovah the Deliverer, the Captain of Israel's national salvation, arose in inspiring vision in Israel's low estate. They felt themselves His to surely work His deliverance for His people. Before Abraham's more spiritual thoughts, the " day seen afar off" shone behind a long undefined foreground of descendants blessed in him; and before Moses, a worldly prospect arose crowned with religious glory; the growth of a nation to be a great testimony set forth among the nations— " Holiness to the Lord." The quieter condition of Abraham and Moses beheld rich sanctification arise from their thinking on the holy Jehovah, before whom they dwelt. Samson, thinking of the mighty Jehovah, was not so freed from the lusts of the flesh, yet neither was David by his higher thoughts; but Samson's ending showed belief in Jehovah's being his sure helper. The catalogue of the cloud of witnesses affords many differences of a less striking kind. It should be heard as a protest against the so human-sighted looking for uniformity in mankind's thoughts of revealed things. These cases are not to be quoted as examples bidding believers seek to differ from one another, but certainly they are barriers to human criticism seeking to condemn diversity that does not appear to have been intentional.

CHAPTER X.

THE CONDITIONS TO FAITH.

1 JOHN iv. 8.—He that loveth not, knoweth not God.

MARK iv. 19.—The cares of this world . . . and the lusts of other things entering in, choke the word, and it becometh unfruitful.

JOHN vii. 17.—If any man will do His will, he shall know of the doctrine whether it be of God.

Ps. lxviii. 11.—Unite my heart to fear thy name.

1. To be able to think habitually, with the continuance of a life habit, and under right emotions, upon the religious things revealed in the Bible, the thinker must be in a certain normal condition, moral, intellectual, physical, and social. This necessity is partly declared to us in the Bible itself, where it describes the "hearing" by which "faith cometh" (*e.g.*, Luke viii. 11-15 ; James i. 21-25); and is partly the closest inference from our own experience of other parts of emotional thinking. A healthy moral state, a conscience neither defiled nor inactive, is an experienced condition of ability to perceive and feel moral truth quickly. The *mens sana in corpore sano* is a condition of correct thinking upon any matters of personal interest. And a lot in life not over-trying is a kindred necessity.

A normal personal condition necessary to faith.

Moral Conditions to Faith.

2. The moral condition upon which faith is possible is not one arbitrarily imposed, but one that is unavoidable under the nature of faith; which is interested and conciliating uniting

Faith and faithfulness reciprocal.

thinking upon God's love to us under our debt to Him. Capability of *faith* and the exercise of *faithfulness* are reciprocal. This reciprocity is only a part of the general law of human religion, whose affections have their authority and ability from the relationships which unite man to God. All the affections and active manifestations of that union are reciprocal. Love is not merely bestowed on God's part or offered on man's, but is interchanged mutually, going between the Father and His child. Repentance and the remission of sins go together, making godly sorrow and the comfort of trust in God concomitant. Dutiful exertion and imparted ability flow out together, meeting one another—"strength perfected in weakness." Faith is eminently after this manner a relative power and possession. Faith and faithfulness are reciprocal — so much so, indeed, that in the best servants of God the comfort of faith, its confidence or assurance, is a fluctuating possession; their faithfulness being a fluctuating condition.

Subjective sources of unbelief.
3. The relation of the power of faith to character is a strong point of Scriptural teaching. Faith and a good conscience are joined together in Paul's descriptions. He speaks of them that are "defiled and unbelieving," to whom "nothing is pure, but their mind and conscience is defiled" (Tit. i. 15) — of "covetous love of money," making men "err from the faith " (1 Tim. vi. 10)—of "men of corrupt minds reprobate concerning the faith " (2 Tim. iii. 8); and reveals, as an explanation of unbelief, that when it follows upon a vicious state of heart, *dislike* of the truth, it is allowed to come in judgment, "God giving the vicious up to a reprobate mind " (Rom. i. 28). These effects of character upon faith, so strongly represented by Paul, are what Christ himself had previously spoken of, contrasting the behaviour to the truth, which would result in unbelief, with that of believers—"This is the condemnation, that light is come into the world; but men loved darkness rather than light, because their deeds were evil. For every one that doeth evil hateth the light, neither cometh to the light, lest his deeds should be reproved. But he that doeth truth cometh to the light, that his deeds may be made manifest" (to his faithful conscience) "that they are wrought in God " (John iii. 19, 20)

Teaching the moral state of soul necessary to faith by contrasting it with the process of unbelief, Scripture bids its readers "take heed lest there be in them an evil heart of unbelief, departing from the living God" (Heb. iii. 12); setting forth the unbelief as having an evil state of heart—being possessed by unfaithful desire, wishing to be separate from the living God, like persons who "*savour* not the things that be of God, but those that be of men" (Matt. xvi. 23)—who "like not to retain God in their knowledge" (Rom. i. 28)—who, beginning with walking in the "counsels of the ungodly" (negatively unfaithful to God), go on to "stand in the way of sinners" (positively, by sinful acts, unfaithful), and at last "sit in the seat of the scornful" (unbelieving) (Ps. i. 1).

The moral states—states of heart—associated with unbelief by the sacred writers, may be classified under two or three separate manners of unfaithfulness, all familiar to experience as incapacitating for affectional thinking in matters of human relationship.

4. Indifference, causing inattention, is in all periods of revelation complained of: "I have called, and ye refused; I have stretched out my hand, and no man regarded" (Prov. i. 24); "They" (being careless or not regarding) "made light of it, and went their ways; one to his farm, another to his merchandise" (Matt. xxii. 5). The seed falling by the wayside stolen away by the fowls of heaven, was the "word heard" as if not heard, and "stolen out of the heart by Satan lest it should be believed"—dwelt upon. This is the "spirit of slumber" which Paul, for its evil effects in turning men away from the truth, sets alongside of gross sinfulness—"They that sleep," and "they that be drunken" (1 Thess. v. 7).

Indifference.

5. Habits of self-indulgent trifling, inducing want of serious thought of anything, are exhibited to us in Pilate's light, somewhat scoffing, scepticism, "What is truth?" and in Herod Agrippa's half-jocular reply to Paul, that he must think him easily persuadable; but in a more widely applicable example, the case of the Athenians, who, occupying themselves with the lightest intellectual pleasures of society—the *dolce far niente* of easy, idle, cultivated life—"spent their time in nothing else but

Self-indulgent trifling.

either to tell or to hear some new thing" (Acts xvii. 21), and jested at Paul's striking declarations, or said pleasantly, "We will hear thee again of this matter." The "seed falling among thorns," the word thought upon for a little, but choked by other thoughts already in strong accustomed possession of the soul—"cares of this life, deceitfulness of riches, lusts of other things"—is the commonest source of want of belief; viz., that ignoring of the truth which as fully shuts it out as resisting it does.

Retained prejudices. 6. Of blindness to observable truth by reason of prejudices of education adhered to, an eminent example appears among the first Christian believers, who, being mistaught and unwilling to let go the worldly notions they had long learned of the Messiah's reign, were "slow of heart to believe all that the prophets had spoken" (Luke xxiv. 25). The same veil of accustomed religious misbelief covered partially or wholly the spiritual sight of the first Jewish Christians as a national peculiarity.

A fleshly mind. 7. Loss of power to think much on spiritual truth, or be impressed with things of that kind, comes upon an unfaithful use of the thoughts in prostituting the imagination to serve sensual lusts, and so turning it into a "fleshly mind." The "natural (fleshly) man" comes to a state of mind that he "receiveth not the things that be of God: they are foolishness to him; neither can he know them, because they are spiritually discerned" (1 Cor. ii. 14). Faithfulness to goodness and to truth is necessary to success in perceiving them. "The path of the just is as the shining light that shineth more and more unto the perfect day. The way of the wicked is as darkness: they know not at what they stumble" (Prov. iv. 18, 19). Blindness through sinfulness is the reverse side of the doctrine of spiritual discernment; in which retention, ready perception, and confident knowledge of the truth is promised to a man "honest and good," "doing truth," "doing the will of God" from the heart to all the extent of his perception of it, while he is "following on to know it more." In him who "obeys not the truth, but obeys unrighteousness," the "light that was in him becomes darkness." The progress in unbelief which

arises in an unbeliever in this way is precisely a stumbling at
he knows not what.

8. Besides, and in advance of these forms of unfaithful un- Antipathy.
dutiful want of readiness fairly to consider the things God has
revealed, Scripture describes and quotes unbelief arising from
conscious antipathy to the truth. An evil conscience may
cause such antipathy: "He that doeth evil hateth the light,
neither cometh to the light lest his deeds be reproved." Pride
may produce it, such as demanded, "Have any of the rulers
or of the Pharisees believed on Him?" (John vii. 48); "Thou
wast altogether born in sin, and dost thou teach us?" (John
ix. 34). A common necessity towards faith is that "imaginations be cast down, and every high thing that exalteth itself
against the knowledge of God, and every thought be brought
into captivity to the obedience of Christ" (2 Cor. x. 5). Undescribed obstinacy, variously caused perversity, was conjoined
with want of faith in the unbelieving Jews whom the apostles
encountered. They were "uncircumcised in heart and ears,
always resisting the Holy Ghost" (Acts vii. 51), "opposing
themselves," "hardened and unbelieving." Our Lord had to
complain of conduct the most "childish" in His hearers, whom
nothing would please—to whom John, for preaching down licentiousness, was as one who "had a devil," and He himself, for
not being austere, was "a gluttonous man and a winebibber"
(Matt. xi. 18, 19). Paul's difficulty among the Gentiles was
much with positive resistance of the pure and humbling truths
of the Gospel. "Strongholds" had to be cast down. Men
"wise in their own conceits" as to religious truth had to be
persuaded to assume the place of the utterly ignorant and
unwise, to prepare them to perceive the truth; and "not many
wise men after the flesh, not many mighty, not many noble,
were called" (1 Cor. i. 26). The rule held, which is so often
declared in religious teaching, that "from the wise and pru-
dent" in their own esteem the truth was "hidden," while it
was "revealed to babes" in self-measurement, whose humble
teachable souls, willing to learn, did not refuse the truth with
the old disdain—"whom would he make to understand doctrine?" (Isa. xxviii. 9), "Dost thou teach us?" (John ix. 34).

9. That faith should, as thus appears, have a reciprocal dependence on faithfulness—that its thoughts and feelings should be a difficult attainment to persons of sensual habits of life, or persons controlled by greedy desires, or persons disposed to indulge unbrotherly temper—is a corollary from the description of faith, that it is an enjoyed habitual thinking on a holy Being, and on man's affinity to Him, the ties which bind them together. "Defiled and unbelieving" is a natural conjunction, if believing be a life's habit of thinking on a history of holy benevolence, and on the grateful holiness which is its reasonable service of acknowledgment. Precisely this doctrine of the moral condition necessary to faith is that declared by John: "He that loveth not knoweth not God" (1 John iv. 8). In the language of the Bible, *love* is often used for the whole life of religion, the right state of the heart, and its outgoings towards God—"the fulfilling of the law;" and the *knowledge* of God is in the same manner used to express the effectual perception of religious truth when the habits of the mind are possessed by, constrained and animated by, the things revealed. John's meaning, therefore, is, that the man who does not make his religion a thing as much of practice in heart and life as the affection of love is, will not attain to anything of that habitual feeling of the assurances of God's love which can be called knowing *them*. The intimation is exactly the inference unavoidable from the practice of faith; under which actual love of God our Saviour is necessary in order to bring into our hearts so abundant and so welcome as is needful all thoughts and recollections of Him and His ways of grace. The history of modern German infidelity illustrates well this connection between inclination and knowledge. Dr McCaul, quoted in 'Aids to Faith' (Essay on 'Inspiration'), has shown that the unbelief preceded in time the learning upon which it professes to rest. The notions of Deism and Rationalism to which the divine authority of the Bible is intolerable were first propagated, and only after that was the biblical criticism undertaken which is now pleaded for those notions. The wish that the grounds of the Christian faith were bad, was father to the thought that they might be found to be so; and the desire to

find them so is very evident throughout the ingenious investigation applied to them. John states largely the moral condition upon which faith is possible: "He that dwelleth in love dwelleth in God, and God in him. Love is of God, and every one that loveth is born of God, and knoweth God. He that loveth not knoweth not God, for God is love." Paul, in his Epistle to the Romans (chap. i.), pursues the darker side of the reciprocal connection to the very depth of religious ignorance, stating the cause of the grossest forms of Gentile idolatry and corruptness to be that mankind, "disliking to retain God in their knowledge," being "unwilling to glorify Him" as they knew Him from His works, having no thankfulness to Him, "became vain in their imaginations, and their foolish heart was darkened." "Professing themselves to be wise, they became fools, and changed the glory of the incorruptible God into an image made like to corruptible man, and to birds and four-footed beasts and creeping things"; and then God gave them up to be led by their own desires into the most awful moral corruption. Christian misbeliefs or failures of faith afford some good illustrations of the necessity of faithfulness to believing. The work of the Holy Spirit, so largely spoken of in the New Testament, has had a pre-eminence among revealed things in not being understood and being misunderstood. His described work of "comforting," "guiding," "helping infirmities" in prayer and desire, is, by its kind, one to be comprehended and valued aright—believed in—only by persons who honestly, with all their heart, striving to do their duties amidst difficulties, feel the need of strengthening comfort and guidance and help to their infirmities. Persons whose consciences have never troubled them, who are satisfied with the strength of their Godward desires and the faithfulness of their life, and the comfort of their prayers, whose self-sufficiency never feels helplessly in need of guidance, protection, strength, and safe-keeping, cannot be expected to appreciate the aid which is expressly called help to the consciously infirm. That is a spiritual discernment requiring some preparation of experience in the spirit. Again, the Holy Spirit's "witness" (Rom. viii. 16) is sometimes misunderstood by religionists who deal largely in consciousness, because, thinking in this matter of consciousness alone, they ignore the practical nature of His testimony. Fanatics of unholy lives have claimed the witness of the " Spirit with their spirit " to their being the children of God, led willingly by their deceitful hearts into thinking of the double witness being given through one channel—that of their own feelings—instead of being two recognisably separate testimonies—the conscious feeling of their own spirit, and the character of a child of God appearing in their conduct the " fruit of the Spirit " (Gal. v. 22). A valuable illustration of the action of spiritual reciprocity—conduct affecting capability *in kind*—presents itself in the fact that *belief in human goodness* is necessary to *belief in the revealed goodness of God.* Liking to think of God's moral perfections—faith's having them ever before the mind—cannot be combined with a liking to think of certain fellow-men's moral blemishes. The love of the first great commandment is inseparable from that of the second, and like unto it; and that love rejoiceth not in iniquity, but rejoiceth in the truth. Its tendency is to large, and not to contracted, belief in its proper objects—" hoping all things " of them, "believing all things " of a brother's goodness (1 Cor. xiii. 7). Recorded deathbed appearances have amply shown that persons who had during all the more generous period of life watched against losing by their feelings, and in progress of disciplining their thoughts to serve worldliness well had acquired the power of thinking all generosity calculated, all good done for selfish ends, all mercy a bargain, have lost the power to think of free loving-kindness coming from God. It is likely that in their first selfish views of life they began, from a subjective sense of comfort in the thought, to contemplate Him as a *just* oftener than as a *good* being; and from that hardened into thinking of Him as a strict exacting master; if they did not, with the progress of their own character, form new and worse notions of Him as a vindictive ruler, at least an inexorable judge. But the end too plainly came to be, that when about to see Him face to face, they had no thought of His *loving* at all, and sought only how to propitiate His anger. The necessity of the true human character—that of charity—to the power of thinking truly of God, appears similarly in the case of the most conspicuously selfish and bitter faiths sometimes indulged in by religious sectaries. Sectaries have often formed to themselves a theory dislocating faith altogether from conduct, professing to think the soul's beholding of God a thing highly exalted above being affected by the circumstances of their human intercourse; but unable to avoid always the feeling of the spiritual connection established in human nature as well as declared in God's word, requiring " him that loveth God to love his brother also," they have begun their defence of their own narrowness of conduct by the old question, " Who is my brother?" and then confining that title to their own associates in creed or in closer communion, they have ended in accommodating their thoughts of the moral nature of God to the dispositions they were conscious of themselves. Their measure of who are included in the second great commandment has formed their faith as to Him who appears in its inseparable companion the first; and they have narrowed His view of His human family to their own. The Pharisees, who failed to recognise in Jesus Christ the express image of God, had a fitting preparation for such failure of spiritual perception in their practice of the " corban," which so depreciated the human family relationship in their service of the heavenly Father.

10. The Apostle John places this part of the spiritual reciprocity in an impressive light in his pregnant question—" He that loveth not his brother whom he hath seen, how can he love God whom he hath not seen?" (1 John iv. 20). Whatever religious conduct towards ordinary unimportant fellow-men is meant here—including *appreciation*—that is made a condition of ability to have the same conduct towards God. And the connection between the practice of it towards man and the practice of it towards God is stated in terms which are used but a few times in the Scriptures, to give superlative consequence to the matter referred to—the language of simple possibility or impossibility. The manner of expression is the same as in the few instances : " Without faith it is *impossible* to please God;" " How *can* ye believe who receive honour one of another, and seek not the honour that cometh from God only?"

The impossibilities of faith.

"The carnal mind is not subject to the law of God, neither indeed *can* be;" and seems to bid us think of an impossibility not arbitrarily imposed by God, but a natural consequence, like those humanly impossible things, which need God's special interposition to make them possible.

Naturally existing judicial element;

11. The expression with which Paul completes his history of Gentile unbelief, "Wherefore God also gave them up to uncleanness" (Rom. i. 24), formally enunciates a judicial element in the reciprocal influence of faith and faithfulness which brings into our view again the great fact of man's union with God—underlying this as all the manifestations of true religious life. In the practice of faith itself, the power to possess and be possessed by its thoughts, as well as in the exertions and enjoyments of faith's outgoings, man is always a fellow-worker with God; and, accordingly, the consequences to be expected from the working of human nature have to be expected also as inseparable from a widely-declared provision of God's government of grace: "To him that hath shall be given, and he shall have more abundantly; but from him that hath not shall be taken away even what he thinketh he hath;" "The meek will He guide in judgment; the meek will He teach His way;" "To the upright there ariseth light in the darkness; the integrity of the upright shall guide them, but the perverseness of the wicked shall destroy them." The reciprocity of faith and faithfulness—righteous life and spiritual discernment, doing the will of God and knowing the doctrine whether it be of God, the eye single and the whole body full of light, the eye evil and the body full of darkness—is discovered to us to be a working of that unavoidable indissoluble relationship of man to God, the effects of which upon man's spiritual condition sensitively follow the fluctuations of his desire after, or his departure from, the living God. The formally-declared government by moral judgment, which extends over all the religious history of man, from Eden downwards, is not any arbitrary thing or positive condition laid by God upon human life which He might not have laid upon it. It is natural, as a father's government of his child by positive laws is unavoidably a natural government, and different in his and the child's ex-

perience from his government of the same form exercised over his horse or his dog, or over a distant and unknown human instrument of his will.   Hence man may perceive but a natural effect following his faithfulness or faithlessness, an effect which speaks to his ear, not from the mouth of God, but of his own consciousness, though it is certainly all judicial also.   So did the effect of sin upon the power of believing in God come, a fruit and a judgment in one, upon them who first bowed down under spiritual death.   It has been the lot of all born in their image ; the nearest, habitually, to God no more exempt from it than those afar off, death passing upon all men, because all have sinned.   David before and David after his great soul-defiling sin seems like two different men in the power of believing in Jehovah's love.   From habitual peace of trust he passed to most frequent despondency, and, as it were, suspiciousness of His providence.   David's failure to keep the comfort of faith has to an observer the form of natural consequence. The loss and recovery by the people of Israel, throughout their history, of influential perception of heavenly truth, as their faithfulness to Jehovah diminished or increased, shows itself to us in the form of judgment.   The source of the change was the same in both—the unavoidable dependence of the human spirit for spiritual life upon God its Father.

12. The judicial connection between practice and perception in matters of revealed truth is no peculiarity of what we technically call the religious part of man's life—no government imposed thereon by God in addition to or apart from the usually seen natural order of human things.   All connection of obedient effort with success in any facility pointed out to us by God's providence, is to be considered a judicial connection established by Him for our moral training ; only our constant propensity is to separate some things which we have chosen technically to call religious from the rest of our life's ways, and think of them as a separate kingdom of God's government—an error which it is the business of the religious exercise of reason to correct.   The connection between faith and works, knowing and doing, in matters of revealed truth, is a law of the same authority with that by which, in learning

one pervading all God's government of man.

R

any art or kind of work requiring mental or manual skill, the practical man, who puts his hand to the work, and is daily grappling with the difficulties of its various tasks obediently to his vocation, has always the clearest, most consistent, and handiest knowledge of the principles that should guide him, and has a persuasion of their truth of a kind which is not enjoyed by one who is merely book-learned in those principles. And abundant religious knowledge gives confidence and breadth to religious practice, just as knowledge of the principles of his art gives its possessor a freedom and resource not in the power of one who has merely learned empirically. Reciprocity rules in both the secular and religious combinations of thought and action, and it is by a judicial arrangement of man's nature—by a governing provision made in his constitution.

Intellectual Conditions to Faith.

A normal state of capabilities.

13. A normal completeness or healthiness of human nature —*mens sana in corpore sano*—is unavoidably a condition to a normal completeness of faith. No one would take a hypochondriac's thoughts of the trustworthiness of human affection as a sound faith or disbelief. There are social Ishmaelites who fancy every man's hand against them. There are mental cases analogous to the want of a musical ear; persons greatly lacking in imagination; others so cold as to be held as unnatural. Persons defective in these ways are no fit judges of emotional things of a profound or delicate kind, and are sure to form an under-estimate of them—perhaps an estimate so defective as to be practical disbelief of them, ignoring them in reasoning upon a subject in which they are of essential moment. Again, acuteness of intellect has sometimes been so without any regulating judgment, as to go upon a clear logical line into the most ridiculous blunders. The undefinable quality of common sense is indispensable to attaining correctly-reasoned conclusions in matters of faith. This mental quality, which seems unconsciously, or without notice, to bring to bear on every point considered many guiding, cor-

recting, testing truths, that come, like a craftsman's experience, spontaneously to hand when they are wanted, is a state of mind seen in correct thinking on all subjects, and is indeed a necessity to correct thinking. The thinking of faith in God's love is a still more composite process and result than any other mental exercise presents. Like its inseparable love, it proceeds from heart and soul and strength and mind,—needing, besides common sense, common sensitiveness, affectionateness, and range of emotional capability.

14. It would be instructive to apply to the various abnormal opinions upon revealed faith which have been most conspicuous this test of the peculiar thinker's personal capability of dealing well with the subject. The readers of sceptical books are by no means in so good a position for judging of their value as the intimate acquaintances of the writer are. The letters or set speeches of a man fond of setting forth his views of controverted or popularly discussed matters, in many cases lead strangers to form at once an estimate of the value of his opinion amusingly different from that formed by those who for some time have had an opportunity of valuing his judgment in other matters. Since it is the case, then, that the opinions set forth in any book must be taken by the mass of readers mainly upon the value of the writer's fitness to form those opinions,—and since, in books on matters of religious faith, this element of authority must so far influence almost all readers capable of following the writer's argument, because reasoning on the matters belonging to faith is not the barely logical work of the intellect upon unexciting, objective ideas, but is a composite process in which moral and affectional sensibility at the same time contemplates those ideas, and judges of them by things which subjective consciousness presents at the same time,—a test is necessary to be applied, like that of intimate acquaintance, in valuing *outré* opinions set forth in books on religious subjects.

It would be a useful book on the value of human opinion which should collate with the strange opinions of celebrated men upon religious matters abundant illustrations, from minute biography, of the moral propensities of the peculiar think-

Value of an opinion affected by peculiarity in the opinion-maker.

ers, and the peculiarities they have shown in other things, and their amounts of common sense, common feeling and affection, and common honesty, and also how far bodily constitution or health had peculiar influence on their ways of thinking. Who would expect to find anything manly or anything morally respectable presenting itself much in the thoughts of Voltaire, after reading even Carlyle's short notices of the despicable facts of his character? Woolston's crack-brained enthusiasm in his university days in propagating new fancies of his own on biblical interpretation, and his extravagant offence at the clergy and speedy abuse of them for not adopting his allegorical theories, deprive of all respectability, all weight which any deference to his judgment might give, his subsequent so-confident scepticism on the subject of the Christian miracles. Hume's dogma, early adopted in his criticism on Leishman's Sermons, that we can only contemplate God intellectually, was of vast aid to him in rendering scepticism easier, as it fenced in the path of his thoughts from the corrective interference of the emotional facts of the Gospel. But we cannot appreciate aright the circumstance essential in judging of the value of Hume's opinion—viz., that a man of his reputed power of judgment adopted, or could adopt, such a maxim—until we come to know Hume's peculiarity of mind. He was very defective in the emotional element of human nature. Mr Buckle's theories upon collective human nature, notwithstanding the immense statistical learning which he brings to bear on his subject, are emptied very much of value as the opinions of one worth following as an authority, when we learn that he was deficient in the power, or practice, of estimating individual human nature, and that he allowed himself to think that so composite a subject could be substantially represented by means of statistics. The 'Philosophie Positive' owes its reputation in the reading world partly, perhaps in great part, to the commanding position assumed by its hierophant, M. Auguste Comte, as being a philosopher who had at his fingers' ends all the history of human knowledge, and who was himself a great discoverer in the honourable field. Dr Whewell exposed how erroneous his history of human thought is, and exposed also the error of his pretences to discovery, or even to great knowledge, in the subjects he claimed upon, and his ridiculous self-esteem, which led him, after receiving temporary aid from his English admirers, upon being cast off by his own more intimate countrymen, to claim it thanklessly in permanence as a just tribute to his philosophical greatness. That exposure, of necessity, followed the worship of M. Comte's opinions by some thinkers of this country, whose voices made him famous in England. Had Dr Whewell's criticism, and some other facts belonging to M. Comte's own history, been presented as a preface to his book, and had thereby his dictation of new philosophy been received at first in connection with these revelations of his own value, the 'Philosophie Positive' would not have been taken so much on credit, as manifestly it had been, as being a true representation of the natural order and limits of human inquiry; but his assertions would have been examined by his English disciples as well as by his English critics, and been seen to be misrepresentations largely of the history of human knowledge, and his *positive* one invented instead of observed, a range of observation arbitrarily confined so as to exclude part of the material to be considered. That his name should continue a name of authority, after his later self-exposure as a philosopher in his new religion of the social goddess—the worship of abstract female excellence in the concrete person of mother, sister, or friend, by a homage consisting in the solemn manipulation of phrenological bumps—makes questionable the hold his followers keep of common sense when upon the Comtean hobby. That their admiration, given, evidently so far upon credit, to his *philosophie*, should be but little affected by such exposure of error and self-exposure of capability, must detract much from the estimate to be formed of their own philosophical judgment. His English representative, Mr J. S. Mill, betrays his own appreciation of the emotional element in human nature by supposing a political economy in which affairs of the heart should be so quietly managed that a large family of heirs would, *in concione*, elect which of them should fall in love and marry.

15. These few cases show that important light can be thrown

Judgment of posterity, why of value. upon the value of *outré* opinions by some knowledge of the *subjective* of the opinion-maker, such as his intimate friends could possess; who are seldomer among the disciples of such a one than strangers are, who only know what he tells of himself in his guarded writings. Minute biography is often not attainable while a writer's opinions are new. It is an acquisition which is in the power of posterity chiefly; and it accords with this, that posterity more frequently forms a truer estimate of an author than his contemporaries do; and the excitement which one generation has felt on subjects of speculation appearing under some new name, has often been looked upon by the next with more of surprise, and something like sympathising pity, than respect. What is the worth which this consideration gives to the fact that posterity has always hitherto returned to hold by the Bible as a true record of a historical religion, and always forgotten abnormal faiths, except as curiosities of speculation, and so generally forgotten them that, when offered to a succeeding generation, they have been widely looked upon as quite new discoveries?

Import-ance of the biography of an opinion. 16. The biography of an opinion is of especial consequence in an age of quick production of books. Popular writers, the chief disseminators of new opinions, are mostly but reporters of less widely - read speculation. Adding no authority to the opinion, they do add the impulse of their own credit, which should not belong to the new opinion, except partially, any more than a story is to be accepted without proof more readily when it has been often repeated than when it was first told on hearsay. In this case, reviewers, able to deal historically with published speculations, become the necessary protectors of public opinion. The history of singular misbeliefs should, for safety, always, if possible, be brought in this way to illustrate their value as the opinions of those who first held them. For sincere belief in uncommon religious doctrines is propagated chiefly by the force of example, conversion to them being often, in most part, a tribute to the personal worth of their adherents; and the secret history of the peculiar creeds would generally be found to be less respectable, and to be owing to separation from a religious body for some mostly personal reason, followed by the necessity of adopting some profession in a state of society which holds necessary a presentable reason for differing in so important a matter from others.

17. The coincidence of one prominent profession of faith with great worldliness is a historical observation. The class of creeds constructed on the notion that man's relation to God is a formal, instead of both a formal and moral relationship— an adoption in arbitrary covenant to a purely forensic position— a union by covenant without being a union of *mutual* affection and of character—stands along the page of history always in some marked way as a faith dislocated from holiness, the origin of which is therefore suspicious, though it may not be traceable. The faith of the Pharisees in whatever they meant by salvation, because they were Abraham's seed and had Moses for their teacher, and their making a religion out of confession without service, was a dissent from the common religious judgment of human conscience ; and was essentially the same, in its want of connection with holiness, as that of the Anabaptists of the Reformation and the Latter-Day Saints of various names—Mormons, &c.—whose uncommendatory origin is so far well known. The progress traceable in the Judaising teaching which obstructed the labours of the apostles in the Gentile cities, is very instructive on this subject of the religious value of an opinion as the opinion of certain persons or classes of men. Judaising Christianity changed its views and its prominent teaching with the exigency of worldly circumstances during the Church's progress. The whole law of Moses, which the Jewish Christians sought to impose upon their Gentile co-believers in Judæa as essential to salvation, was given up, all but circumcision and the doctrine of meats, in the disputes raised in the heathen cities, where to hold the whole law would have endangered the continuance of the Jewish leadership of the quickly-extending Christian Church. With the same worldly ambition, the Judaising teachers soon diverged more from their first essential principles. Paul was the great preacher of the spirituality of the Christian law; and his teaching of that doctrine, which removed from the faith all

Worldliness of one historical class of creeds.

authority of Mosaic institutions, the cherished grounds of Jewish supremacy in the Church, made it the policy of polemical Judaism to undermine his influence, even by outbidding him in what they thought his advantage over them—viz., freeing religion from burdensome conditions.   To have the lead of the new faith, evidently rising to dominant influence in the communities of the empire, and to keep in view thus the means of perhaps accomplishing the never-abandoned national hope of supremacy, was a necessity that overruled all other considerations.   Accordingly, we find the Judaising teachers, by the time of the later Epistles, strangely changed in their teaching from advocating bodily austerity—the extreme development of the restraint on meats and drinks and days—and become the leaders in a libertine interpretation of " the liberty of Christ," representing it as freedom from all law, social and moral.   By this doctrine, so well adapted to lay hold on the originally more corrupt Greek, Roman, and Asiatic Christians, they were evidently succeeding in leading Christian communities on to seditious notions.   Hence the strong inculcation which we find in the later Epistles of the duties of social subordination, " obedience to the powers that be," as " ordained of God," and the marked change to stern teaching of the moral law in place of the early proclamations of freedom from the law of ceremonies.   (See Stanley's ' Apostolic Age.')

Circum-
stances of
Councils
producing
famous
creeds.

18. To understand well the value of the leading creeds of the Church as conclusions come to at famous assemblies of the eminent men of their times, and to appreciate the weight of that authority as a proper guide of opinion, would need extensive historical matter of illustration of the same kind ; exhibiting the peculiarities, mental, moral, political, &c., of the leading persons in those councils—the political difficulties of the times, and the state of morals—the particular history of the deciding council—the facility of comprehending each other's language, and sympathising with each other's sentiments, which existed—and the private interests which were moving influences in the plan or the conduct of the discussion.   The first great council—that of Nice—is itself a large study of this kind. Many later councils have the strongest likeness to the political

parliaments or states-general of modern days, for the kind of moving causes which they recognised or concealed.

Social Conditions to Faith.

19. Among the things which influence an individual's habits of thinking upon the essentially emotional subjects of religious faith, are included, besides moral habits affecting his willingness to think justly or at all of these things, and his natural peculiarities, spiritual or physical, affecting his capability or propensity in dealing with them, the peculiarities of his social condition, which may either confine the range of his religious thoughts, or constrain them to take some special direction. A condition needful to faith, to affectionate universally-sanctifying thinking on the things of Christ, is accordingly freedom of spirit—freedom from the oppressive confinement of overbearing society, and freedom from too great trial of heart. *Freedom of spirit.*

20. The state of intellectual society in France which was produced by the "philosophers" of Louis XV.'s time, exercised such a social oppression upon all conversation respecting questions of revealed religion, that few had the courage to talk anything but scepticism on the subject. Some in the leading ranks of society in France are understood to have practised Christian worship in such secrecy as idolators in Israel occasionally had to keep. Where the whole talk of educated persons upon the subject which cannot be extruded from mankind's conversation, was matter-of-course scepticism enlivened by universally appreciated sallies of wit against "the old superstition," faith must have become nearly an impossibility to the many. That habitual spontaneous arising in the mind of emotional life - controlling thoughts upon the facts and assurances communicated in the Bible was prevented, by the mind being already filled with borrowed thoughts and sayings, with which the philosophical part of society was perpetually flooding the public ear as the only true wisdom. To break through the confinement of such an overbearing weight of authority, constantly imposing itself and zealously *France in the 18th century.*

circulating its representations, would have needed a degree of independence, or rather originality and courage of thinking, which is very uncommon, and was at that time shown by but a few thinkers in Europe. Hume's learning days fell in the brightness of that misleading light; and it is not unreasonable to connect with that the early bent of his intellect. He did not retain in maturer life all his first philosophical notions, nor wish to propagate his peculiar theories as the philosophers did. Even his clerical contemporaries were at least so far kept down by the dominant voice of scepticism; and if some of them even joined in the light talk of his school, all were less outspoken on behalf of what they believed the truth than a state of society, in which truth has the popular side, would think natural. Perhaps the infidel school of the Encyclopædists arose out of the same want of freedom to think which it afterwards imposed upon the thinking world. They had been educated in the schools of the Jesuits, in which their thoughts were confined to reason always to a dictated result; while the training in reasoning which they received, of course exercised them in the desire to have all freedom, and induced as well as prepared them to throw off confining guidance; and they, as is common, sought their first freedom in bounding away into the region of theories antagonistic to that in which they had been imprisoned.

Perverts to Romanism. 21. Perhaps we might fairly connect with the same social repression of free thought on religious things many of the cases of what are called perversion to the Church of Rome which have occurred in the higher classes of English society. Most of the "converts" in that rank from Protestantism have been females. How many of them were individuals who from early life had been as much taken possession of, their thoughts, sentiments, and anticipations as much engulfed in a closely-confining artificial life of gaiety first, and family interests afterwards—from which religious reading, and perhaps all but frivolous or enervating reading and knowledge of the ways of ambitious life, was absent—as the upper French society a century earlier was held in possession, and its thinking imprisoned by the philosophers? To not a few of them it is likely their first thoughts on Christianity, causing them any emotion—that is, their first thoughts of faith—were experienced in the new excitements they had removed into, and they were not perverts from any faith, never having had freedom, or enough of it, or strength of mind to form a faith, a habit of religious thinking for themselves.

22. Within the range of Christian profession, and especially where greatest diversity of profession might be assumed as indicating greatest freedom of thought, the same repression of thought by dominant social influences produces an imitative or dictated faith as little respectable as the imposed scepticism of the last century. In times of party excitement, few have ever had freedom to think except within the limits and even the very form adopted by their section—a thinking mostly by book, hardly knowing diversity of expression. Of course, it is no merely religious disability, being only part of the general law of social control and confinement, which produces the phenomenon, exhibited by all political parties, that all facts of a political kind present themselves naturally in the importance and logical connection which suit the particular opinions of the thinker's party. A religious example of social repression of thought, and of the harm done by it to the comfort of faith, is supplied by the history of artificial codes of morals. The practice of certain customs or abstinences as essential to a religious character, is a frequently recurring peculiarity of religious sects or coteries. Widely, in America, membership in a temperance society is the essential and sufficient stamp of religious worth. To question the sinfulness of dancing, reading a novel, or seeing a play, would offend or perhaps shock not a few religious teachers in the Church or in the family in our own country. Preceptive restrictions of this kind imposed on the young, with the argument of authority alone, have the effect afterwards of obstructing the comfort of faith's thoughts, when seeking to enjoy themselves in the spiritual largeness and freedom of the Saviour's gladsome service of all holiness, in the same way as prejudices of other kinds, grown part of personal nature, render truth when it is perceived less comfortable, though they may not

Sectarian and political confinement of thought.

suffice to exclude it. As these peculiar artificial points of
conduct have no general, though sometimes a personal, connection with the spirit of Christ's service, advancing experience of His service, and of personal requirements of discipline, rejects the feeling of their importance; but yet, long
habit of reverencing them, combined, perhaps, with the religious feeling of filial loyalty to the teacher, makes the conscience uneasy in not giving obedience to them—and in the
mental contest they have a hardening effect, not designed by
those who taught them. They are related to the "letter which
killeth," not to the spirit which giveth life. Sometimes they
have had a "killing" effect on Godward thinking; for it is this
kind of moral confinement—the "inventions" of men's well-
designed but ill-executing zeal, and not the divine dictations
of preceptive morality — that produces those rules of "too
strict upbringing," emancipation from which proves so often
a fatal crisis in life.

Heathen
society.
23. Social confinement of thought is the main hindrance to
the conversion of highly civilised heathen peoples. Actively
protecting the lifelong habits of thought from the aggressive
influence of Christian truth, society all but prevents conversion in adults; and both the growth of personal habits of
heathen religious and moral thought has to be forestalled,
and the social pressure of those habits to be evaded, by taking
the young into Christian homes to be trained up in the way
in which they should go. Such is the rule of conversion in
India.

Technical.
education.
24. An education which has confined the perceptive and
appreciative faculties to one class of objects must confine and
may reduce the power of appreciative thought in essentially
different things. Minds developed closely on the study of
solely physical cause and effect, such as most of the clever
mechanic class in England, and not a few medical men who
have had a purely technical education, are said to be materialistic in their turn of thought. Even the faculty of being
charmed by pictures and music is lost by most of our labouring population in the same way—capacity being starved by
diversion of the thoughts to perfectly different occupation.

Religious materialism may be a habit of thought no more respectable.

25. A condition to the comfort of faith, shown widely by experience to be necessary, is a moderate degree of peace of heart—freedom from strong trial—a soul possessed in patience. In the great record of the practice of faith, the Psalms, distraction of heart by overburdening troubles appears among the stumbling-blocks in the path of faith as instructively as moral backslidings. In the perfect teaching of faith, the " cares of life " are set forth as dangers to faith, as well as " deceiving riches " and " worldly lusts," and the comfort of peace of heart is recognised as a necessary one. " Let not your heart be troubled," is the sympathising caution given by the Saviour, as in the older word of faith the prayer, " Unite my heart to fear thy name," was recognised as needful to the joy of faith (Ps. lxxxvi. 11). It is a comfort which needs divine help sometimes in order to let the soul have " delight in the multitude of its thoughts within itself" (Ps. xciv. 19). It would be instructive to ascertain by instances the history of such abnormal faiths as conventual life could supply most largely perhaps, but which occur beyond the pale of the Romish Church, and seek escape from the burden and correction of society in other ways of seclusion or separation. How much, for example, would it be found that the lack of human sympathy, caused by loneliness in the midst of social life through bereavement or disappointed affection, has had to do with the materialistic way in which some nuns think of Jesus as their husband and the Virgin Mary as their mother, as is betrayed by their language, in some cases more suitable for purely human relationships than for that of earthly beings with a heavenly one ? How much does a desolate thirsting after some definite future of personal enjoyment of affection make some peculiarly circumstanced Christians embrace with avidity materialistic notions of the second coming of our human-hearted Lord, and think of a worldly kingdom, a worldly visible city, a home among the homes of earth, into which He will take them, His own outcast, troubled, weary, heavy-laden ones to live a thousand years of love with Him—a crown of life recompensing them in kind

Peace of heart.

for the cross they have had to bear from the "coldness of the world"? How many, who give way to this belief, bringing heaven down to earth in another than Scriptural sense, have passed to it through the way characteristic of human thoughts —the wish being father to the hope—because they have been suffering under the oppression of unaccustomed and unprepared-for desolation of affectional life—left out of a place in family life by time's changes, with a heart yearning for social happiness, and perhaps sorely made hopeless of attaining the share of it they had fondly looked forward to and come to need? Prolonged excitement and tension of courage in a succession of dangers have had strange effects, in some cases producing a spiritual hypochondria as manifest as the bodily derangement. Aberrations of reason upon some religious thoughts have come upon overburdened spirits in solitude, in the case of individuals whose amount of rational faith much exceeded that possessed by any of their acquaintance, or perhaps their time. Luther was a marked example of this, and ascetic life must have furnished many more than are on record. The being that is to enjoy the thoughts of faith—to be sensitive to their light—to have his whole nature moved harmoniously by them—is not only a compound of body and spirit, each susceptible of disorder sure to affect the whole, but the working of his faith is to be an action of heart and soul and strength and mind, in which all his affections, sympathies, activities, and reasonings are to be complete, needing therefore to be healthy and unburdened.

26. The relation of man's subjective condition to the objective faith offered to him in the Word of God tells two ways in the Christian argument. Agreement between the subjective and the objective is a condition to faith as freely recognised and expressly taught in the Bible as it is claimed by unbelievers; and while they wish to take advantage of that necessary connection to defend their unbelief, God's Word uses it to condemn such a state of mind. The disagreement may arise from faultiness in the subjective as freely as in the objective; and the immense variety of mankind's subjective states, giving rise to propensity or affecting ability to think in certain ways, makes that *prima facie* more likely to be the place of

Value of the subjective as a defence of unbelief.

the faultiness than the confessedly consistent teaching of the books of Scripture. But the disagreement is intolerable to the spirit of man, and will be sought to be got over, by modifying either the subjective habits of thought and feeling, or the objective truth accepted. The former is the demand of the Bible —the latter the liberty claimed by unbelievers. This felt necessity of concord between a man's own feelings and the religious truths offered to him, which helps any impulse to faith or unbelief, gives us a starting-point in considering the value of the subjective in the question of faith.

Christianity, the disputed religion, is not a speculative invention, but a historical matter from the very foundation; and its first fact in the order of observation is man's own nature—what he is conscious of being. The God who is to have the worship of man's nature—his reason, feelings, and energies—his heart and soul and strength and mind—must be a being who is fitted to command man's homage, and to attract his love and constrain his inclinations. The qualities and conduct man is to have trust in God for must be such as he can feel the value of. No amount of external evidence of the supernatural origin of an objective faith would make it of sufficient value to man, without this recognition of it by his own spirit as his needed, desired, and appreciated religion.

But the correlative argument arises directly from this, that if the history and teaching of Christianity, including under that name all the introductory revelations unfolding Christianity proper, have commended themselves to the nature of mankind in general of all races and degrees of civilisation, that body of truth is truth that belongs to man's religious condition. Evidently, it is man's peculiar faith, however a different system of contemplations may be " the truth " for an order of beings differently constituted and in different circumstances. Now, it is a historical fact that the great moral and spiritual features of the religion of the Bible have been generally recognised by all differences of mankind as face answers to face; and that the diversity characteristic of their thoughts, turning to choice selected favourite subjects of chief contemplation, has been as much manifested to be a uniformly occurring diversity, turning, with the human diversity of selection seen in all other things, only to different features of one person, different points of view of one character, different episodes of one history always.

Persons, therefore, who say that their consciousness does not recognise a Saviour suited to it in the Bible, and that they cannot see there the divine excellence and the grace man should be constrained by, have the burden laid on them of accounting for their peculiarity by differences, in their condition of mind from the common condition, of a kind which makes their mental sight more true. At first sight, at least, their exceptional disability seems more likely to need correction than to deserve copying. And if claim be made by exceptional persons of respect for the judgment of the few against that of the many, which is frequently a just award, two barriers arise to that respect: the first, that besides intellectual judgment, moral and emotional completeness and health are needed to appreciate the Bible's doctrine—an average human subjective; and the second, that the great mass of men of judgment, acknowledged leaders, "the few," in all intellectual departments, have been believers. This historical position of unbelief with respect to belief takes away materially the insinuated value of the plea—one generally made as in the interest of superior intellect — that "a man is not accountable for his belief." That plea assumes that the man has been both honest and capable in his consideration of the offered faith. A defect in the honesty makes the unbelief blamable; a defect in the capability, the subjective moral or emotional fitness for appreciating the offered truth, makes the unbelief of little weight to influence other men's judgment. The plea is only fully applicable in the subject when used as the language of medical jurisprudence—as an excuse, not a recommendation.

Human subjective ignored by Hume and Comte.

27. The existence of an average subjective in mankind—something not definable, but so well known and universally recognised as to be freely spoken of as "human nature;" the fact of there being in every ordinarily healthy and capable individual a composite constitution of mind, the action of which is predicable within pretty definite limits—makes the exclusively intellectual process asserted by Hume in religious reasoning,

and the peculiar "positive" assumed as exhaustive by Comte, both inapplicable. Man's religious logic not only uses his reason upon outside facts as matter of observation, but appreciates these by comparing them with moral and emotional facts, also matter of observation, within himself. Hume, ignoring the emotional part of this observed human nature, ignores part of the first matter of observation upon which *man's* religious reasoning is to proceed. He leaves out the human term of the connection partly, and therefore cannot come to an understanding of all that enters into the action of that connection. M. Comte's true theory, that all knowledge must begin from observation of facts, takes as such only the facts of written history, and of external observation, and theorises on these as if there were no light thrown on them by facts of human nature. If written history be full enough to exhibit the individual characters of it in recognisable mental and moral distinctness, the reader, conscious himself of certain common "human" propensities and needs, takes these into account, and cannot help doing so, in understanding the conduct of those individuals and the turns which human affairs take in the history he is studying. In reading even the history of the early myth-constructing period of Greek life, graphically written by Mr Grote from the positivist point of view, we can realise in the rough the religious propensities and needs of "human" reasoning constructing these myths as a form of thought to hold by, just as we can divine the springs and forming influences of thought in modern growths of peculiar opinion. The *Philosophie positive* establishes its groove of reasoning by ignoring this nearest of positive facts, man's peculiar nature, which is the fundamental fact of any theory of human philosophy upon which a theory of human religion is to be raised. The Apostle Paul *observed* more thoroughly than M. Comte when he argued that "*we*" (conscious of what our own nature is) "ought not to think that the Godhead is like unto gold, or silver, or stone, graven by art or man's device" (Acts xvii. 29).

28. In the subjective plea for unbelief a deduction of value The subof fatal amount has to be made from opinions which bear the jective plea

a foretold
phenome-
non.

character of old objections revived before in various forms, and the more if ingenuity of a solicitous kind appears in their reproduction—such objections, in fact, as are most likely to have the respectability of subjective difficulties arrogated to them. That deduction is the fact that resistance, of this special kind, to the truth is distinctly given warning of in the Christian Scriptures as certain to arise from sources named. The subjective plea is, in fact, anticipated, and the manner and matter of its arguments described beforehand, and assigned to sources well known in human experience as powerful in making human opinions diverge in other subjects from obvious right. Among these sources are the characteristically subjective motives of self-interest, self-importance, and desire to preserve self-respect notwithstanding questionable inclinations. For example, the plea of " advanced views," " the opinions of thinking men," asserted at present with some assurance against the common faith, is deprived fatally of its arrogated respect by its kindred to the eighteen-hundred-year-old argument, " Have any of the rulers or of the Pharisees believed on Him ? " The demand of a faith that shall accommodate itself to man's alleged subjective necessities is no philosophical discovery made by modern superiority of intellect. It is the common and old way of heathen theosophy, into which Jews of early ruder times, exactly like Christians of imagined mature times, were apt to wander, the wish to think God such a one as themselves. That leaders of opinion should always arise, " builders " of new fabrics of human civilisation, who should " reject the corner - stone laid in Zion," is a phenomenon of human philosophy to be as surely expected, and to be of as little authority, when it appears, in affecting man's thoughts of revealed truth, as any other foretold recurring phenomenon of the moral history of man ; and manifests not the master skill of the *new* builders arising to reject the truth, but the comprehensive grasp which revealed truth has taken of all human things—that to it there is nothing new under the sun.

CHAPTER XI.

THE LIVING BY FAITH; OR, THE EDUCATION OF
THE INDIVIDUAL TO FAITH.

GAL. ii. 20.—The life that I now live in the flesh I live by the faith of the Son of God.

LUKE xix. 13.—Occupy till I come.

JOHN xvii. 22.—That they may be one, even as we are one : I in them, and Thou in me.

1. "BELIEVING IN," as it is represented by the term in Gen. xv. 6, which was etymologically constructed to describe the experience of the father of the faithful, is essentially different from philosophical contemplation of a creed, system of truth, or what we call a belief. It is the feeling of connection with a person. Accordingly we find the practice of faith, as described in the New Testament, is not intellectual contemplation of truth, but "living to Christ," living by His life—a state of human experience requiring this language: "I am crucified with Christ: nevertheless I live; yet not I, but Christ liveth in me: and the life which I now live in the flesh I live by the faith of the Son of God, who loved me, and gave Himself for me" (Gal. ii. 20). It is the circumstance of this life having to be lived under an indescribable complication of worldly and fleshly conditions that makes faith, as believers experience it, not susceptible of exhaustive definition; and renders the study of faith one that must be undertaken from the practical and not from the theoretical side; and produces the phenomenon in religious teaching, that intelligible exposition of faith is never generic but specific, describing faith in some one or other of its diverse exercises.

Original and latest description of faith : living in a person.

Training
contact of
faith's
thoughts
with cir-
cum-
stances.

2. In living by faith, a believer's emotional thinking of Christ and the things of Christ has perpetually to come into contact with his own propensities, and with the circumstances of his condition in the world; and to exercise and encounter influence by the contact. His thoughts of earthly life, planning and valuing the different things which it presents, meeting its emergencies, dealing with all its varying elements, take inspiration from his one unmovable "treasure in heaven," with which "his heart is also," and judge or suspend judgment, cleave to or give up, avoid or tolerate, plan or wait events, all relatively to that.

Phases of
living by
faith.

3. In accordance with the diverse exercises and experience of human faculties and affections which must thus arise, we find this life of believing spoken of in the Word of God under very different descriptive figures—the walk of faith, the fight of faith, the work of faith, the patience of faith, the obedience of faith, the trial of faith, &c.—indicating the varying forms and feelings which the intercourse of heavenly thoughts with earthly things may take. And, corresponding to these phases of living by faith looked at from the human side, we have, looking at it from the divine side, the appropriate helps described, of light to the path, armour and strength for the fight, tasks for the work, experienced help and deliverance to the patience and trial, grace to give the obedience,—a universal comfort of faith fitted to the exigencies of its living, and the living made throughout a connection with a personal Saviour, faith a living to and by Him.

Unifying
element—
"Occupy
till I
come."

4. Divergent, however, into many branches, as the subject of the worldly life of faith is, there is presented to us, by one of the expository sayings of Christ, a view of a believer's manner of life here which unites them all; as in those frequent sayings of His who was the wisdom of God we find the key-note to most or all of the harmonious unities in diversity presented by God's comprehensive ways with the "world" of mankind whom "He so loved." In the parable of the pounds, He, the Master going into a far country to receive a kingdom and to return, directs His servants in what thought they are to labour, or wait, or strive, or endure. They are, every one, to make their worldly

lot keep Him in their thoughts; and it is by constant looking unto Him that they are to accomplish their tasks, becoming desirously sanctified to Him by their diverse peculiar services. All their thinking and working and self-discipline are described in the direction, " Occupy till I come."

5. The declared analogy of the heavenly relationship to those of earthly homes is as satisfactorily instructive as to how the difficulties and duties of God's children are to be the means of keeping Him in their minds, as when it makes us understand the nature of family faith in Him, either the emotional nature of all its thinking, or its habitual, or its reciprocal character. How better could a mother, leaving little children alone for a time, help them to keep her in their minds a guarding and assuring thought, than by giving them some little task and bidding them " occupy till I come"? A servant, who is also a son, occupying, till his father's return, some selected portion of a work the whole of which his father only is capable of dealing with, is kept by the occupation in the right position of soul towards his father, by having to think constantly on former exercises his father put him through, to connect every success with his direction and anticipated approbation, and by every insurmountable difficulty to feel his needed sufficiency and the certainty of his help. How could the saviour of one in a position of greatest danger so well keep the needful reliance upon him in the feelings of the exposed person, as by dealing out his guidance and help step by step, hold by hold, for him to " occupy till he come" farther to his aid? Now these are the very positions in which God our Saviour stands to us, and in which He links our consciousness of self to Him, by perpetually-recurring feelings of dependence, of confinement to one way, and of appropriate help being at our hand or at our request. He is our Father, the Father of " little children," whom He trains in the way they "should go;" whom He feeds with " food convenient" for them, not food chosen by themselves, but selected by Him; and who feel His loving restraint, and give themselves to it. He is the Master of servants, whom He leaves to await His return, they know not when or how, knowing only that they have work

Analogy of inter-human faith.

allotted by Him to take themselves up with, and keep His coming and inspection, as well as His first kindness, constantly in their thoughts—the absolute Master who alone knows what is good for His servants, and has not left them to look out for work to do for Him, but has distributed portions of work, or care, or husbandry, of kinds and quantities which He has arranged—ten talents, or five, or two, or one—and has set them to their distributed tasks to labour for times He may choose— some for a full day of life, some but a portion, some but a short one like an hour (Luke xix., Matt. xx., xxi., and xxv.) So does He in His providence set and support the life of faith, that has to be lived "unto Him," "by Him," "in Him," "living, moving, and having its being in Him," who "is in all its thoughts," "ever before it," "seeing whom though He is invisible it endures."

Providence the Master's distribution of tasks, &c.,

6. Providence, the guiding finger of the Father, Master, Saviour, directs each individual—master, servant, husband, wife, parent, child, brother, sister, friend, neighbour, pastor, ruler, each different age, rank, sex, relationship, &c.—to his own allotted set of little or great cares, opportunities, difficulties, and helps; in whatever part of the vineyard it lies, no part of which is to bring forth unripe or wild grapes, be it the household task, the trading industry, the opportunity of general helpfulness, or the close watchfulness of an individual charge ; and under whatever burden the duty has to be done, whatever weight has to be borne or laid off in running the race —many cares of the family or of the world, seductions of riches or of poverty, besetting tempers or lusts, weakness of courage or too much self-confidence, "fightings without or fears within." Amidst all these—our tasks, helps, troubles, and disabilities which individualise our lot—we are set in a selected circle of things which are arranged to be associations bringing and keeping Him in our faith's thoughts, and keeping or making us united to Him, reliant, content, loving, desiring, expecting, "occupying till He come."

making a life of union to Him—

And this description of faith, that it is a life, necessitates what was before set forth, that its thoughts are not of philosophical propositions, doctrines however true, but of facts. It is reliance in difficulty on a person, comfort in a history, guidance by looking constantly to an example, rest looked forward to in a described home, not an indefinite state of blessedness. Every present labour, or self-discipline, or difficulty, or enjoyment, is represented in the Word of God as made to link the future to the present, the unseen to the seen. Each one is *lived through*, as the task confided by an absent father, or master, or friend, to keep that absent one before the eyes of the mind and of the heart ; more helpfully, more enjoyably, more naturally feeding the new life with healthful diversity of food, than set formal thinking of Him by doctrines or attributes would.

> "Labour is sweet, for Thou hast toiled ;
> And care is light, for Thou hast cared."

7. Just thus does the Bible's general language respecting the living by faith connect it with express thought of Christ always: *the historical Christ.* "To me to live is Christ" (Phil. i. 21); "We thus judge" (have in our minds the feeling), "that if He died for all, . . . they which live should not henceforth live unto themselves, but unto Him who died and rose again for them" (2 Cor. v. 14, 15) ; "Who is he that overcometh the world, but he that believeth that Jesus Christ is the Son of God?" (1 John v. 4, 5); where believing must mean thinking on Jesus himself, and the love that He, the Son of God, has taken God's other children into in Him. "Purifying their hearts by faith" (Acts xv. 9) is a co-operative work containing God's gracious help to will and to do, but in which His servants, "having this hope, purify themselves, *even as He is pure*" (1 John iii. 3). As hereafter, so here they become like Him, "seeing Him" (looking upon Him) "as He is." They put off the old man, and are renewed in the spirit of their minds, putting on a new man "created after God" (Eph. iv. 22-24). Faith working by love works by the same connecting of personalities : "We love Him because" (thinking of how) "He first loved us" (1 John iv. 19).

Personal connection, union of living, of the believer with the Object of faith, is the common idea in all the diverse phases of living by faith ; which are described as a fight, a race, &c.

8. In describing the fight of faith, when Paul enumerated "the whole armour of God" (Eph. vi.), he placed faith in the position of the *protector* of protective habits of holy life; and the connection requires us to understand by faith this habit of looking to, living by connection with, a person and facts and relative promises of saving love which surround the thought of him. Wrestling not merely against flesh and blood, but against spiritual wickedness in high places, he that fights "the good fight of faith" is to protect himself from dangers of human origin by acquired, "put on," *habits* of "truth," saving him from entanglement among the risks of the double-minded, keeping the multitude of his thoughts, his heart's desires, united to fear God's name, as "a girdle" binds loose garments close from catching in a wrestling fight; —*habits* conscious and manifest too, of all "righteousness," protecting him as by a breastplate from the solicitations addressed to those frail in honesty by tempters or by their own hearts;—and *habits* of "preparedness," obtained from "the gospel of peace," against the stumbling-blocks which bring that destruction of brotherly love which makes love of God impossible. Those *habits* are acquired by a long continuance of the thoughts faith presents, and they suffice to protect from, or to repulse, contamination or attack by ordinary human sinfulness. But their growth of human habit is not strong enough to protect from "fiery darts of the wicked one"— thoughts of evil cast by the father of lies into the soul, like the poisoned or ignited arrows of ancient warfare; and to protect from these superhuman dangers the "shield of faith" is to be extended over the good soldier's acquired habits of truthfulness, righteousness, and peace. What is it that can be a shield, consisting of thought and feeling, to cover habits of all goodness of thought from being suddenly invaded by some evil thought coming like a fiery dart into the soul, but another life habit, a habit of living with the eyes of the mind looking continually to "the Lord and the power of His might," the helps promised in His salvation—having Him, the Captain of the soul's salvation, the very present help of His soldier's need, ever before the eyes? Attained truthfulness, righteousness, and

brotherliness, passing along life's dangerous path under a
habitual glad thought of God our Saviour—a felt union of
the life to Him, giving assurance of His ever-present help—is
the life of safety; enduring as seeing Him who is invisible. It
is even like the living of a virtuous child who, on his first
exposures in the world of strangers, is protected from ill by
the thought of home, in constant conscious addition to the
good habits of home. Thus, evidently, in the fight of faith,
the soldier, "strong in the Lord"—having armed himself after
His direction—with habits which He has given him power to
acquire—"occupies" his post of danger "till He come." He
occupies it looking to His coming, as we must yet more distinctly understand by the succeeding description of "the
whole armour,"—he "having for an helmet the *hope of salvation*," taking also "the sword of the Spirit, which is the word
of God," and "praying always with all prayer and supplication." The fight, which formally is a struggle, is, in this
"living by faith," practically a help to growing closeness of
union with the Object of faith.

9. The work of faith—trading with His talents, occupying The work
His pounds, labouring in allotted spots of His vineyard, of faith.
serving in His house in watchful readiness for whatever work
may be to occupy the time until He appear (Luke xii. 32-40)
—is, like the armour of God and the fight of faith, another
name for perpetual helps to faith to endure as seeing Him,
in a union of spirit to Him. Every willing work, every faith-
fully desirously accomplished task, great or little in "profit-
ableness" to Him, is to bring a fore-echo of His approaching
steps and His coming words, "Well done, good and faithful
servant!" Every consciousness of faithfulness unto the end
of a task is a joy-giving light from the Master's heavenly
chamber, whose coming reward is described thus: "Blessed
are those servants whom their Lord when He cometh shall
find so doing. Verily I say unto you, that He shall gird
Himself, and make them to sit down to meat, and will come
forth and serve them" (ver. 37). It is the helping foretaste
promised to the faithful by John: "Beloved, if our hearts condemn us not, then have we confidence towards God" (1 John

iii. 21). *Every* work well done is thus to bind the life of the believer to the Object of his faith :—

> "The trivial round, the common task, will furnish all we need to ask—
> Room to deny ourselves, a road to bring us nearer God."

The patience of faith. 10. This contact within the soul of future things with the things that have to be "endured" now, making one *life* of them all, is the very explanation of the patience of faith in which believers are to possess their souls, "occupying" their troubling position "till He come." That is an exercise that is constantly bringing (Rom. v. 3-5) experience of the spiritual "living," in a consciousness of support which the thought of God our Saviour's faithfulness of help gives—a consciousness producing fresh hope, settling into confirmed stable hope, a *state of hope* in Him. It is an experienced appreciated dependence and support which, bringing no ashaming disappointments, enables present life to "rejoice in looking for the glory of God" (ver. 2)—"living" with a life which is fed from a divine as well as a human source, "because the love of God is richly taught to our hearts," "poured out" on them "by the Holy Ghost which is given us" (ver. 5)—that "Spirit" promised to "comfort" us, and fill us with the glory of Christ Jesus by "taking of His and showing unto us." Every act of patient endurance, like every accomplished duty and every successful fight, is made to bring Jesus, *our* Saviour, closer to the soul in some degree of joint-life—"Jesus, who endured such contradiction of sinners"—Jesus, who instructed patient faith in these words, "In the world ye shall have tribulation: but be of good cheer; I have overcome the world" (John xvi. 33).

The race or walk of faith. 11. The close connection of faith's consciousness with Jesus personally, not doctrines or theories of God's love, but the historical Object of man's faith—Jesus, who saves His people from their sins—is prominent in that other leading representation of living by faith, its progressive character, in which it is called a race. Even the subordinate guidance and encouragement given to the progress of faith is not the thought of principles but of persons, living examples — not philosophical reasonings affording motive and hope, but the sight of "men of like passions with ourselves, who have through faith and patience inherited the promises." Faith's subordinate help is the thought of the notables of faith recorded in the Word of God: "Wherefore, seeing we are compassed about with so great a cloud of witnesses, let us lay aside every weight, and the sin which doth so easily beset us, and let us run with patience the race set before us" (Heb. xii. 1). But the continual centre of faith's thoughts seeking guidance, sympathy, strengthening courage, is to be one singled-out object—"Jesus, the author and finisher of our faith, for the joy set before Him, enduring the cross, despising the shame" (ver. 2). Of the same significance is the fact that the guiding knowledge of a believer's race, or walk, or way, is not the truth in the abstract, but the truth in closest personal connection with Him; viz., His words—"If ye abide in me, and my words abide in you, ye shall ask what ye will, and it shall be done unto you" (John xv. 7). The expression, "author and finisher of our faith," which critics have felt obliged, one after another, to understand in a pregnant rather than an exact sense, may cover a truth which is necessary to the practice of faith, and corresponds to much of the language of Scripture respecting Jesus; viz., that He is the beginning and the ending of every believer's thinking of faith, as He is seen to have been historically the first, and will be the last, object of the world's true religious faith. Beholding Him, the first and the last, the author and the finisher of the earthly episode in universal life abbreviated in the words "God so loved the world," believers are to feed their thankful motives upon the past, as the early love of Jesus, and anticipate with desire thus instructed His trusted promises not yet received, and "occupy" the progressive present, until the unrevealed hour when the Son of man cometh —looking unto Him, and finding each trying portion of the race, or walk, or pilgrimage, passed over in His steps, bring Him, ever "this same Jesus," in saving comfort to His disciple's side, one with Him in the difficulties and joys of the way.

12. In the obedience of faith Jesus Christ is placed in the

same uniting nearness to the soul, to be its felt support in that
conscious living to the heavenly Father's commandments which
has "its meat and its drink to do His will." This condition of
a child-servant's obedience is to be "occupied," looking upon
Him, learning of Him continually, "who, though a Son, learned
obedience by the things which He suffered" (Heb. v. 8). Our
Object of faith is set before us carefully in this connection with
our living by faith : " In the days of His flesh He offered up
prayers and supplications, with strong crying and tears, unto
Him that was able to save Him from death, and was heard in
that He feared ; and being made perfect, He became the cause
of eternal salvation unto all that obey Him " (ver. 9). What is
meant by "obeying Him" amidst all this association of thought?
—what but "occupying" till He come the tasks assigned by
Him, whatever His word generally or His providence specially
gives to be done—thinking of His coming we know not when,
but having that coming future our life's future—an "eternal
salvation " of union to Him, which is begun here in our experience of these uniting things. That obeying Him is a state of
"living," whose consciousness is to become fuller evermore of
emotional thoughts of Him, and growing likeness to Him ; both
which shall be perfected in indissoluble personal union to Him
in the "inheritance," " the joy of our Lord," into which He ,
shall bid His own enter with Him, when He shall call them
"good and faithful servants "—" servants " who are "friends,"
—friends who are children of His Father and their Father.

13. There has been much exemplified in the recorded and
unrecorded experience of faith a sense in which human life
itself—the talent of human estate and its affections—is a living
by faith, a visible thing, which is yet not a life of sight but of
faith, lived in the faith of the Son of God, who loved us and
gave Himself for us. What must the inner life of Hezekiah
have been in those fifteen years (Isa. xxxviii.) in which he had
not to "go softly in the bitterness of his soul," but Jehovah,
" the life of his spirit," "recovered him and made him to live "
—"redeemed him from the pit of corruption, and cast his sins
behind His back " ? It was a life filled with thoughts of faith
which united him in peace and happy safety to Him "who is

ready to save "—a "life singing songs to the stringed instruments all the days of his life in the house of Jehovah"—saying evermore, "The living, the living, he shall praise Thee
as I do this day: the fathers to the children shall make
known Thy truth." What occupied the soul of Lazarus in his
second life? The restored happiness was precious, no doubt,
of Martha's and Mary's love; and their happiness in him was
as great, though diverse by a strange diversity of circumstances from his: but did not another love and union, known
before, dwell then in their souls more than those once their
nearest affections—a love and union which was felt by them
to be *life*, which their own helpless love and union had not
been? The trial of faith which had to speak the unanswered
words, "Lord, behold, he whom Thou lovest is sick," had been
in reality the help of faith to a union closer than was known
before, and never to be broken after—a life in which the bitterness of death was indeed past for ever. Abraham's case was
nearer that of common trials, in which He who is our invisible
life comes most solemnly near to us to help faith by unforget-
able experience. When the old man's heart was breaking—but
his spirit rose up in that awful obedience to offer up his son a
burnt sacrifice to Him from whom he received him the child of
promise the seed of many nations—his soul was helped to be knit
to Jehovah, his declared "shield and exceeding great reward,"
by a new intensity of thought, a life felt in a new feeling, looking to Him, holding fast by Him, its only sure portion amidst
all other things of thought or sight. Abraham's temptation
was the type of an often-repeated trial-help to faith in the
same Object of faith—our Jesus, his Jehovah of Mamre. That
trial-help is the unforgotten event of many a human home,
when parents, standing by the bed of death, called up their
hearts to say, "The Lord gave, and the Lord taketh away;
blessed be the name of the Lord;" and yet He did not take
but gave again the resigned life, a new uniting bond of
faith between present and immortal life, to be occupied "till
He come." Such family experiences are a congruous help to
"believing in" (Gen. xv. 6)—*i.e.*, resting, having peace and
strength like Abraham's—in that so great love which gave

up an only and well-beloved Son for man. They also help the eyes of the soul to recognise the specialty of uniting faith given to homes full of human affection—"Children are a heritage of the Lord;" and that given to other homes which have been emptied—"Them that sleep in Jesus will God bring with Him." The domestic experience of life in another has, as its eminent religious fruit, not the symbolising of heavenly life by earthly, but the maturing of the one by the other. Many a parent can use Hosea's language of fatherly sorrow and yearning over children lost but not abandoned. The trial is to open to their eyes the heavenly home of so great salvation, and bring to their feelings the uniting assurance of the heavenly Father's fellow-feeling with their pain. The contrasted blessing of good children, in like manner, makes the language of salvation "My well-beloved Son," and every believer's position in God's sight, which is assured thereby, more keenly appreciated. To those good children the reciprocal happiness of that domestic union also brings a uniting exercise while they pass their days "obeying their parents in the Lord." They learn filial love to the heavenly Father through the happy training of its earthly counterpart, made thus a foretaste of it also. The relation of master and servant is no mere worldly tie and earthly position. The old religious care confided to His chosen people by Jehovah, in His many charges as to "the stranger within their gates," is, in the Christian life of faith, the master's feeling evermore that he is the servant of the "Master who is in heaven," and the servant's blending feeling that he is serving not his human master merely, but him and "the Lord" together. Conjugal union is the closest earthly type of spiritual oneness with the Lord. Its experience is not only to make that oneness appreciable, but to be a training towards it. The thought of all a husband's cherishing love is to bring to the trustful wife's reasoning heart appreciation as well as confidence of God's so great grace, promised in association with that human gift of it—"Thy Maker is thy husband." To both members of the foretasting union their own faith and faithfulness are to be suggestive ever of the sure blessedness in which believing souls shall be "the bride, the Lamb's wife." And conjugal sorrow, the desolation of its widowhood, is to unite the faithful and solitary heart, not to the dying only, but, with him, to the undying One.

All these helps of domestic experience are His language, saying, "Occupy till I come;" and the answer He desires is the same for them all—"In Thee we live, and move, and have our being." "To me to live is Christ."

14. Man's living by faith of the Son of God includes the "occupying" of a special help of that living "until He come." The means of grace, called collectively the Word of God, is the help given to keep up faith's conscious association of earthly occupations with the personal heavenly Saviour, and it has to be occupied with that help till He come. The "light of the feet," the "lamp of the path," is called to us a light shining in a dark place, to which we "are to take heed until the day dawn and the morning star arise" (2 Pet. i. 19). The personal connection is inherent in all the means of grace. It is not as *truth* or *wisdom* or *light* only that the Word is to be thought of by us, but as *help—His Word*. David exemplified this practice of faith, using the Word as a provided help to live present occupations for God—"*Thy* word have I hid in my heart, that I might not sin against *Thee*;" and he exemplified at the same time the divine co-operation which is assured to man's living by faith—"Blessed art Thou, O Lord; *teach me Thy statutes.*" The whole practice of the means of grace, both the human and the divine use of them, looks to this end of storing His words or a very sight or presence of Himself in the heart that is living by faith—the believer "hiding His words" there (Ps. cxix. 11); God "writing" them there (Jer. xxxi. 33); the heart "forming" the glad tidings of Him within itself into "Him dwelling in it by its faith, the hope of glory" (Col. i. 27, Eph. iii. 17); "His comforts" causing the "multitude of its thoughts" to give it "delight" (Ps. xciv. 19); out of which, again, the mouth speaketh, or the conduct exhibits, a "living epistle of Him, known and read of all men" (2 Cor. iii. 2, 3). Hence the peculiar manner of instruction in "the truth" practised by believers and arranged by God to "stablish, strengthen,

The word of faith.

and settle them in the faith." No philosophical system which could be stored in the memory in logical abbreviation of propositions that reason could take up at convenience and expand into fulness, "the faith" is a *life* lived in thinking of Christ Jesus, looking upon or rather *to* Him, as numerous and minute facts about Him, or varying spiritual circumstances in the beholder, produce endless variety and riches of expression. It comes, therefore, to be the practice of believers to read anew and anew, as the constantly fresh food of their thoughts and affections, the same things of His which they have often read before; and His help comes to them in the same form of renewing the thought of Him. A day in every seven comes *His day*, to break afresh, but in no new way, the hurry of worldly work, and give a repetition of the same needful contemplation. Faith is promised to come by hearing, when the hearing is no new thing, but old things of His Word heard again and again, or only in changed connection; a change of light merely, but the same things of Christ brought afresh to the mind to establish His presence by another hold of thought. The training influence of prayer is of the same manner and design. It is a frequent repetition of the same thought and feeling of His presence with the soul's living, uniting more and more in conscious feeling the believer's spirit with Him, as "daily," or "seven times a-day," or "without ceasing," it sets the Lord before him, putting Him in all his thoughts. This design of storing in the heart thoughts and sights of Jesus, growing riches of precious things for the soul to treasure, might have suggested the very terms in which the Lord's Supper was instituted—"Do this in remembrance of me;" and its remembrance, its showing forth of His death, is expressly "till He come." To the same life of thought the Spirit is to minister; who is promised to take of the things of Jesus and show them unto believers in Him, and to bring all things to their remembrance whatsoever He spake to them, and to "strengthen them with might in the inner man," to "know the breadth, and length, and depth, and height of His love, which passeth knowledge, that they may be filled with the fulness of God" (Eph. iii.) "Occupy till I come" is the practice of the means of grace. The sight of Him—looking back on His human manifestation, looking up to His fellow-feeling, looking forward to His prepared places in the "Father's house"—the vivid sight evermore of Him in the facts of His life and the words of His grace they make so credible, that sight which yields an all-adapted help suited to every work, race, fight, patience, obedience, &c., of faith—is evermore the gift bestowed by God, as it is the use sought by man, in the means of grace. "To know the only true God, and Jesus Christ, whom He hath sent, is man's eternal life" (John xvii. 3).

15. Living by faith comprehends, besides the distinct open training of the means of grace, an inscrutable spiritual discipline, which also the believer has to "occupy till He come," of whose grace this is a part more than of man's practice. The prayer, "Lord, increase our faith," has had, and will continue to have, a comprehensive answer; every part of which he is to school and chasten his soul by as occasion may arise. Sometimes strong trial, as in the case of the Canaanite mother, is needed to draw out and fix in consciousness a deep belief in Jesus, which does not yet know itself. Persistence in faith was one of the most prominent lessons taught by Him directly, and by such examples as that woman's, and Abraham's, and Jacob's. A sense of utter helplessness, bordering on hopelessness, may be a needed experience. "Be not afraid, only believe," was an exhortation He needed to address in another illustrative case. The experience of exceptional trouble, suggesting exceptional diffidence, may be needed to open the eyes to the real extent of His grace; as the leper, greatly daring to break all bounds of religious rule to come to His presence, yet needed to be taught that he was welcome, and had his hesitating words, "Lord, if Thou wilt, Thou canst make me clean," answered on the moment, "I will; be thou clean." Reproof may be needed for a half-unconscious seeking the help of some sight to believe in Him: "Except ye see signs and wonders, ye will not believe." Entire help to speak the words of prayer may be needed, as when He drew out supplicating but silent desire to an expression which would strengthen desire and faith both: "What will ye that I should do unto you?" And

Spiritual discipline.

T

suspense may be needed, sending His suppliants away without a distinct promise, to exercise their faith in Him in absence, and find the answer of peace they know not when nor how, but to recognise it and Him when it comes (John iv. 52, Luke xvii. 14). Such discipline, when it comes "food convenient" for the living soul, must be used as the means of grace are, to help it to abide in Him, and keep His words abiding in it; and the records of such training passed through by believers who have passed within the veil are to be anchors of the soul's peace to yet-enduring believers in their living the life of faith, helping them amidst the needful discipline to "occupy till He come."

LIFE.   16. The review now taken of the trial-helps of man's living by faith of the Son of God prepares us to ask, with some guidance to a comprehensive answer, What is the life of man's spirit that is nurtured and exercised by this *living*? These ways in which believers in Jesus "occupy till He come" are ways in which He is coming to them continually now, "that they may have life, and may have it more abundantly." Peter tells us that living this (temporal) life in Him, "whom having not seen we love, in whom, though now we see Him not, yet believing, we rejoice with joy unspeakable and full of glory, we receive the end of our faith, the salvation of our souls" (1 Pet. i. 8, 9). What is that purpose of our faith, the salvation of our souls which we "receive"—*i.e.*, are receiving now? Evidently what believers do receive in the various exercises of living by faith of the Son of God is that which in a previous chapter was collected from a comparison of Scriptural examples as the essential feature of faith's experience, —*a consciousness of union with Him.* That union is logically the essential feature of a life which is described as lived "in Him," "by Him," "unto Him," "abiding in Him," and "He abiding in us"—a conscious union, containing reciprocal action, the disruption of which was Adam's immediate death, and in all Adam's race is the condition of the evil heart of unbelief, "departing from the living God." Thus clearly described, both in the practice required of believers and in

God's gift, is *Christ Jesus himself* "all in all things." "He is our life;" "because He lives, we shall live also;" "when He shall appear, we shall appear with Him in glory." And He himself is "the way, and the truth, and the life" of that present new life, revealed to us as a life of union in kindred and nature, a life of sonship, in which "man cometh to the Father." Believers are not pupils, servants of a law, but children, brothers and sisters of an individual. And they are living, not in a state of self-regulating trial—not separate and independent even in the sense of guiding themselves by principles which they are to work out into practice—but are living in the habitual consciousness that they are left by Him, the Object of their faith and love, and repentance and obedience, at a defined task—in a home, or place of work, or of trial, chosen for them by Him—with selected talents He has committed to their husbandry, to "occupy till He come." They are left in a state of bodily separation from Him, which is to constrain them to seek constantly a union in spirit with Him, in which they look forward to His coming, not as to a state of indefinite happiness or holiness, but to be "absent from the body and present with the Lord," "to be with Him," and "to become like Him, seeing Him as He is." The spiritual life whose present consciousness is described in the phrases, "Occupy till I come;" "I live, yet not I, but Christ liveth in me;" "to me to live is Christ," &c., is the same life which when perfected is spoken of in these terms of the Son's own life: "As Thou, Father, art in me, and I in Thee, that they also may be one in us" (John xvii.)

17. "Till I come;" "I am the way, and the truth, and the life: no man cometh to the Father" (to the life of sonship) "but by me;" "I, if I be lifted up, will draw all men unto me;" "Abide in me, and I in you." This "I"—the sole subjective Ego, the "I AM" of revelation, "the life," in which human time is an episode, the single origin of all distributed life, "of whom, and through whom, and to whom are all things"—must be contemplated in religious thought as the end, good, object, design, and desire of moral life, even as He is of all natural life; its source also from which, and to which, all

Conscious union with Christ.

its thoughts and their works radiate and converge. Consciousness of self and of Him is to be the unifying practice and experience of the soul, the *life* it lives, having been dead and living now " not itself, but He living in it." To bring on this consciousness of union, the discipline of the walk and fight and patience and obedience of faith, the doctrine and reproof and correction of the Word, and the whole troubles and comforts, exercise and guidance, of providence and grace, are needed and are fitted. They educate the soul in the sense of helplessness looking unto Him, of difficulty absolutely needing Him, of comfort, health, and necessary enjoyment of which He is felt to be the source and treasure ; that sense which the fruitful branch might be supposed to have of its need and its possession of the richness of the vine, or the members of their need and possession of the whole life of the being to whom they belong ; that uniting sense of dependence and assurance first chosen to explain " believing in "—the infant's *life* in its nursing mother's arms.

The conscious union of helplessness to all-sufficing help, of emptiness made full, weakness made perfect of strength in His strength, is the life that living by faith gives even now ; and how thoroughly does it gather home to itself all the metaphors of the life of salvation !—the recovered prodigal's life in his father, the brother born for adversity, the friend closer than a brother, the refuge, the shield, the sure portion, the habitation, rock, and fortress, the sheltering wings, the one lost sheep brought back to the broken flock, the little child's life in its mother, the wife's in her husband.

Union making oneness is the essential existence, the eternal life, which the present exercising living by faith is to lead up to, and accustom, and feed to more abundance. The oneness of that perfected life is expressively represented by two metaphors of the Christian Scriptures—" the living stones built together in Him a spiritual house," " a habitation of God ;" and " the members of Christ" growing together connected by joints and bands, making increase of the body growing up into Him " in all things, who is the Head" (1 Pet. ii. 4, 5 ; Eph. ii. 20, iv. 15, 16). And the consciousness of that eternal union takes into clearest unifying connection the metaphors used of heaven—the "rest" of home, which is reunited love; the servants' entering into the joy of their Lord; the life freed from all separating influences of night or hunger or tears; the perfection of human life's essential happiness—that of living in the light of some "believed-in" one's countenance—when there shall be no need of the sun, for the Lamb shall be the light of the *city of the Father's house of many mansions.*

18. Some passages of Scripture open up to faith a glimpse of the union of salvation wider than perfected human nature's consciousness, one extending beyond and around the healed life of the original lord of earthly creation—a foresight comforting much, and congruous to the thoughts now dwelt upon. It is of a universe of healed life, which is to be the home of that perfected life of man. Human restoration is to behold the union, into harmony and health and joy, of all nature's living elements which were made discordant and "subject to vanity," in connection with, perhaps because of and in curative anticipation of, man's fall into discordance of being. "The whole creation groaneth and travaileth together in pain until now," "waiting for the manifestation of the sons of God" (Rom. viii.), "when He shall gather together in one all things in Christ, both which are in heaven and which are on earth, even in Him in whom we have obtained an inheritance" (Eph. i.) *The healed universe.*

19. The different features of the practice of faith dwelt upon in the preceding chapters are evidently necessary to and accordant with our understanding faith as pervading and making all this life of union. This unifying living by faith must be the habitual contemplation of a personal Object of love, thinking of Him not by the medium of a philosophical system or theory, but through the boundlessly-diversified facts of a rich history of love; in which feeble babes in Christ may have their powers of contemplation filled with but one or two things of Christ, and be perfectly blessed therein; and those of full growth may revel in a world of knowledge, yet only learning still the one joy of faith—His all-filling love. This unifying living by faith in the Son of *Agreement with preceding statements.*

God must be a mass of feelings to which no exhaustive definition could be applied ; for sometimes it may be—oftenest it is—a state of unconscious resting in Him in peace and happiness, that does not individualise its thoughts or feelings ; and when it is conscious, it is a thinking in which there commingle in perpetually-varying life, and in mutual influence and nurturing, all the spiritual fruits and sources of that new-hearted thinking—" love, peace, gentleness, goodness, trust, meekness, temperance." This unifying living by faith in the Son of God will evidently have its diversities according to the feature of his Lord's manifested character, or the things of His history with which the believer feels himself most in union of heart. It will have its conditional changes, too, corresponding to the fluctuations of the feeble mind's and unstable heart's union of faithfulness to Him.

Adam's death " in the day that he ate " of the tree.

20. Does not this " new life " of union resulting in oneness, as the grafting of a branch into a tree makes what had been separate not merely united but *one*, shed a light on what was man's first life in his heavenly Father, and what the death was that he died " in the day " he ate the fruit of disobedience ? He did not taste of bodily death for nine hundred years ; but all his history shows that he was one with his Father no more, not near Him in possibility of loving Him or even of appreciating Him, but afar off, and having to be brought nigh by slow degrees and much painstaking, compassionate, forbearing nursing of the smoking flax to heat and flame through thousands of years—all things of the world's education, through multiform providence and revelation, working together to make him let his eyes observe his Father's ways, and his heart return to Him. This same death has never ceased to pass afresh—" an evil heart of unbelief " —" upon all men," every child of Adam's race who in like wilfulness " departs from the living God."

God's impossibilities and man's omnipotence.

21. The fact that union is the essential form of spiritual life in God sets in their true force of meaning the famous Scriptural expressions of faith's necessity and its efficacy—the impossibilities predicated of God, and the omnipotence offered to man : " Without faith it is impossible to please

God;" "He could not do many mighty works there because of their unbelief;" "Be not afraid, only believe;" "If thou canst believe, all things are possible to him that believeth;" "Because I live, ye shall live also," &c. The broken union means suspended help and life; the renewed union means renewed power.

22. If spiritual death was from the first *disunion*—the disunion in which the evil heart of unbelief departed from the living God, seeking to be independent of Him, to be a god to itself knowing good and evil—the death of family life which the prodigal son always suffers—it sets in a clear light the connection of never-suspended present faith with the assurance of life. All faith's forms of habitual thought, soul-possessing feeling of the Saviour's presence, conscious reasoning trust, and less conscious musing of Him in reveries of affection, spontaneous outgoings of joy in Him, or sorrow towards Him, or desire after Him—all are simply pulses, life-throbs, peaceful or agitated breathings of a new life of union to Him. And there can be no assurance of being His apart from this conscious union to Him. No first sufficient act of faith can be, in the sense assumed by some religionists—no act which, once done, assures all succeeding life in Christ to the human thinker. In the counsels, or active love, or whatever we may call it, of God, the act may be written in which the everlasting life of a human child of His began; but that is not our point of view, from which we are able to look, who know not these counsels and that book of remembrance; and in that child's comfort of faith, or sureness of God his Saviour's love, it is not any one introductory act of the heart's believing that is sufficient for his comfort, but acts of heart-faith repeated evermore in abiding continuity of union to Him—the *new life,* not the *new birth*—not Paul's one experience on the road to Damascus, but Paul's daily living unto Him who died and rose again for him. So the comfort and the conditions of faith are set down by that largely-experienced believer: "Let the peace of God rule in your hearts, to the which ye are called in one body; and be ye thankful. Let the word of God dwell in you richly in all wisdom; teaching and admonishing one

[margin: Condition to assurance of salvation.]

another in psalms and hymns and spiritual songs, singing
with grace in your hearts to the Lord. And whatsoever ye
do in word or deed, do all in the name of the Lord Jesus, giving thanks to God and the Father by Him" (Col. iii. 15-17).
When, like the great example of conscious faith, Peter walking
on the sea to meet his Master, a believer's emotional thoughts
of reliance or apprehension turn aside from Jesus, he loses
hold of comforting assurance; and while he is looking with
constraining feelings, not to Him, but at the things seen and
temporal, he is *one with Him* no more, and he "begins to
sink."

Sceptical reasoning primarily disuniting. 23. Scepticism, as previously noticed, has its measure of
success partly accounted for by the psychological fact that
"believing in" Jesus has in it one element of union to Him—
viz., constant beholding Him as He is—and that the "departure" in thought and inclination from that "occupation" of the
mind, the suspension of that beholding, brings suspension of
strength to resist evil thoughts of unbelief. Wiling away the
thoughts from the facts of revelation as they are given in the
Word of God, in the position, colours, proportion, shape, connection, and all that gives their real life to them in the narrative
—to consider the possibility and the affirmed grounds of bold
and disloyal metaphysical or other questions about some one
or more of those facts taken out of connection with the whole,
or about man's power to be sure about anything—all sceptical
reasoning has as its first work, incidental or designed, but of
exceeding importance, induced a habit of the thoughts which
breaks that union of man's spirit with the things of his own
Father, which is constitutionally natural to him to feel. By
the suspension of that conscious contact with the things of
God, the soul is put into a state in which its needed comfort
of faith is withdrawn for the time, like Peter's; and, unlike his
case, it may be the beginning of an evil heart departing from
the living God. The continuity of the living by faith is broken—its consciousness is suspended—as when a child, who is
to be seduced from faith in a parent, is first drawn away from
that parent's presence, the sight of whom would be the answer
to all insinuated doubts about him.

24. We have before contemplated the individuality of the Heavenly life united individualities. life reserved for man in the inheritance of the sons of God. The language of the 12th chapter of Hebrews, if not also such expressions as "the greatest and the least in the kingdom of heaven," and "the stars differing in glory," point to individual life in heaven, as well as in the preparatory spiritual life. The life being one life of all, even in its preparatory state—"as Thou, Father, art in me, and I in Thee, that they also may be one in us,"—is also an essential feature of it; the mystery of which is approximately comprehensible by the habits of human love's thoughts in the family life of united individualities, which is man's fullest life and best happiness, and the completest development of his nature. The education given by human relationships is to a life of united individualities, beginning with that of a child's life in his parents; followed by that of brothers in each other, of sisters together, and a varied development of their united life, when brother and sister each finds in the diverse sensibilities of the other an appreciated complement of his or her own; and culminating in the conjugal union of two separate lives making one life, which is quoted by Paul as illustrative of the one life of Christ and His Church.

25. A thought has arisen in various heathen religions, which Heathen thoughts of a future life. is connected with the true faith of man's eternal union unto oneness with God. It is the Hindoo thought that the end of good men is absorption into the being of Brahma. The notion appears in other religions as a retributive transmigration of souls, in which the good shall be elevated, as they continue good, to higher and higher states of being through a succession of lives, and the bad find themselves, unless they repent, passing through progressive degradations of existence. If we are to regard error in speculative thought as "the shadow cast by truth," we should be glad to recognise by this one the existence of a strong light upon human consciousness which could cast widely so well-defined a shadow of mistaken thought. Could the notion be regarded as a remnant of pristine true thought, it would be invaluable. Is it much less valuable regarded in the only alternative light of being a subjective necessity of our nature, that divine nature which God

gave us—some consciousness belonging to a being who was made in the image of God, that God is his, and he is God's, and, therefore, leading the soul to "feel after Him"? (Acts xvii. 27). Our revealed light of life and immortality—"the light which came into the world, the life of man"—assures us of a life which is oneness, and yet not absorption—a life one with God, yet contemplating Him—a life of the same well-ordered dependency of parts as we have experienced in human spiritual life under the same grace in our present state—a life of unity in individuality, of harmony in diversity—the sameness, yet variety, of all united human life, multiplying the emotions in which life consists, making them full and perfect, each filling the others with power and blessedness.

CONCLUSION.

AN attempt to set forth historically the practice of faith
might appropriately conclude with what history would often
seem to call the failure of faith, but which is truly to be
named the waiting, the patient waiting, of faith for the fulness
of the promise. Christian teachers weary at times of their
fruitless-looking labours, and light thinkers, looking on the
experience of years or of a generation, undervalue the means
of faith, and say, "Where is the promise of His coming?"
The law of faith's great history has been, "One soweth, another reapeth." Let us place ourselves at any point along
the line of history of the undoubtedly unbroken advance-
ment of the truth, and it shall be, that while the past always
shows progress, the present will always seem to show failure.
What are the figures we there behold whose spirits needed to
pray all along in the words, "Lord, I believe: help Thou mine
unbelief"? Abraham childless, who was promised countless
seed, standing alone on the plains of Canaan, looking wistfully,
often wearily, into the never-clearing future;—Moses gazing
from the top of Pizgah upon the promised land, near at hand
at last, but afar off from him, never to be trodden by his feet;
—fugitive Elijah on a pinnacle of Horeb, his face wrapt in his
mantle, answering Jehovah's words, "What doest thou here,
Elijah?" "I have been very jealous for the Lord God of
hosts, because the children of Israel have forsaken Thy covenant, thrown down Thine altars, and slain Thy prophets with
the sword; and I only am left, and they seek my life to take
it away;"—Isaiah at the head of the scattered prophets, all in

the midst of hopeless signs, standing with their faces Zionwards, looking for an approaching but never-coming time of the salvation of the Lord, and complaining all, "Who hath believed our report?" Souls living in vain, as they think, on the earth for their Master's service, dying in vain, and leaving the world, not having received the promises, to go complaining into the presence of the Lord, and cry before the altar, "How long, O Lord, holy and true?" (Rev. vi. 10)—with one grandly-impressive uniformity in this respect, diverse in all other circumstances of their history—these stand along the first great history of faith foreshadows only of the attitude and the depression of soul of an awfully more august figure; even The Only-begotten Son, enduring the contradiction of sinners against Himself, complaining in weariness, "O faithless generation, how long shall I be with you? how long shall I suffer you?"— His miracles called Beelzebub's,—the Holy Ghost blasphemed, —the Saviour despised and rejected of men,—the mocking hill of Calvary in view.

Who shall look forward and expect to see, or wait to receive, the supports of worldly promise, when those could but look to Heaven's promise alone; and, upheld by that, endure, patient and unfainting—in the morning sowing the seed, in the evening withholding not their hand—until they all "died in the faith"? But who shall look back on that past story of the truth's reception, and see faith's life and growth written in the Church's and the unbelieving world's history of salvation, and not be helped by the sight to turn with strength of heart and lift its eyes to the future with patient waiting—"troubled, but not distressed; perplexed, but not in despair"? Had the mighty prophet Elijah to leave his labours to be taken up by his servant Elisha? Did he think himself alone faithful in Israel, while the Lord had seven thousand who had not bowed the knee to Baal? Had the wide sowing of the thoughts of faith in David's reign to perish in the idolatries of Rehoboam? Had the grand moral proclamations, the protests, rebukes, and exhortations, of the later prophets, and their glorious visions of the latter days of salvation, to sink into the mire of the drunken filthiness of the nobles and priests of Jehovah's own chosen people? and yet the Messiah, when He came, came the desire of all nations. Is the manner of this world's history broken? Is it not the same to-day that it was in that long-back yesterday? If the morrow be as far separated from to-day, is there anything in experience to make the promise unstable? Is this the end of the world, as sowers of the living seed eighteen hundred years ago thought their day was; or is the world of man but little past its beginning, needing many ages yet for its recovery to uniting faith in God from the destroying effects of sin? Whenever that destined future may be, he that soweth and he that reapeth shall rejoice "together." To look from the height of Christian ages over the field of the world is the best rebuke to slowness of heart to believe in the efficacy of the teaching of the glad tidings for the recalling of the heathen now, and bringing the evil heart of unbelief into captivity to Christ; the better a rebuke that it is a rebuke likewise to reports of speedy success attending man's schemes in that work of God.

THE END.